WALKING TOGETHER

WALKING TOGETHER

Christian Thinking & Public Life in South Africa

Joel Carpenter

Editor

Abilene Christian University Press

WALKING TOGETHER
Christian Thinking and Public Life in South Africa

ACU PRESS

Copyright 2012 by Joel Carpenter

ISBN 978-0-89112-315-6
LCCN 2011022899

Printed in the United States of America

Scripture quotations noted NRSV are taken from the Revised Standard Version of the Bible, copyright 1952 [2nd edition, 1971] by the Division of Christian Education of the National Council of the Churches of Christ in the United States of America. Used by permission. All rights reserved.

LIBRARY OF CONGRESS CATALOGING-IN-PUBLICATION DATA
Walking together : Christian thinking and public life in South Africa / Joel Carpenter, editor.
    p. cm.
ISBN 978-0-89112-315-6
1. Christianity and politics--South Africa. 2. Christianity and culture--South Africa. 3. Church and social problems--South Africa. 4. Democracy--Religious aspects--Christianity. 5. Democracy--South Africa. 6. Christians--Political activity--South Africa. I. Carpenter, Joel A. II. Title: Christian thinking and public life in South Africa.
BR115.P7W25 2011
261'.10968--dc23

2011022899

Cover design by Zeal Design Studio
Interior text design by Sandy Armstrong

For information contact:
Abilene Christian University Press
1626 Campus Court
Abilene, Texas 79601

1-877-816-4455
www.abilenechristianuniversitypress.com

12 13 14 15 16 17 / 7 6 5 4 3 2 1

To three public theologians

Tinyiko Maluleke

Nico Koopman

John De Gruchy

We are grateful for your guidance

Contents

Part I: Identity and Culture

Part II: Churches and Social Problems

Part III: Christianity and Politics

FOREWORD

John De Gruchy

By all accounts, the Football World Cup tournament held in South Africa in July 2010 was a resounding success. South Africa captured the attention of the media in a way that was reminiscent of that bright and sunny day in 1994 when Nelson Mandela was inaugurated as President of the new post-apartheid republic. But the serious issues facing South Africa's public life, many of them part of the legacy of apartheid, others more recent in origin, were sidelined from public attention for those brief and magical moments when the "beautiful game" took center stage.

At the time I write these words, however, somber issues have resurfaced with a vengeance. Widespread protests about government service delivery in poor communities and massive strikes by civil servants in the educational, health, and justice sectors have highlighted the problems that beset the country. Together with the historic burden of racism and landlessness, the HIV/AIDS pandemic, and periodic outbursts of xenophobic violence, these issues threaten the well-being of South Africa. They also provide the raw material for the case studies documented in this book. But the book is of more than South African relevance. Many countries across the world, whether in the global South or North, face similar challenges, though their character and contours may be different. And many churches and Christians in these countries are seeking insightful resources to inform their engagement with the issues. This book is a contribution to this public and ecclesial discussion and a prod to action.

The authors come from Africa and North America. They do not claim to be experts on South Africa, although a few are citizens here and some have lived or studied in this country. Only a handful would claim to be theologians by training and vocation, though all are theologians, I would insist, by virtue of their commitment to think and live in the public arena from the perspective of Christian faith. Together they represent a diversity of Christian and cultural experiences, and they are skilled in a variety of academic disciplines. For a brief two-and-a-half weeks, they were brought together as a community of Christian scholars concerned about public life, and they plunged into the deep end of South African reality. For most of them, this was a new experience and no matter how well-briefed beforehand—they all read intensely before arriving—nothing could have prepared them adequately for what they experienced both individually and as a group. It is this experience, filtered through theological reflection and social analysis, and the narratives that emerged in the process, that gives the book its coherence and value.

There were many places the group could not visit and key people with whom they could not converse, so there are perspectives and positions to be taken on issues that they did not encounter. Given the constraints of time and the nature of the seminar, such limitations were inevitable. As a result, some of the nuances that South African specialists might want to find in the essays may be absent. But the issues they discuss are complex, defying simple analysis or easy solution, and there are many books written on the subjects by the experts. The strength of this book lies elsewhere—in the freshness of engagement, the difference of perspective, and the immediacy of experience that characterized the seminar, whether in Johannesburg, Soweto, and Pretoria, or in the Western Cape. Daily immersed in situations where they encountered the issues firsthand and entered into conversation with those dealing with such issues at the cutting edge, they learnt more about South Africa than many South Africans learn in a lifetime.

The media did not report the events of this seminar, but its outcomes both personal and shared, both lived and written, are important for anyone who has at heart the interests of South Africa and their own countries, together with the public life and witness of the church. Among the outcomes is undoubtedly the impact of the experience itself on the participants and the way in which this will shape their futures as faculty and church members in their home contexts. But this book is a further substantial outcome of the process, one that shares the experience and the insights it engendered with a much wider constituency. I can anticipate its use in the college or seminary classroom and church study group, for it is a resource that is worthy of good use.

I was privileged to help prepare the way for the seminar, to shape its structure and monitor its progress. My task also included facilitating the writing and preparation of this book at a three-day concluding workshop held at Volmoed, a Christian retreat center situated near Hermanus in the Hemel en Aarde Valley, about 120 kilometers from Cape Town. The participants arrived exhausted but exhilarated. We worshipped together and shared stories of encounters along the road, some tragic and others full of courage and hope. We engaged each other in debate, sometimes heated, often critical, but always collegial. Gradually we discerned the way forward. The result, I submit, is a volume of thoughtful, creative, and multi-disciplinary essays that provoke, inform, and challenge us to respond in ways that are pertinent to the issues at hand and appropriate to Christian faith, hope, and love in public life.

ACKNOWLEDGMENTS

This book bears the fruit of an international faculty development seminar held in South Africa during June 2009. It was sponsored by the Council for Christian Colleges and Universities (CCCU). The CCCU's operating partners for this seminar were the Nagel Institute for the Study of World Christianity, a research and projects agency of Calvin College; and the Plowshares Institute, a peace-promoting organization based in Simsbury, Connecticut. The project also was co-sponsored by the Paul B. Henry Institute for the Study of Christianity and Politics, another research and projects agency of Calvin College.

We are grateful to these agencies and their leaders, notably Mimi Barnard, vice president for research and professional development at the CCCU, who assisted in the planning and fund-raising for the seminar, and who walked with us for two weeks in South Africa. Likewise, Claudia Beversluis, provost of Calvin College, accompanied the team and contributed her wisdom to its discussions. The support and advocacy of these two leaders in Christian higher education have been invaluable.

The staff of the Plowshares Institute capably handled the lion's share of logistics for this seminar. We are especially indebted to Plowshares' directors, Bob and Alice Evans, who coordinated the team's visits and conversations in South Africa. Their many contacts throughout the churches, community organizations, and government of that nation gave us unsurpassed access to leaders at all levels. Even more, Bob and Alice gave from their great stores of energy, good cheer, networking talent, and wisdom about group dynamics. They showed us amazing grace, and vision brimming with hope.

Three South African theologians were our guides. First came John De Gruchy, professor emeritus of religious studies at the University of Cape Town, author of many outstanding works on theology and a key leader in the "public theology" movement in South Africa. John laid much of the intellectual ground-work for the seminar and conducted a time of reflection and writing at its end, near his home in Volmoed. Next came Nico Koopman, dean of the theology faculty and director of the Beyers Naudé Centre for Public Theology at the University of Stellenbosch. Nico finalized plans for the seminar before bowing to health concerns, and was able to host us for a morning in Stellenbosch. And then there was Tinyiko Maluleke, dean of research at the University of South Africa and president of the South African Council of Churches, who was our convener throughout the seminar. These able guides showed us how to engage in Christian thinking about public life, in South Africa and beyond. We dedi-cate the book to them, without whom it would not have appeared.

Projects like this one do not pay for themselves. We are deeply grate-ful to several generous partners. Walter and Darlene Hansen provided major financial support for this seminar, and from the start, Walter helped to shape the very concept of an international faculty development program. Corwin Smidt, director of the Paul Henry Institute, lent his agency's financial support and advised us on recruiting participants. It was good to have him with us for the seminar's first week. And finally, this project would not have been possible without the support of the academic officers of all of the North American and several of the African institutions whose faculty members were on our team. They came through, on late notice, with travel funding for the team members.

Making books is deeply labor intensive, and often is a very lonely endeavor. What a delight it is, then, to have cheerful, encouraging, and expert colleagues to walk with on the long march. Donna Romanowski, program coordinator of the Nagel Institute, has been engaged in this project from the very start, and has handled every detail of the work with good humor and great expertise. She arranged the initial visits and planning, guided the project's promotion and selection process, managed its budgets, tracked the book's various edit-ing stages, and finally, formatted and cleaned the text. She is the consummate professional and a steady and supportive colleague. Here at the end of the process I am grateful to Heidi Nobles, Robyn Burwell, and Leonard Allen at the Abilene Christian University Press. They believed in the book and helped me get it across the finish line.

Finally, this book owes its existence to all of the members of the seminar, those who stayed on to write chapters, and those who did not. Each one contributed to the thinking here, which could not have happened were we not walking together.

CONTRIBUTORS

Godwin Akper is a senior lecturer at the National Open University of Nigeria, in Lagos, and a research associate in the department of Systematic Theology and Ecclesiology at Stellenbosch University. Dr. Akper has published essays and articles on a wide variety of topics that address Christianity's role in contemporary Africa.

Charles Awasu is professor of sociology at Nyack College, United States. He has researched the role of microfinance institutions in Ghana and political and economic liberalization in Sub-Saharan Africa. He has also led faculty development seminars for Central University College, Ghana. One of his more recent works is "Salt and Light: The Social Value of the Church in the Post-Industrial Inner City." *Integrite Journal*, 7:1 (Spring 2008): 48-57.

Bernard Boyo is senior lecturer in Bible and theology as well as dean of community life at Daystar University, Kenya. He has written on the role of American fundamentalist missions in creating "an underlying skepticism" about the value of politics in Kenya.

Paul A. Brink is associate professor of political science at Gordon College, United States. He writes on political philosophy and the role of religious language and argument in politics. He is currently doing research on what makes democratic communities hold together, particularly in pluralistic societies.

Joel Carpenter is the director of the Nagel Institute at Calvin College. For many years, his major field of inquiry was American religious history, and his best-known work is *Revive Us Again: The Reawakening of American Fundamentalism* (New York: Oxford University Press, 1997). More recently, he has been studying Christian movements in the global South, and his most recent book is *The Changing Face of Christianity: Africa, the West, and the World* (New York: Oxford University Press, 2005).

Sophia Chirongoma is a doctoral student and lecturer in the Humanities Access Programme at the University of KwaZulu-Natal, South Africa. She is also a research consultant with the Ecumenical HIV and AIDS Initiative in Africa, sponsored by the World Council of Churches. She has published a variety of essays and articles on women's health, environmental concerns, and the church and politics.

Rhonda M. Collier is associate professor of English at Tuskegee University, United States, where she teaches in the areas of American, world, and African American literature. She has also taught in Uruguay, done research in Brazil, and written on the literature of Equatorial Guinea. She is deeply involved in writing and community action. She is the author of a variety of works, ranging from poetry to the blues to women in the arts and the role of poetry in political protest. Her most recent work has been on how "Hip Hop music has ignited young people to be politically involved and spiritually connected."

John De Gruchy is emeritus professor of Christian Studies, University of Cape Town, South Africa and extraordinary professor in the Faculty of Theology at the University of Stellenbosch. He is the author of numerous books, including *Christianity and Democracy: A Theology for a Just World Order* (New York: Cambridge University Press, 1995); *Christianity, Art and Transformation: Theological Aesthetics in the Struggle for Justice* (New York : Cambridge University Press, 2001); *Reconciliation: Restoring Justice (Minneapolis:* Fortress Press, 2002); and *Confessions of a Christian Humanist* (Minneapolis: Fortress Press, 2006).

Alice Frazer Evans is the director of Writing and Research at Plowshares Institute; former senior fellow at the Centre for Conflict Resolution, University of Cape Town, South Africa; advisor to the Research Center for Management of Social Risk and Public Crisis, Nanjing University, China; senior trainer for the Center for Empowering for Reconciliation and Peace, Indonesia; adjunct faculty at Hartford Seminary in theology and ethics; and the author of numerous books, including *Peace Skills: Leader's Guide* (Malden, Mass.: Jossey-Bass 2001).

Robert A. Evans is executive director of Plowshares Institute; professor of ethics at Hartford Seminary and Centre for Christian Muslim Dialogue; special researcher at Jiangsu Academy of Social Sciences (Nanjing, China); senior trainer for the Centre for Empowering for Reconciliation and Peace (Jakarta, Indonesia); former professor and senior fellow for the Centre for Conflict Resolution (University of Cape Town, South Africa); and author of numerous books including, with Alice Evans, *Human Rights: a Dialogue between the First and Third World* (Maryknoll, NY: Orbis Books,Books, 1983).

Tracy Kuperus is associate professor of international development studies at Calvin College, United States. She is interested in democratic transitions and political development, with a focus on the role that civil society agencies play in these transitions. She has published a variety of works in that area, including a book on the role of the Dutch Reformed Church's relations to the South African state.

Stephen W. Martin is assistant professor of theology at the King's University College, in Canada. He works in the field of political theology and has a variety of publications on the role of the church in the reconstruction of South Africa. He is now investigating the role that liturgy plays in constructing an alternative view of life's aims and purposes to those of global capitalism. He is particularly interested in exploring this theme within the African Instituted Churches.

Scott L. Moeschberger is assistant professor of psychology and higher education at Taylor University, United States. He has done research and written a variety of articles on forgiveness and reconciliation among former combatants in Northern Ireland, and the complex relationship between forgiveness and justice. He is also interested in how communities build cultures of peace, and how such aims apply to the counseling professions.

Tinyiko Maluleke is dean of research at the University of South Africa and president of the South African Council of Churches. He is the author of many theological essays and articles on mission, culture, politics, and social issues in southern Africa.

James Nkansah-Obrempong is associate professor of systematic theology and of theology and culture at Africa International University and dean of Nairobi Evangelical Graduate School of Theology. He has written and published on a wide variety of topics in these fields, including angels, demons, ancestors, sin, the problem of evil, and African theology. He was a contributor to the *Africa Bible Commentary* (Grand Rapids: Zondervan, 2006) and the *Global Dictionary of Theology*, ed. William A Dyrness, (Downer's Grove, IL: InterVarsity, 2008). His most recent work is *Visual Theology: Some Akan Cultural Metaphors, Proverbs, Myths, and Symbols and their Implications for Doing Christian Theology* (Munster, Germany: VDM Publishing House, 2010).

Sara Shady is associate professor of philosophy and director of the Honors Program at Bethel University, United States. Her main field of expertise is twentieth-century European philosophy, but she also studies and writes about social and political philosophy and ethics, with publications addressing issues of fear and trust in society, interfaith dialogue, and educating students for constructive participation in diverse societies.

Rothney Tshaka is associate professor and chair of the department of philosophy and systematic theology at the University of South Africa. He has taught theology in Zimbabwe and in the United States. He has written a variety of works on the encounter of Reformed confessionalism with African culture, and is now working on the role of race and racism in South Africa.

WALKING TOGETHER

Christian Thinking and Public Life in South Africa

Joel Carpenter

Across the world—in sub-Saharan Africa, Latin America, and southern and eastern Asia—two historic winds are sweeping across the social and political landscapes. One of these is the struggle for democracy in civic life, politics, and governance.[1] The other trend, which until recently was nearly invisible to most public affairs experts, is Christianity's dynamic growth and development in these regions. The great majority of the world's Christians now live outside of Europe and North America, and Africa in particular has become a great heartland of Christian belief and practice.

Given the huge scope and importance of these two revolutionary trends, it is surprising that few have asked what they might have to do with each other.[2] Timothy Shah, an American political scientist, assembled an international team to address that question, and in three broad-ranging studies, they bring some answers. All over the world, Shah and his team of scholars have discovered, members of surging Christian movements who once were uninvolved in public affairs are now engaging social concerns, civic life, and even electoral politics. Too often, however, these Christians enter politics to address a crisis or one burning issue, but they lack the depth and breadth of vision to sustain long-term, faithful service. Too often, once engaged, they have been co-opted by the established powers and patterns and have not sustained a consistent Christian political vision.[3]

Christians in the global South and East have been more effective, generally speaking, at directly engaging needs and concerns close at hand. As Donald Miller and Tetsunao Yamamori documented in their broad-ranging study of Pentecostal social engagement, emerging Christian movements in Africa, Asia, and Latin America are finding myriad ways to put their faith in action.[4] They are not only founding churches, but also starting schools, organizing poor and vulnerable workers, strengthening and encouraging fellowships of women, combating child abuse, starting loan cooperatives for small businesses, running basic health and addiction recovery clinics, operating feeding programs, and advocating for basic civil rights. Some scholars and activists disparage such "social work" as, at best, "indirect resistance" to social injustice and social misery, when what religious groups really need to provide is "direct resistance" in the form of protest and advocacy for political change. But both Shah's research teams and Miller and Yamamori show that very often, more direct and local responses to need lead to organizing, advocacy, and even campaigns for political reform. Indeed, the "civil society" school of democracy argues that all of these grassroots initiatives have positive roles to play in the creation of democratic values; they are the seedbeds of democratic culture building, the needed "deep structures" of values, achievements, and expectations that sustain political democracy. Christian movements' main contribution to democratization worldwide is in their penchant, like the early Methodists, for "organizing to beat the devil"—responding quickly to perceived needs by creating new voluntary associations.

What is true in the global South and East, where democratic institutions and values are often young and fragile, is also remarkably true in North America, where democratic institutions are old and fairly stable. In the United States, evangelical Protestants in particular have increased their political engagement over the past three decades, but it has been rather unstable. American evangelicals have learned to address moral issues with great vigor and to mobilize millions of concerned citizens. But they have produced relatively few long-term perspectives or public servants who can apply a comprehensive biblical view of public justice to a variety of concerns in a religiously plural society. Only a few of the more than one hundred evangelical Christian colleges and universities in North America have departments of political science, or even some philosophers and theologians who focus on political thought. So the need among evangelical Christians in particular for close and careful reflection on their faith's role in advancing public justice is fairly universal, especially among recently emerging movements. Such Christian thinking is as needful in Kansas as it is in Kenya and South Korea.

This book arises, then, out of an effort to encourage some fresh Christian thinking about public life. Its authors—North Americans and Africans alike— were participants in a team effort to learn from people of faith in a setting where Christianity is dynamic and influential, and where democracy is emerging, but still fragile. So they sojourned together in South Africa, a nation where Christian adherence is more pervasive than the United States, and where a remarkable democratic experiment is underway. Against all odds, South Africa has made a largely peaceful transition from an overtly racist and repressive regime to a multi-party, interracial democracy. The South African situation is both hopeful and fragile, with signs of positive change, but some deeply troubling social, political, and economic problems as well. South Africa straddles two worlds: the technologically driven and affluent world of Europe and its overseas settlements, and sub-Saharan Africa, which is still largely agricultural and economically struggling. At a time when democracies are fragile and even regressing in parts of Africa, and when democratic values are being tested in Europe and North America, South Africa also reflects some of the political traits of both the West and of greater Africa.

Over the past three decades, South Africa has become the home of some of the most profound and influential expressions of Christian public thought. Its first democratic president, Nelson Mandela, who repeatedly described himself as not being a very good Christian, nevertheless championed a politics of reconciliation and solidarity that clearly drew on Christian values.[5] Theologically gifted public intellectuals, most notably Anglican Archbishop Desmond Tutu, the Nobel peace laureate who chaired the Truth and Reconciliation Commission (TRC), have done much to shape public policy and outlook.[6]

And there are many other remarkable public leaders—black and white, colored and Asian, Afrikaner and British—who as preachers, community activists, jurists, professors, business leaders, and philanthropists sustained hope for a new commonwealth, even in some very bleak times.

So our team, which included nine scholars from North America and nine from African nations, came to South Africa to learn more about Christianity's public role by seeing it in action, among both grassroots activists and national elites, in a setting that was familiar to only a few of them. One premise behind this experiment was that Christian scholars in North America need to reorient their interests and outlooks toward the global South and East, which are the new heartlands of their faith and the front lines of its mission in the world. Simultaneously, Christian scholars from Africa, one of these new heartlands, need some basic opportunities to transcend their local contexts and understand what their counterparts elsewhere are doing and thinking. They know all too well what the intellectual and cultural trends are in Europe and North America, but they have had surprisingly little opportunity to compare notes with each other and to see Christian ideas and values being put into play in a relevant context. So we North Americans invited them to join us in a place that is both familiar and strange to us all: South Africa.

This book communicates what we learned in South Africa about Christian ways to address some of the most important public issues of our time. Its chapters address matters of personal identity and collective peoplehood, the deeply cultural dimensions of conflict resolution, the role of churches in addressing vexing social issues such as immigration and HIV/AIDS, the use and abuse of power, the nature of legal and governmental authority, the political voice and role of churches in deepening democracy, and the political nature of the church itself. Our team was broadly interdisciplinary, featuring not only theologians and political scientists but a sociologist, a psychologist, a philosopher, a historian, and a scholar of arts and media.

These topics and disciplinary approaches are all valuable for learning some fresh ways to engage in Christian social, cultural, and political thought. But it is also instructive to see how much this group learned from their interactions, both with each other and with the South African scene. In the first section of the book, on culture and identity, Sarah Shady, an American political philosopher, gained a fresh appreciation for the power of public monuments, back home as well as in South Africa, to perpetuate destructive mythology. She hopes that they might also prompt new dialogues that will confront and overcome these legacies. For Scott Moeschberger, an American social psychologist who has studied conflict and peace-making in Northern Ireland, the South African scene looked remarkably more complex, but amenable to similar kinds of analysis. Rhonda Collier, an African American scholar of arts and media, was impressed by the resonances between South African and African American popular cultures. And Godwin Akper, a Nigerian who had studied in South Africa and knew firsthand its problems with xenophobia, discovered the astonishing universality of alienation among native South Africans, black, white, and brown.

In the second part of the book, on the churches and social problems, we see fresh discoveries as well. Bernard Boyo, a Kenyan theologian who was visiting South Africa for the first time, wonders how a nation could work so hard to protect its migrating wildlife yet have such an aversion to its human immigrants. No doubt these contrasts brought to mind similar ones in his homeland. Sophia Chirongoma, a Zimbabwean theologian currently studying in South Africa, helps us understand the sources and scope of the current immigration crisis. Yet she ends up urging the church's people to rediscover and re-express, in deeply Christian terms, the traditional African value of "walking together" with strangers. Charles Awasu is a Ghanaian sociologist who has taught in the United States for many years while researching West African community values and economic development. He found that South African churches' contributions to social capital while dealing with HIV/AIDS were more ambivalent than he anticipated. And Rothney Tshaka, a South African ethicist, applies some theories and research about racism that he had recently discovered on a visit to the United States. They help him understand the anti-immigrant riots in the black communities during 2008, and the ongoing anti-foreign tensions.

In the realm of Christianity and politics per se, James Nkansah-Obrempong, a Ghanaian theologian teaching in Kenya, responds to one of the more salient topics we heard about in an election year: abuses of governmental power. His exposition demonstrates the freshness of the biblical drama for Africans and the direct relevance of biblical stories and precepts to the continent's politics. Yet he finds wisdom for the way forward from a surprising source—American feminist theologians. Paul Brink, a Canadian political scientist, gains fresh insights from the South African constitution for addressing a common Western political dilemma: how to anchor governmental authority in a secular and radically plural age, when both divine mandates and liberal consensus-building have eroded. Tracy Kuperus, an American political scientist who previously researched church-state relations in South Africa during the apartheid years, is surprised to see today how the former "priestly" and "prophetic" postures of the churches have been transformed under the new regime. And Steve Martin, a Canadian theologian, sees in the huge, African-founded Zion Christian Church (ZCC) a radical alternative to modern political ideologies. The church is inherently political, he says; it is a rival to the state as a kingdom and seat of authority. If Jesus is Lord and Savior, then Caesar is not. Martin finds much for Western churches to learn from the ZCC's resistance to being co-opted by the powers of this world. And in a powerful afterword, our team's convener, the South African theologian Tinyiko Maluleke, shows how African-American poetry has inspired him in his struggle to understand who he is and how South Africa can ever become his home.

In sum, this book shows that as Christian scholars of the North awaken to the concerns of their faith's new heartlands in the South, and Christian scholars from the South awaken to their faith's public imperatives, they gain fresh insights from engaging each other. Together we discovered South Africa's greatest contribution to social and political thought, *ubuntu*—the power of belonging—or as Sophia Chirongoma puts it, the power of walking together. So we invite you to accompany us, and to learn some of what we learned on our South African sojourn.

Notes to the Introduction

[1] As we go to press, an "Arab spring" of popular democratic uprisings sweeps North Africa and the Middle East.

[2] But see a pioneering world survey by Paul Freston, *Evangelicals and Politics in Asia, Africa and Latin America* (New York: Cambridge University Press, 2001).

[3] Shah's team produced three volumes of nationally focused, chapter-length studies: Terence O. Ranger, ed., *Evangelical Christianity and Democracy in Africa* (Oxford: Oxford University Press, 2008); David H. Lumsdaine, ed., *Evangelical Christianity and Democracy in Asia* (Oxford: Oxford University Press, 2008); and Paul Freston, ed., *Evangelical Christianity and Democracy in Latin America* (Oxford: Oxford University Press, 2008).

[4] Donald E. Miller and Tetsunao Yamamori, *Global Pentecostalism: The New Face of Christian Social Engagement* (Berkeley: University of California Press, 2007).

[5] Anthony Sampson, *Mandela: The Authorized Biography (New York: Knopf, 1999)*, ch. 36, "Forgiving," 512–525.

[6] Desmond Mpilo Tutu, *No Future without Forgiveness* (New York: Doubleday, 1999).

Part I

IDENTITY AND CULTURE

CHAPTER ONE

BEARING WITNESS TO HOPE

Personal Identity and Public Memorials

Sara Shady

"Hope, after all, is not knowledge of future events,
but living out of the conviction that there is meaning in history
and that our actions do in fact make a difference."[1]

O n our first morning in South Africa, we toured Soweto. I was instantly immersed in the contrasts that are South Africa. In Soweto is it possible to simultaneously feel anger—at the injustices of the Afrikaner regime during Apartheid; compassion—for the poor who live with the ongoing effects of structural injustice; and joy—for this vibrant community that has emerged and continues to grow on the outskirts of Johannesburg. These conflicting moods began to affect me more deeply as our large tour bus turned onto the small roads where people piece together homes out of cardboard and tin. Unable to process the guilty discomfort of voyeurism, of being merely a passive spectator of someone else's life struggles, I stopped looking out the window. The weight of privilege sat heavily on my shoulders, and it would grow as the day continued.

At the Hector Pieterson Memorial, I learned that I was born exactly ten days before Hector Pieterson died. The contrasts became more personal. Born into the world of middle-class, white America, I experienced a childhood free of evident oppression. There were no issues personally pressing enough in my youth to drive me, like Hector, to risk my life for a political cause. Apartheid was a distant system I learned about in school, but evidently it never affected me personally. Now, however, as a political philosopher, I learn, write, and teach about oppressive systems. I have learned to identify the ways in which race, gender, class, religion, sexuality, age, and ability intersect to create structured systems of privilege and oppression. While I continue to live in a world that is easy for me to navigate without much personal contact with structural oppression, my studies lead me to ponder the responsibilities I have as a beneficiary of racial and economic privilege.

The goal of this essay is to reflect on the personal and public responsibilities we have to address systems of oppression. *How can an individual avoid being an aloof and passive spectator into the world of the oppressed and use personal power to be a voice for justice? How can we collectively point toward the hope of reconciliation and unity in the midst of fear of what we do not know or understand? How do we promote social change in spite of the things that we cannot change about ourselves?* Using the work of Martin Buber and Eboo Patel, I will argue for the need to forge lives that bear witness to truth and to hope. Using the visual and ideological tensions between the Voortrekker Monument and Freedom Park as a background, I will explore the relationship between public memorials and personal identity to demonstrate how the stories we tell can shape the worlds in which we live.

Bearing Witness: The Stories We Tell

In his famous work, *I and Thou*, Martin Buber argues that human beings are fundamentally relational. We can never be completely severed from our relationships with God, the natural world, and other human beings. The nature of these relationships, however, fluctuates between the mode of relating to other as I-It, where the self maintains the power to analyze, categorize, define, and determine the value of her experience with the other, and the mode of relating to other as I-Thou, where the self is a "receptive beholder" of the other in a manner that allows the other voice to speak to the self. Essential to Buber's argument is the notion that either mode of relation affects not only the other, but also the self. When I relate to the other as I-It, I impose myself as the subject of the relationship and the other is defined as an object—of my use, my action, and my experience. When, on the other hand, I relate to the other as I-Thou, I actualize my whole personhood. I am not merely a rational subject, instead I am conscious of myself as co-existing and deeply interacting with other persons who can both confirm and challenge my view of the world and of myself. For Buber, the mode of being in relation as I-It is not necessarily wrong, but it is limited. And, a limited perspective that only reflects my view of the other can easily become passive observation, or unilateral "doing unto," or even harden into hatred for and oppression of the other. I must navigate the world of It in order to make rational sense of my experiences and accomplish my goals. If this is the only world I encounter, however, I will fail to see the world for what it really is, a place where God is always present and pushing back. I will also fail to see myself for who I really am, a person in relation not only to objects and things, but to a lively creation. As Buber famously writes, "Without *It*, man cannot live. But he who lives with It alone is not a man."[2]

According to Buber, every meeting between I and Thou provides a portal through which we can glimpse the Eternal Thou. Since every I-Thou encounter is a temporary and fleeting moment, gone as soon as I reflect upon it, the question that must be answered is how these meetings affect my life in the world of It. According to Buber, these encounters are never merely for my own spiritual benefit. As he explains, "Meeting with God does not come to man in order that he may concern himself with God, but in order that he may confirm that there is meaning in the world."[3] The problem, as Buber recognizes it, is that "Again and again man brings about, instead of realization, a reflexion to Him who reveals: he wishes to concern himself with God instead of with the world."[4] The task, therefore, is to bear witness in one's everyday life to those moments of meaningful encounter that reveal the world of Thou. Buber describes the person who takes on this task as one who "knows well that he cannot simply confront the people with whom he has to deal as so many carriers of the You, without undoing his own work. Nevertheless he ventures to do this . . . he serves the truth which, though supra-rational, does not disown reason but holds it in her lap."[5]

This person is "a man who knows that he cannot actualize the You in some pure fashion but who nevertheless bears witness of it daily to the It."[6]

What would it mean to be people who bear witness to the truth of privilege and oppression in daily life? Eboo Patel, founder and leader of the Interfaith Youth Core, addresses this issue in his work on the challenge of religious diversity in the contemporary world. In many of his speeches, Patel emphasizes the importance of the narratives we choose to tell. Patel often tells the story of a community of Egyptian immigrants in Jersey City, New Jersey, half of whom are Christian and half of whom are Muslim.[7] For decades, the Christians and Muslims lived together peacefully and collaboratively, until a day in January 2005 when a family of four Egyptian Coptic Christians were brutally murdered, execution style. Before anything was known about the identity of the killers, a leader in the Christian community said, as Patel tells the story, "This looks like something that Muslims would do." According to Patel, the community leader "chose to define reality for the community" in the sense that he "chose to tell a story of Muslims and Christians in perpetual and inherent conflict." Since that day, the community has remained fractured, even though the persons eventually charged with the crime were not Muslim. Patel goes on to imagine that instead of defining reality in a divisive manner, the community leader had publically said, "We as the citizens of Jersey City stand tall and proud and together as a community of pluralism against whatever extremists who might violate that effort." For Patel, this positive story would have had the power to preserve community and prompt a positive response to the violence.

Patel emphasizes the importance of storytelling because it "moves the encounter from competing notions of 'Truth' to varied human experiences of life, which possess the unique quality of being both infinite and common."[8] This approach emulates Buber's contrast between I-It, where I speak my view of the truth and label the other to fit my perspective, and I-Thou, where our relationship bears witness to the truth beyond us that unites us.

On the level of public discourse, Patel maintains that it is not enough for us to tell stories within our own traditions, we must share those stories as well. By building bridges between different faith communities, we affirm "the identity of the constituent communities while emphasizing that the well-being of each and all depends on the health of the whole." Sharing stories reflects "the belief that the common good is best served when each community has a chance to make its unique contribution."[9] The model of pluralism he envisions is "neither mere coexistence nor forced consensus."[10] Rather it actively encourages an ongoing dialogue between citizens from various perspectives.

Our visits in South Africa brought us into contact with a variety of communal stories and self-revelations, and here are two of the more striking ones. I can only guess how the ongoing dialogue implicit between them might play out in that nation, but they prompted me to think about similar dialogues we need to have in the United States.

A Tale of Two Memorials

A famous African proverb states "until lions have their own historians, tales of the hunt shall always glorify the hunters." In light of the persistent question of how to overcome the divide between oppression and privilege, I believe we must tell complete stories and develop new narratives in order to point to the truth and the hope beyond the structural systems that divide us. The Voortrekker Monument and the contrasting Freedom Park both provide illustrations of Patel's emphasis on the power of narrative to unite or divide. Even more powerful, however, is the third narrative that emerges from the fact that both monuments are intentionally held together in the midst of their separate and contrasting stories. Noting the parallel here to the movement between I-It and I-Thou, we can reflect on ways in which public memorials can either reify limited and harmful views of the world or bear witness to truth and hope.

Both the Voortrekker Monument and Freedom Park tell stories. Of the two, it is much more obvious that the Voortrekker Monument does not bear witness to the full truth. According to the monument's official website, "The majestic Voortrekker Monument is situated in the northern part of South Africa in the Pretoria (Tshwane) region in a nature reserve. It is a unique Monument which commemorates the Pioneer history of Southern Africa and the history of the Afrikaner and is situated in a beautiful setting."[11] But what we discovered at the site was that the pioneers, and their victory over the Zulu, are commemorated in a manner that uses power and Providence to rationalize and justify oppression. The Voortrekkers' side of the story is told; the voices of the Zulu are silent. The Voortrekkers are depicted as both the recipients and bearers of God's goodness while the Zulu are portrayed as violent savages who deserved to be suppressed.

To enter the monument, one must past through an iron gate with assegais motifs, a gate that "symbolises the might of Dingane who blocked access to the country's interior. Once through the gate, the visitor stands inside a big wagon laager that symbolically protects the Monument."[12] Inside the monument, friezes and tapestries graphically represent the "Great Trek" from Cape Town to the area surrounding Pretoria, including Zulu attacks on pioneer women and children as well as the decisive defeat of the Zulu at Blood River on December 16, 1838. The monument is built so that the sun will shine directly through the dome on top of the building each year on December 16 and illuminate and venerate the "cenotaph," or tomblike memorial to the Voortrekkers.

The Voortrekker Monument continues to be one of the most visited tourist sites in South Africa. For many, it remains an important celebration of Afrikaner life and culture. At times it is still used as a stage for radical white supremacists' political rallies. There is nothing at the monument site that attempts to present alternative stories of South African history or apologize for the wrongs of apartheid. Everything about the monument seems contrary to the emerging progressive democratic narrative of the new South Africa. This raises an important question about why the monument remains standing, when it memorializes a story the nation is trying to overcome.

The monument's existence has been challenged in many ways since the end of apartheid. Originally, some called for it to be taken down, defaced, or superseded by the construction of a nearby new monument—an initial proposal imagined a bronze sculpture of Mandela's fist pushing into the sky.[13] Others have challenged the power and meaning of the Voortrekker by reinterpreting its symbolism. For example, when ANC politician Tokyo Sexwale's visit to the monument was published in the *Sunday Times*, he responded to the sixty-four-wagon laager by stating, "Now I understand the laager mentality. But I'm glad there is a gateway, or the whole Afrikaner nation would have been trapped inside."[14] And speaking specifically about this assegais gate he maintained, "It was precisely the assegais at its height that turned the tide . . . the spear of the nation, opened up the path of civilization."[15] Ultimately it was decided that the Voortrekker Monument should be preserved, but juxtaposed with Freedom

Park, a contrasting monument and symbolic form of reparation. This decision bears witness to the hope that is promised in South Africa's emerging democracy. By allowing the Voortrekker Monument to remain a visible part of the national heritage, South Africa has actually opened up the possibility for the monument itself, and the story it tells, to be called into question. These questions open up dialogue that can bear witness to a more inclusive truth.

Officially, Freedom Park is described as "a monument to democracy, which was founded on the values of human dignity, rights and freedom. It serves as a symbol of the tortuous journey to and the sacrifices made for freedom."[16] In contrast to the very limited perspective offered by the Voortrekker Monument, Freedom Park tells a story that both honors the oppressed and celebrates all of humanity. Freedom Park points beyond a history of struggle to the plurality of peoples and perspectives that must be held together in order to move forward.

The construction of Freedom Park began in 2000, as one of eleven Presidential Legacy projects undertaken by the South African government's Department of Arts and Culture to establish public symbols of South Africa's history and heritage. The park attempts to commemorate the history of all peoples in the story of Southern Africa, dating back 3.6 billion years. The park is truly inclusive in this attempt. One of the hallmark features of the park is S'khumbuto Memorial, which remembers all of the conflicts in South Africa's past. The Wall of Names in this area of the park commemorates seventy-five thousand who have died for freedom in various conflicts throughout South African history, including Afrikaners who died in concentration camps at the hands of the English during the Boer War. Other features include a resting place for the dead comprised of materials from all of South Africa's provinces, an eternal flame for unknown heroes, and a hall of leaders in the struggle for democracy. Freedom Park also symbolically represents the cleansing and healing that must continue to take place for the new democracy of the "Rainbow Nation" to thrive.

While walking on Mveledzo, the spiral path that "links all [segments of Freedom Park] into one unified whole,"[17] it is possible to see the Voortrekker Monument. Hence, the existence of the other is confirmed in the world of Freedom Park. But the distant Voortrekker is experienced as one small part of the larger story encountered along the Mveledzo. It is only by bearing inclusive witness to all of the truths of South Africa that Freedom Park is able to accomplish its mission: "To provide a pioneering and empowering heritage destination in order to mobilise for reconciliation and nation building in our country; to reflect upon our past, improving our present and building our future as a united nation; and to contribute continentally and internationally to the formation of better human understanding among nations and peoples."[18] Notice that the mission statement itself redefines the term "pioneer." In fulfilling this mission, Freedom Park opens a relationship of I-Thou, calling the Voortrekker monument into question, while at the same time confirming its presence in a way that actually enhances the story and power of Freedom Park.

The paradox of the two monuments together provides a glimpse of the power we have to transcend and transform difficult histories. The construction of Freedom Park in tension with the Voortrekker Monument does not by itself solve the problem of finding meaningful unity in South Africa. It does not exclude the possibility that some will unapologetically continue to celebrate Afrikaner heritage without contextualizing that heritage amidst competing stories. Nor does it appease the voices of those who continue to experience pain from the existence of the Voortrekker and the ideology that it symbolizes. Additionally, the existence of these two monuments does not prompt critical reflection on South Africa's relationship to the rest of Africa. Yet, in the midst of these limitations, however, the ongoing dialogue between the two monuments, standing in tension, bears witness to the potential hope of the new South Africa. The robust democracy emerging in South Africa itself bears witness to the rest of the world of the hope and possibility of reconciliation. The paradox of the monuments pushes us to extend our thoughts beyond the stories that they represent to other stories, including contested views of the American past.

Bringing the Stories Home

If my experiences in South Africa stay in South Africa and do not affect my life in North America, I fail to bear witness to the truth. If I am to avoid the all-too-common academic posture of voyeurism, these reflections on the process of reconciliation in South Africa must also call into question the challenges to find unity amidst diversity and address issues of privilege and oppression at home. Peering into the world of South Africa in order to analyze, categorize, label, and evaluate limits me to the mode of I-It. A genuine encounter with South

Africa as Thou must necessarily influence the I. So the questions I must ask include: *What sort of person must I be to bear witness to the hope for reconciliation at home as well as abroad? How do I overcome my own prejudices and privileges?*

While walking along the Mveledzo path that winds through Freedom Park, I was overcome by the memory of America's own history of injustices. As I wrestled with the idea that the Voortrekker Monument is still allowed to stand only a few miles away, I realized anew our failure to question and challenge the celebration of the American pioneer. In most small towns in the Midwest, festivals celebrating pioneer life and culture are annual events. Native American culture is typically not represented, or it is represented without any attempt to provide a meaningful story that contests the celebration of pioneer culture and narrates how these cultures came to overlap. Even though we have museums and monuments that bear witness to the truth of Native American culture and history, the stories they tell are not prevalent in public discourse and they rarely challenge the dominant paradigms. One of our most celebrated holidays, Thanksgiving Day, tells the story of "pilgrims" and "Indians," but we do not have a national conversation about the rest of the story. We do not talk about or try to visually represent the oppression, theft of land, loss of life, and cultural destruction.

The analogy between American Pioneers and Voortrekkers can be striking, both in terms of the similarity between historical events and how they have been represented as well as the contrast in public response to the events and their visual representations. To illustrate this, it is helpful to reflect on an example recently debated in American government.

The Ariel Rios Federal Building in Washington, DC, houses several murals created in the 1930s as part of the New Deal Era federal arts program. Six murals in particular have come under concern for their stereotypically negative representation of Native Americans. There is a strong visual analogy between the Voortrekker reliefs and tapestries and these murals, notably Frank Mechau's "Dangers of the Mail" and William Palmer's "Covered Wagons Attacked by Indians," both of which portray white men, women, and children under attack by natives and using their guns to fight off the enemies. The visual contrasts between white settlers'"innocence" and Native Americans'"savagery" are impossible to miss. The Ariel Rios Building is on the National Register of Historic Places and now houses the Environmental Protection Agency (EPA).

A few years ago, both visitors to the building and employees of the EPA began to complain about the public display of these images, and the U.S. General Services Administration (GSA) held a series of hearings on the issue. The GSA has chosen to resolve the issue by building a screen in front of Mechau's "Dangers of the Mail" mural, so that individuals can choose whether or not to view the mural. Along with the screen, interpretive materials will be designed and installed to help contextualize and interpret all of the murals housed in the building.[19]

In spite of the clear comparison between the Ariel Rios murals and Voortrekker reliefs, the GSA's decision regarding the murals provides a stark contrast between how the American and South African governments are choosing to deal with a difficult past. The GSA has chosen to resolve the issue by building a screen in front of Mechau's "Dangers of the Mail" mural, so that individuals can choose whether or not to view the mural. Along with the screen, interpretive materials will be designed and installed to help contextualize and interpret all of the murals housed in the building.

This decision illuminates a glaring difference in how both nations have responded to a history of oppression in a contemporary democracy. In the United States, reflection on and reconciliation with our imperialist past remains optional. The South African government, on the other hand, has decided that this reflection and reconciliation must be intentional. This difference is reflected in the preamble to South Africa's constitution, which states: "We, the people of South Africa, Recognise the injustices of our past; Honour those who suffered for justice and freedom in our land; Respect those who have worked to build and develop our country; and Believe that South Africa belongs to all who live in it, united in our diversity." Contrast this with the preamble to the United States constitution: "We the People of the United States, in Order to form a more perfect Union, establish Justice, insure domestic Tranquility, provide for the common defense, promote the general Welfare, and secure the Blessings of Liberty to ourselves and our Posterity, do ordain and establish this Constitution for the United States of America."[20]

It seems implausible, if not impossible, that Americans will be able to form a "more perfect union" out of a history of oppression if we do not actively recognize, reflect upon, and dialogue about that history. As the African-American philosopher, Cornel West, argues, until we acknowledge the "painful truth . . . that the enslavement of Africans and the imperial expansion over indigenous peoples and their lands were undeniable preconditions" for the making of America, we cannot mature as a democracy.[21] Arguably, we will not be able to have a robust and truly pluralist democracy until we wrestle with this past.

American culture is not entirely void of examples of public critical engagement with our past. For example, the Crazy Horse Memorial stands in dialogue with Mount Rushmore. The National Museum of the American Indian (NMAI) in Washington, DC, is situated between the Smithsonian's National Air and Space Museum and the U.S. Capitol Building. The architecture of the NMAI itself, constructed to symbolically represent Native American views of space, time, and nature, offers a visual contrast to the celebration of Greco-Roman civilization provided by the other buildings. But, for the most part, public and private discourse about our national identity and heritage still neglects and ignores the fact that the United States has been an aggressive empire from the very beginning of its nationhood. In addition to reflective conversations about our relationship with Native Americans, we also need to sustain a variety of "truth and reconciliation" dialogues, private and public, with fellow citizens of African, Latino, Pacific Islander, Caribbean Islander, Filipino and East Asian descent whose stories have been stamped by Euro-American aggression.

Hope beyond Privilege and Oppression?

This reflection on American history in conversation with the South African past highlights structural challenges that must be addressed if we are to move together beyond the legacies of oppression and privilege. It also raises important personal questions about taking on the role of a witness versus that of a voyeur, about being a participant, not merely an observer.

One of the most important things that I learned as a participant in the seminar is that I have a responsibility to bear witness to my encounter with both the Voortrekker Monument and Freedom Park by continuing to wrestle, in visible ways, with America's imperial past and my own status as a beneficiary of that past. Where I can and when I can, I must bear witness to the truth by challenging limited, assumed, or false views. I must avoid the temptation to consider myself the perennial subject surrounded by a world of objects at the mercy of my definitions, descriptions, and evaluations. Instead I must allow my encounters to define, describe, and evaluate me in a manner that transforms my understanding of the world. Where I can and when I can, I must bear witness to hope by living a life that gives testimony to reconciliation and positive change. I must choose to tell the stories of hope emerging in spite of fear and the stories of unity forged even amidst real and significant differences. I must live out the truth to which I testify. Patel recalls that "the great rabbi, Abraham Joshua Heschel, once said, 'First we begin in sound and then we must move to deed.' Stories are just the beginning. They provide a powerful call to action, to a better self, for each of us individually, for our religious communities, for our nation, and for our world. However, without action their full potential for social change remains unrealized."[22] Echoing this idea is Buber's statement that "what one believes is important, but still more important is how one believes it."[23]

More specifically, my experience in South Africa has reminded me that it is often easier to care about problems and issues that are distant from us. I can reflect on the challenges faced by South Africa's emerging democracy with some amount of comfort, because I am not responsible for implementing the changes I might envision. To genuinely bear witness to what I have learned in South Africa, I must turn my attention as an educator and scholar to the problems in my own country. For example, how can I integrate Native American narratives into my teaching of structural systems of oppression and privilege? How might reflections on the relationship between the State of Minnesota and the Ojibwe and Dakota tribes inform my thinking about finding unity amidst diversity and fostering healthy civic societies?

Just as there remains much to be done to open a more complete dialogue about American history and culture, so also we must remember that South Africa's story is also in progress. We should not imagine, of course, that South Africa has found a way to resolve all racial and ethnic tensions and bridge the divide between the privileged and the oppressed. But the story of South Africa points to a path we have not yet taken. South Africa's public decision to hold all pieces of its past and present in tension bears witness to the possibility of new, inclusive narratives that tell the story of both the lion and the hunter, and the existence they share.

Notes to Chapter One

[1] John De Gruchy, "A Theology for a Just Democratic World Order," in *Christianity and Democracy: A Theology for a Just World Order* (Cambridge: Cambridge University Press, 1995), 232.

[2] Martin Buber, *I and Thou*, trans. Ronald Gregor Smith (Boston: Charles Scribner's Sons, 1958), 34.

[3] Ibid., 115.

[4] Ibid.

[5] Martin Buber, *I and Thou*, trans. Walter Kauffmann (New York: Simon & Schuster, 1970), 98.

[6] Ibid., 99.

[7] See for example, Eboo Patel, "Is Interfaith Understanding Possible?," speech given at the Westminster Town Hall Forum, Minneapolis, Minnesota, May 7, 2009, accessed December 3, 2009, http://minnesota.publicradio.org/display/web/2009/05/08/midday1/.

[8] Eboo Patel, "Storytelling as a Key Methodology for Interfaith Work," *Journal of Ecumenical Studies*, 43.2 (Spring 2008): 35–46.

[9] Eboo Patel, *Acts of Faith* (Boston: Beacon Press, 2007), xv.

[10] Ibid.

[11] Voortrekker Monument and Natural Reserve, accessed December 1, 2009, http://www.voortrekkermon.org.za/index2.html.

[12] Ibid.

[13] Annie Coombes, *History After Apartheid* (Durham: Duke University Press, 2003), 22.

[14] Andrew Unsworth, "Tokyo's Groot Trek," *Sunday Times*, 15 December 1996. Sexwale was the premier of Gauteng province at the time of the visit.

[15] Ibid.

[16] Bathandwa Mbola, "South Africa's Freedom Park," September 23, 2008, http://www.southafrica.info/about/history/park-230908.htm.

[17] Ibid.

[18] Ibid.

[19] More information on the Ariel Rios murals, along with information about the murals, artists, and public debate can be found at "Ariel Rios Murals," U.S. General Services Administration, last updated June 30, 2011, http://www.gsa.gov/portal/content/104979.

[20] This issue is discussed at length by Eduard Fagan, "The Constitutional Entrenchment of Memory," in *Negotiating the Past: The Making of Memory in South Africa*, edited by Sarah Nuttall and Carli Coetzee (Cape Town: Oxford University Press, 1998), pp. 249–262.

[21] Cornel West, *Democracy Matters* (New York: Penguin Press, 2004), 41.

[22] Patel, "Storytelling," 46.

[23] Martin Buber, *Pointing the Way*, trans. and ed. Maurice Friedman (New York: Harper and Brothers, 1957), 104.

CHAPTER TWO

DIVISIVE SYMBOLS IN A POST/CONFLICT SETTING

Scott Moeschberger

Among developmental psychologists, the term "schema" describes the filter through which one views the world and makes sense of it. From Jean Piaget's early theorizing to the findings of modern-day cognitive research, there is a fundamental agreement among psychologists that we use significant events, memories, and symbols as ways to organize and make sense of the world around us—this is our schema. Upon introduction to the Voortrekker Monument, I realized that I was experiencing a cultural icon that contributes to a schema. Sitting on a hill, dominating the landscape, reaching high above the tree line, the monument is more than a building; it is a living memory, a collection of memories that shape a cultural identity. This impression was strengthened as I listened to the history of the monument, witnessed cultural events taking place that day that gave the experience breath, and walked through the dark story of blood and covenant oaths that is told within the walls.

My understanding of the import of this living monument continued to grow as I spoke with South African residents about my visit. When mentioning the Voortrekker visit to others, I heard reactions and descriptions that ranged from national pride to deep anger. It was almost as though I visited with a long-time enemy or a close family friend. Even within the ambivalence conveyed by Piet Meiring, the retired theology professor from South Africa who introduced us to the monument, there was a depth of emotion that spoke to the challenge surrounding any attempt to make sense of the monument in the current climate of reconciliation in the country. Even among our international delegation of scholars there were varied responses, from the gloom of oppression to a sympathy for a one-time powerful culture that is clinging to its past.

The range of reactions reminded me of my own experience living and working in Ireland and Northern Ireland, surrounding the issue of parades. Parades in Northern Ireland remain one of the most contentious and emotionally explosive issues facing the peace agreement today. Every 12th of July, a celebration of Protestant Unionism (those who wish to remain in the United Kingdom) unfolds in bonfires, the prominent display of the "Union Jack" flag, and marching. This date marks the Battle of the Boyne, in which the Protestant William of Orange defeated the Catholic King James II for the throne of England. The battle took place in Ireland. The defeat of James gave rise to what is often referred to as the Protestant Ascendency in Ireland, ultimately resulting in the colonization of the whole of Ireland, with a particularly strong population in the Northeast corner by Scottish Presbyterians.[1] The transition of power brought with it a redistribution of land and wealth from Catholic (at that time the majority) to Protestant landowners. Many Irish historians note that these events marked the shift in what became a three hundred-year conflict between the Irish and the English.

As a symbol of Protestant Unionism, the parades often use the imagery of William of Orange and several prominent Protestant reformers such as Martin Luther and John Calvin. It would not be uncommon in these parades to see large banners depicting William's likeness on one side and Luther on the other. In addition, the parades traditionally attempt to follow routes that pass through neighborhoods that would be predominantly Catholic. Historically, this would often lead to tensions that would escalate from verbal taunts and rock-throwing to riots and larger scale violence.

Not surprisingly, the Republicans or Nationalists, who seek a united Ireland and are typically Catholic, view the parading of Unionists through their neighborhoods as triumphalism. They resent the blatant reminder of Protestant control over their society, despite the Catholic persuasion of the majority of the population of the broader island. While this perspective is understandable, many Protestants within Northern Ireland view the parades and the celebrations surrounding "the 12th" as part of a cultural heritage that is focused on connecting with faith, family, and nation.

While living in Ireland, I was struck by similarities to an American symbol that, like the Voortrekker in South Africa and parades in Northern Ireland, elicits strong reactions. Somewhat oddly and perhaps related to the close relationship between the countries, this symbol is commandeered in Ireland as a tongue-in-cheek way to comment on geographical rivalries. In Armagh, while waiting for a bus, a lorry pulled up that was flying the Confederate battle flag with the inscription "the South will rise again." Similarly, the Confederate flag is featured prominently by fans of County Cork (known by some as the "Rebels") when they show up to support their hurling and Irish football teams. This irony was not lost on some of my white American students who bristled when they viewed so many Confederate flags. It is an uncomfortable reminder of the complicated oppression found in our own heritage.

Traveling to both the Slave Lodge in Cape Town and to Goree Island off the coast of Senegal has increased my own recognition of how the Western world benefited from three hundred years of slavery. It is tempting to examine other divided symbols and miss the ones at our doorstep. The powerful symbol of the Confederate battle flag still today evokes strong (and opposing) reactions by various groups. Some link the flag to white supremacy, but others claim it as a powerful representation of their broader Southern heritage.

The symbolism of the Confederate flag seems to overstep the simple association with the geography of the civil war. Many of my students in Grant County, Indiana, have observed with some confusion the use of the Confederate flag in this area. Assuming that there are not an unusual amount of émigrés from the South, why do so many homes and trucks fly the Confederate flag? Is it a statement supporting the cause of Southern slave owners and the oppression of blacks or an indication of some kind of solidarity with states' rights and the desire for independence from the federal government? It is not unreasonable to see racist overtones in a Northern area where the Confederate flag is commonly flown. Grant County was the location of the last lynching in the Northern States (in the year 1930) and still harbors racial tensions. The sight of the old courthouse where the lynching was held still holds power for many black citizens in the city of Marion.

Friends from the South would be appalled at this implication of racism and assert that, no, it is simply a part of being a Southerner, and taking pride in that geographical heritage. This very topic was hotly debated in regards to whether the South Carolina state capitol building ought to fly the Confederate flag.[2] (The flag continues to fly today, and to face regular public protests.) The example of the Confederate flag illustrates that America, too, is faced with some of these powerful schematic symbols that elicit both pride and oppression. Does the Confederate flag represent a cultural heritage that has been neglected by historians and media, or does it symbolize hatred, discrimination, and white supremacy? This raises broader questions about how to remember the American civil war appropriately. How is that aspect of history taught in schools? Was it a Northern crusade against slavery or Southern resistance to imperial aggression? These are not questions with easy answers. Nor is there a simple answer to the question of how one treats schema-forming cultural symbols that elicit such powerful but polarized responses.

More Than a Symbol; Part of an Identity

There seems to be little disagreement as to what the Voortrekker represents. Dedicated in 1949, at the beginning of the National Party's rule and of apartheid, the monument serves as a reminder of the vow that the Afrikaner people made, which they believed was honored by God. The South African theologian, John De Gruchy, explains: "The vow or covenant thus became a cornerstone of the ideology of apartheid, the heartbeat of Afrikaner civil religion as celebrated in the Voortrekker monument in Pretoria. It (the vow) provided divine justification for maintaining a separate Afrikaner nation, for the policy of apartheid and the entrenchment of white power."[3] As a symbol, the monument serves as not only a memorial to the events of Blood River but as a visual marker to a people's cultural, religious, and political heritage. As Donald Akenson reflects on his experience with the Voortrekker "it is an extraordinary structure, not only a monument to a culture's past but also as a map of a collective mind. The monument is a national museum for the Afrikaners, but it could just as well serve as a defensive outpost."[4]

The Voortrekker undoubtedly is one of the remaining "hot places" in South Africa. Psychologist Vamaik Volkan notes that a "hot place" is a "physical location that individually and collectively induces (or reinduces) immediate and intense feelings among members of an ethnic or other large group."[5] These hot places serve as an identity marker for a people group. They become a mental representation of events that connect members of a group in an invisible way. These identity markers serve as a symbol of collective memories that have evolved through traditions and stories passed down from generations.

Zdzislaw Mach provides a helpful anthropological analysis of the use of symbols in conflict and identity development. In short, Mach highlights the importance of context in understanding symbols when he notes "the same object can symbolize two quite different ideas and emotions, and the particular meaning depends on the context within which the symbol is used."[6] This is certainly the case in seeking to understand the Voortrekker.

The power of the Voortrekker lies in its simplicity. Inside the walls is a large space, surrounded by twenty-seven ornate, bas-relief marble carvings that convey the story of Blood River. The sarcophagus commemorating Voortrekker leader and martyr Piet Retief lies bare with minimal decoration. The monument's vast size almost overshadows the stories that are told, as they are eclipsed by the open space. Initially, I felt almost disappointed by the inside. After looking from the outside, I expected more. As I stood inside and reflected, this changed. While it might seem that this layout would almost minimize the stories, the opposite somehow occurs. The massive structure has a singular, simple message: one story, one people, one God, one covenant. This is what gives this identity marker its power. The design allows for the collective memories of the people to further the story in ceremony and celebration. A consciousness is born that expands past ideology to create a symbol that represents a heritage. This evolution from ideology to heritage is the breath that gives these markers sustainable life. In the case of our visit, a costumed dancing troupe of children at the entrance was a sign that this monument represented more than just a memorial. A culture was being celebrated and taught to children. A heritage and a piece of their identity were being formed.

Again, I refer back to my experience in Northern Ireland with the parades. Although the parades are not a physical marker or monument, they certainly would classify as "hot places." For many in the Unionist communities, the festivities on the "Twelfth" would be viewed as a celebration that represents more than ideology. It would be a family event in which children and relatives enjoy bonfires, cultural events, and pageantry. As one young man from a Unionist community in Northern Ireland commented, "Growing up I didn't even know what we were celebrating, but that it was a time to celebrate, eat candy, and watch the bands."[7] Parades serve as transgenerational events that connect individuals to their families. This Unionist young man went on to describe the great sadness he would feel if the parades and celebration were taken away. He recalled the fond memories he had with his father, brothers, and uncles in the parades and other events. He too wanted to share these memories with his son.

From another community, a Nationalist man recalls how his family would either leave town or lock themselves in their house as the parade would pass by. For him, the event was simply "triumphalism" and "symbolic of the oppression of Nationalist communities for the past 300 years."[8]

In both cases, the symbols have become more than an ideology. They are a way to connect with past generations, celebrate a heritage, and to some degree, express their religiosity. They have become part of the individual's social identity. Tajfel and Turner's seminal work on "Social Identity Theory"[9] is helpful in understanding the social dynamics that seem to be demonstrated in these symbols. Tajfel and Turner hypothesized that our individual sense of self is represented in the larger group's identity. Individuals tend to categorize and identify with some large group identity and make comparisons to other groups (out-groups) to establish the group identity to which they belong (in-group). Most relevant to this discussion is the personal sense of self that is drawn from these categorizations and comparisons. Ultimately our own self-esteem and personal identity are influenced by this process. This is the danger in the identity markers or "hot places." They are, to some extent, a source of identity and connection for every individual who claims membership to the group.

This is the great challenge in answering the question of what to do with these deeply dividing symbols in a post-conflict society. How do we begin the process of healing and reconciliation when so much of group identity and personal identity is represented in the symbols? Following the logical steps in Social Identity Theory, an even greater danger lies in the removal of such significant symbols when there are no replacement symbols or markers. The individual sense of self that has drawn strength from such membership is left with an uneasy void. This void creates a sense of anxiety, fear, and resentment that could ultimately lead to people aggressively taking up symbols and "causes" that attempt to recreate nationalist ideals. The combination of loss, fear, and bitterness becomes a fertile environment for extremism and hyper-nationalism. To some degree, this would be the case in post-WWI Germany, where a cultural void led to the rise of the Third Reich.

If straightforward removing or banning the symbol is not the answer, what option does society have to deal with such powerful symbols of cultural, religious, and social identity? This question is particularly thorny in a setting in which these symbols signify oppression, triumphalism, and an ideology that was used to inflict pain on so many.

Possible Future Directions

When faced with the prospect of future decisions, three options seem to emerge: Dismantle, Complement, or Transform.

Dismantle: This option entails the removal of the symbols from society. The dangers of this approach are discussed above, however there are times when symbols are considered too divisive or are eliminated by a conquering group. A prime example of this would be the banning of the swastika following the Nazi regime in Germany. The symbol is essentially so divisive that the only option for healing is complete removal. One important caveat with this approach is the risk of eliminating the cultural history of groups.

Complement: Here society attempts to "complement" the symbols with other symbols that balance or tell a different story. This approach seems to be used ineffectively in the Voortrekker monument with the creation of the Zulu museum, which presents a re-interpretation of the battle of Blood River from a Zulu cultural perspective. It is perhaps more effective with the Freedom Park peace museum that sits on the next hillside. When viewed together, the monuments tell a larger story that depicts a fuller history and identity. A possible drawback of this approach (though a downfall avoided by Freedom Park) is the potential that the symbols would become rivals, increasing a sense of separateness rather than an integrated piece of identity.

Transform: The last option can turn a painful symbol into a powerful piece of reconciliation. This approach is empathy-focused, encouraging reconciliation with "others" as well as reconciliation within the "we." In a sense, groups must look inward and deal with their past to determine how to move forward. The most difficult piece of the forgiveness puzzle is the thorny question concerning how the oppressed group can value the oppressor when the culture is tied closely with the oppression. One perspective is to give them space to make changes themselves. Ultimately, the issues of the Voortrekker and parades can only be decided by the Afrikaners and Ulster Protestants, respectively.

Sometimes a changed context can be an effective route to transform the meaning of a symbol.[10] In attempting to achieve transformation, the symbol can be re-interpreted in a new or altered context. If the once oppressed group can highlight and affirm the positive cultural aspects with a condemnation of the negative, it is possible to redeem the usefulness of the symbol. A wonderful illustration of this is highlighted in the recent film *Invictus*. Despite the initial disapproval of his friends, family, and party, Mandela wears the national rugby jersey—a symbol of Afrikaner pride and therefore of white oppression. Ultimately, he helped create a context that permanently changed the symbol. It is important to note a significant difference here. Unlike parades and the Voortrekker, there is nothing inherently oppressive in the jersey, making it easier to shift what it symbolized. However, this example provides an important and hopeful model of an altered symbol.

Another route to transformation is through the development of empathy for the "out-group." Empathy rehumanizes the "other." The greater understanding that one group has for the experiences of the other, the more able they will be to broaden their view of the events of the past and its associated symbols. There is some empirical evidence for these links, derived from my research in Northern Ireland.[11] Empathy has a strong link to forgiveness of the other community following violence or oppression. Increased levels of empathy and forgiveness create an environment where the possibility exists for healthy dialogue about contentious symbols. The challenge for the social scientist is discovering how to create an empathic experience that fosters understanding. This can happen in a variety of ways, but it is important for communities and leaders to find ways in which mutual dialogue can occur, whether through mixed education, sport, or reconciliation programs.

Covenantal ideology is embedded in the rhetoric of both South Africa and Northern Ireland. Akenson discusses the view of covenants or vows in people groups who view themselves as exclusively chosen by God.[12] We see this scenario in apartheid theology where the Voortrekker Monument celebrates a vow to God that if He will provide victory to the Boers over the Zulu, then they will honor Him. In Ulster in 1912, the Solemn League and Covenant was signed by nearly the entire population of Protestant males.[13] James Craig, Prime Minister in Northern Ireland some two decades later, publicly advocated this ideology, noting his objective of "carrying out a Protestant government for a Protestant people."[14]

John De Gruchy advocates a returning of the notion of Covenant to a true biblical context: "For the idea of covenant, truly understood both theologically and politically, can provide the framework within which we can think and act together to overcome and heal the past, restructure power relations, restore justice, and develop a common vision for the future."[15] This view of Covenant moves beyond the idea of select people groups and places all of humanity on equal footing, made in the image of God. The ability to recognize both our own propensity to sin and our own value to God allows us to see both of these in our fellow humans, and therefore to empathize with them. De Gruchy goes on to note that a covenantal relationship is more concerned with reconciliation than co-existence. One can hope that a post-conflict society can develop a peace that is more than the absence of violence. Relating this peace-making to symbols, a complementary approach (e.g., adding a balancing monument) may facilitate a peaceful co-existence. A transformative approach hopes for the next step of creating a shared identity, or at least one that takes into account the experience of the other.

An obvious difficulty in this endeavor of transforming the symbols is that it is ultimately up to the group to which the symbol "belongs" to decide what must be done. For instance, Robben Island is a clear example of a powerful symbol that is used as a source of remembering and healing. Ultimately it was up to the black South Africans and former prisoners to decide the fate of the old prison. Likewise it remains up to the one-time oppressors to reckon with their culture. My experience and research in Northern Ireland has shown me that when the former power holders begin to lose power, or have lost power, the tendency is to cling to the cultural symbols more than ever before, and to become defensive. And indeed, the Voortrekker, with its ramparts and laager (circled wagons), looks like a defensive fort. The Protestants in Northern Ireland often refer to this as siege mentality. There is a strong sense of fear that if Catholics are in power, then all sorts of bad things will happen to Protestant freedom and rights.

This is where the true notion of restorative justice begins. In a sense, the oppressed group has the right to dismantle the symbols of oppression that serve as a reminder and potential catalyst for hate. However, healing occurs when a society can move past justice and seek the embrace of the other.[16] Ironically, such actions and attitudes will likely give the symbol less power as well. In contrast, a direct threat to the symbol can increase its power. The celebration of parades increased following the Ulster peace agreements. Participants noted how they valued the marches even more. A nonthreatening environment gives space for reconciliation within the "we" to experience guilt or develop new ways to communicate.

The concept of restorative justice has also become an important feature of South African's thinking about reconciliation. In such foundational writings as Archbishop Tutu's *No Future without Forgiveness* and John De Gruchy's *Reconciliation: Restoring Justice*, the theological and sociological underpinnings of restorative justice are explored with passion and precision. I believe that restorative justice is the best place to start in a discussion on how to react to and deal with these dividing symbols. In essence, the concept of restorative justice in the South African context is founded on a Xhosa principle called *ubuntu* or oneness, the idea that we, as humans, are interrelated and need to be in relationship with each other. At the core of this relationship is the principle of forgiveness in the midst of justice—embracing the idea that we as humans hold the capacity to forgive those who have wronged us. Many contemporary theorists have observed that forgiving is moving away from retaliation and hatred to a pro-social response that is based on empathy for the transgressor.[17] It is in this empathic response that the rehumanizing of the offender takes place. It is providing a response that is not deserved nor always accepted. The great difficulty in this process is the burden that the forgiver bears in doing this.

This empathic response might be an important dynamic in reckoning with divided symbols. Given the apartheid ideology that is so deeply reflected in the Voortrekker monument, a case could be made for its destruction as a symbol of oppression and supremacy. Likewise, an empathic response could easily conclude that the site is a source of culture and history for so many Afrikaners, illustrated by the children's dance troupe that proudly performed their traditional dances. This seems to be the fundamental tension, and to some degree ambivalence, in the discussion regarding what to do with the Voortrekker monument.

Within the empathic response that represents forgiveness and reconciliation, the importance of dialogue and mutual understanding emerges. It is in this direction that I am leaning in my response to the Voortrekker and other divided symbols. De Gruchy illustrates this dialogue: "Reconciliation begins to become reality when, without surrendering our identity, who we are, but opening up ourselves to the 'other,' we enter into space between, exchanging places with the other in a conversation that takes us beyond ourselves."[18] It is in this "space between" that the Voortrekker can shift to becoming a transformative symbol rather than a divided symbol. The primary route to this is by South African society creating a space for the Afrikaner community to celebrate its heritage and culture in safety with the freedom to explore a new identity. From this position of safety, the Voortrekker can serve as a space to educate the world about the rich traditions of Afrikaners. Likewise, the ensuing dialogues would ideally enhance a mutual understanding in which all South African cultures exchange perspectives and confront the wrongs of the past.

This "safe space" for dialogue allows for the healing hand of history to take hold. In our near-sightedness, such powerful symbols fill us with confusion and deep emotions. But history seems to have a way to judge such symbols differently over time. Ironically the cross of crucifixion served as one of the most powerful symbols of oppression for many in the Roman Empire. How unfathomable would it be to Roman subjects that the cross would be adorned around our necks today as a symbol of our union in Christ? However, it has become one of the most prominent symbols today and reflects the ultimate sacrifice and avenue for forgiveness and reconciliation.

This is not to say that the Voortrekker monument will take on a redemptive meaning, but neither does it need always to be a painful symbol of apartheid theology. I have mentioned reasons that I do not think the answer lies in removal of the symbol. However, the best case scenario may be to situate the memorial in a cultural context that celebrates what is good in culture while not ignoring evil. Martin Luther King Jr. describes the importance of this in individuals. "We must develop and maintain the capacity to forgive. He who is devoid of the power to forgive is devoid of the power to love. There is some good in the worst of us and some evil in the best of us. When we discover this, we are less prone to hate our enemies."[19] Similarly, all cultures have a mixture of good and bad in their histories. We must find a way to acknowledge what has happened, when we have been wronged and oppressed, as well as when we have oppressed others, or benefited from their oppression. Then we must adjust our sense of identity to embrace both our culture—including the religion, values, experiences, and ethnicities that have shaped us—and our shared humanity with other groups.

Final Thoughts

These conflicted symbols serve as a gauge for how much a society is "at ease" with itself. When use of divisive symbols stirs such strong emotional responses between two communities, it is a signal that a movement toward reconciliation is still needed. With the intense debate involving the Confederate flag and the recent racial tensions surrounding the election of a Black president in the United States, it appears that we Americans still have much work to do. We still have not come to terms with our own past, with slavery and the Civil War. This unfinished business in our social psyche seems to be highlighted in the (mostly tandem rather than reconciled) co-celebration of King/Lee Day in Arkansas, Alabama, and Mississippi, in which both Martin Luther King Jr., and Confederate General Robert E. Lee are honored and revered.[20] Did we just "move on" from slavery in our collective memory? Did the Civil Rights movement create equality in hearts and minds or simply allow black and white to coexist in public, while we still inhabit our separate neighborhoods and churches? If we are attempting to embark upon a covenant relationship, we must not be satisfied with a relatively peaceful co-existence. Rather we must begin the process of an actual "embrace," in which redemptive empathy for our black or white neighbors is fostered.

The new South Africa seems to exhibit strength in its willingness to embrace multiple cultures and wrestle with its past. Out of a painful history, in forging a new democracy, South Africa has chosen to seek a way to redeem what has gone wrong in the past while making room for a better way forward. Instead of focusing on hunting down the offenders and punishing them, the TRC represents another way of speaking truth, while simultaneously seeking healing and forgiveness. I think that Freedom Park is a physical reflection of this cultural attitude. Rather than allowing the Voortrekker monument to stand as a solo statement—painful to some and uplifting to others—it is becoming one piece of a broader history. Across from it stands Freedom Park, with its embodiment of South Africa—symbols of history, culture, life, and the cleansing renewal of water, rebaptizing a broken nation into a new way of relating to itself.

Notes to Chapter Two

[1] Robert Kee, *Ireland: A History* (London: Abacus Books, 2003), 57.

[2] Cooper Christopher & H. Gibbs Knotts, "Region, Race, and Support for the South Carolina Confederate Flag," *Social Science Quarterly* 87 (2006) 142–154.

[3] John De Gruchy, *Reconciliation: Restoring Justice* (Minneapolis: Fortress Press, 2002), 182.

[4] Donald H. Akenson, *God's Peoples: Covenant and Land in South Africa, Israel, and Ulster* (Ithaca: Cornell University Press, 1992), 3.

[5] Vamik Volkan, *Killing in the Name of Identity* (Charlottesville: Pitchstone Publishing, 2006), 137.

[6] Zdzislaw Mach, *Symbols, Conflict, and Identity* (Albany: State University Press, 1993), 25.

[7] Scott Moeschberger, *Forgiveness in Northern Ireland: A Qualitiative Approch to Building a Theoretical Model* (Dissertation Abstracts International: Section B: The Sciences and Engineering, Vol 67[3-B], 2006), 1749.

[8] Ibid.

[9] See Henri Tajfel and John C. Turner, "An Integrative Theory of Intergroup Conflict," in *The Social Psychology of Intergroup Relations*, edited by W. G. Austin and S. Worchel (Monterey: Brooks-Cole, 1979), 33-47.

[10] Mach, *Symbols, Conflict, and Identity*, 52.

[11] Scott Moeschberger, David Dixon, Ed Cairns, and Ulrike Niens, "Forgiveness in Northern Ireland: A model for peace in the midst of the Troubles," *Peace and Conflict: Journal of Peace Psychology* 11 (2005): 199-214.

[12] Akenson, *God's Peoples*.

[13] This document denounced the campaign for Irish "home rule" as a threat to civil liberties, especially religious freedom. It insisted on remaining subject to the British Crown and having equal citizenship in the United Kingdom. Its title echoed *A Solemn League and Covenant for Reformation and Defence of Religion, the Honour and Happiness of the King, and the Peace and Safety of the Three Kingdoms of England, Scotland and Ireland* (1643), drafted by Parliament during the English Civil War. For Ulsterites to sign it was to affirm their covenantal ties to British Protestant hegemony in their region.

[14] Sir James Craig, Unionist Party, then Prime Minister of Northern Ireland, 21 November 1934, reported in *Parliamentary Debates, Northern Ireland House of Commons*, Vol. XVII, Cols. 72–73.

[15] De Gruchy, *Reconciliation: Restoring Justice*, 183.

[16] See for example Miroslav Volf, *Exclusion and Embrace* (Nashville: Abingdon Press, 1996), a profound theological study of encounter and reconciliation.

[17] Everett Worthington, *Steps to REACH Forgiveness and Reconciliation* (New York: Pearson, 2008), and Michael McCullough, *Beyond Revenge: The Evolultion of the Forgiveness Instinct* (San Francisco: Jossey-Bass, 2008).

[18] De Gruchy, *Reconciliation: Restoring Justice,* 153.

[19] Martin Luther King Jr., *Strength to Love* (Philadelphia: Augsburg Fortress, 1981), 49.

[20] Associated Press, "Arkansas, Alabama, Mississippi continue to honor Robert E. Lee on Martin Luther King Day," January, 21, 2008, http://www.msnbc.msn.com/id/22768207.

CHAPTER THREE

FROM HIP HOP TO HIP HOPE

Art and Public Theology

Rhonda Collier

South Africa is quite a trip, I have to say, for any American. Yet "trip" is a truly troubling term, which makes it the perfect metaphor for my experiences in Johannesburg and Cape Town, South Africa. My embrace of my African descent, Christian values, and feminist worldview shaped the nature of my trip to South Africa in meaningful ways. The parallels between South African and American race relations are glaringly obvious, and for someone who must live these realities every day in the U.S., experiencing them in South Africa was quite disturbing. But my time in South Africa had major repercussions for me in another important way, as well. As a professor and scholar of global literature and popular culture, I found that the language I had previously studied in hip hop seemed to make what I perceived as surreal, real—and what at times seemed hopeless, hopeful. In essence, hip hop gave my trip a rhythm and a soundtrack, and it inspired me as I hope it will inspire you.

Purple Rain

As if he were a DJ on the radio, Keith, our South African guide as we encountered Cape Town, told us about something that happened in that city during the struggle against apartheid: it was "the purple rain riots of 1989." When Keith explained that the purple rain riots were a result of police using water hoses to spray purple dye on the people's peaceful protest march in Cape Town, I thought, now this is a 1980s Prince song if I ever heard one. In September 1989, at the height of the non-violent movement against apartheid in South Africa, of which one of the leaders was Archbishop Desmond Tutu, the people were protesting and calling for an end to a segregated Parliament. Since I am deeply attuned with all things purple, including the work and life of the U.S. pop icon Prince, who penned and sang the multi-platinum soundtrack album *Purple Rain* (1984), it only seemed natural for me to connect Prince's image of the judgment day with South Africa's tumultuous history. Prince's hit song "1999," released in 1982 on the album entitled *1999*, relates to his apocalyptic view of red blood dropping in a blue sky on judgment day: literally purple rain.[1] Like many people, Prince believed that 1999 would be the end of the world and that we would all face the judgment day. He sings about signs and portents in a purple sky, of people trying to "run from the destruction," a scene of chaos and panic.[2]

Prince's lyrics, written just a few years before the purple rain riot of 1989, provide a prophetic image of what happened in Cape Town on September 2, 1989. A photo from the *Cape Times* shows "one lone resister jumping the roof, grabbing the nozzle of the hose, and turning the jet of purple water on the police."[3] The photo is emblematic of hip hop culture in that there is no hip hop without resistance. News journals also chronicle that the purple rain riots produced revolutionary purple graffiti that read: "The purple shall govern." In the U.S., graffiti art is considered one of the original manifestations of hip hop culture; a few of the other classical manifestations of hip hop culture are rap music, deejaying, emceeing, break dancing, hip hop clothing, and hip hop language.[4] Art is a powerful tool for demonstrating the relevance of public theology in a democracy, and Prince's famous song captures the urgency of self-reflection and change that we saw in South Africa.

According to urban legends, Prince, born Prince Rogers Nelson, grew up a mix-raced child of a black Seventh Day Adventist family in Minnesota.[5] His *Purple Rain* album, released two years after the *1999* album, became the soundtrack for the 1984 autobiographical film that shows his struggle as an artist and a black man. His music is avant-garde. It is soul, jazz, rock-n-roll, funk, gospel even, and border-line hip hop. Prince's "Purple Rain" lyrics, like the South African peaceful "purple" protestors, encourage us to look to the sky and to change. Prince sings of people anticipating a new beginning but fearful of the decisions they must make. Time for closure, he urges; time to embrace the purple rain.[6]

South Africans, like North Americans, are reaching out for something new. South Africans are still teenagers in their democracy; and for the first-time in its history, the United States has elected an African American president. For Prince, purple rain is baptism into new relationships and trusting in new leaders. It involves embracing national sorrow and pain, but also moving forward. It is a very emotional process, so much so that it requires personal and collective bravery. It's absolutely frightening to think of a blue sky becoming purple because of mass bloodshed. Prince asks us whether or not we can find the truth underneath all that purple.

Like my colleagues and the many people we encountered on our trip to South Africa, we can move away from the anger, sorrow, and tears of our shared past. Jesus can light the path. Prince sings of never meaning any sorrow, harm, or pain, but only wanting to bring joy in the coming of the rain.[7] He makes the struggle for justice and positive change sound easy, and he makes the purple rain sexy like the blues.

During our time in South Africa we didn't see easy, or sexy, but we saw people on the move, finding some joy beyond their pain.

Justice under a Tree

Blues singer Billie Holiday is known for her performance of "Strange Fruit," written by Jewish-American Abel Meeropol; after Holiday's continued blues rendering, her song became a protest against racism and lynching in the United States.[8] When our group had the opportunity to visit the Constitutional Court, established in 1994 by South Africa's first democratic constitution,

I could not help but deconstruct the phrase "justice under a tree," which is the motto for South Africa's Constitutional Court. Sadly, I reflected on how many times the U.S. justice system had failed African Americans—particularly members of my own family.

I was extremely excited to meet our host, the Honorable Deputy Chief Justice Dikgang Moseneke; I was the only one in the group literally jumping up and down, and shamelessly locating myself for a photo opportunity. As the honorable judge presented our group with lapel pins featuring South Africa's "justice under a tree" logo, I felt a little hopeful. I remembered that the tree does not always have to be a negative symbol. After all, the tree is the symbol of death, burial, and resurrection of Christ, and at the same time, a symbol of forgiveness. For South Africans, the "justice under a tree" logo "depicts people sheltering under a canopy of branches—a representation of the Constitution's protective role and a reference to a theme that runs through the Court, that of justice under a tree. The idea comes from traditional African societies: this was where people would meet to resolve disputes."[9] Like everything else about the Constitutional Court, from its location to its artwork to its architecture, a lot of thought had gone into the logo and the phrase.

The location of the Constitutional Court was once the home of the Old Fort, the high security prison that once held such activists as Mahatma Gandhi and Nelson Mandela, among many other political prisoners. "Justice under a tree" represents democracy and the voice and power of the people: instead of the purple rain—the purple reign. Massive wooden entrance doors were carved with South Africa's eleven official languages, as well as sign language and Braille. The welcoming doors seem to suggest the new court is not only in a place of judgment, but a place of reconciliation. In "Drawing the Line: Justice and the Art of Reconciliation," Carrol Clarkson argues that the forces of law and the forces of art can converge towards reconciliation.[10] Clarkson cites a conversation between Angela Breidback and South African artist William Kentridge, whose work I discovered is also featured in the art collection of the Constitutional Court. In the conversation, Kentridge claims, "I come from a very logical and rational family. My father is a lawyer. I had to establish myself in the world as not just being his son, his child. I had to find a way of arriving at knowledge that was not subject to cross examination, not subject to legal reasoning."[11] Surely art has the ability to merge what public theologian Max Stackhouse calls the quadrilateral touchstones of authority for constructing and reconstructing public theology: scripture, tradition, reason, and experience.[12] Kentridge's work, "Sleeper," is one of the many compelling works of the court's art collection. It shows "a man in isolation, lost in himself and disengaged from the world."[13] The "Sleeper" represents the guilt and conscience of the character King Ubu (often compared to Shakespeare's "Macbeth") in the 1888 French play, "Ubu Roi," by Alfred Jarry. In 1998, this same play was adapted and renamed "Ubu and the Truth Commission," by South African playwright Jane Taylor, and directed by Kentridge.[14] His director's notes to the play claim:

> The Commission itself is theatre, or at any rate a kind of ur-theatre. Its hearings are open to the public, as well as being televised and broadcast on the radio. Many of the hearings are presided over by Archbishop Tutu in full purple magnificence. The hearings move from town to town setting up in a church hall, a school auditorium. In each setting the same set is erected. A table for the witnesses (always at least as high as that of the commissioners so the witnesses never have to look up to the commissioners.) Two or three glass booths for the translators. A large banner hangs on the wall behind the commissioners, TRUTH THROUGH RECONCILIATION... How to deal with a guilt for the past, a memory of it. It awakes every day the conflict between the desire for retribution and a need for some sort of social reconciliation. Even those people (and there are a lot) who will have nothing to do with the Commission and who are in denial of the truths it is revealing are, in their very strident refusals, joining in the debate.[15]

Archbishop Tutu presided over many of the hearings in "full purple magnificence," and the people were never far from the theatre of events that shed light on the many horrific accounts of the injustice of apartheid in South Africa. As the director's notes indicate, even those who remained silent and refused to confess their sins were a part of the drama of truth. The silent atonement of the sleeping man in Kentridge's painting mirrors King Ubu's guilt for his excesses and sins. As Prince sings in "1999," uneasy sleep calls for bad dreams of a judgment day in which red blood falls in clear blue sky, especially for those who claim not to care—essentially purple rain. Kentridge's art is not concerned with legal response, but emotional response.[16]

Art, as in public theology's "experience" category, allows us to experience God through love and compassion for other members of society. In U.S. hip hop and the U.S. black church, this emotional response is called "call-and-response," "testimony," and "witnessing." Ironically, these words also have legal implications; there is a fine line between the creative process and the legal process. This intersection corresponds to Stackhouse's notion of the intersection between reason and experience. Furthermore, art challenges tradition and the status quo. In the words of DJ Mister Señor Love Daddy, in Spike Lee's 1989 hip hop film, *Do the Right Thing*, art is supposed to make you "WAKE UP!"

As our group toured the art collection of the Constitutional Court, I was inspired by a triptych work featuring a stunning blue dress, by South African artist Judith Mason. When I looked at this work, I knew there was a blues story behind the painting. The piece was called *The Man who Sang and the Woman who kept Silent* (1-3).[17] The work was conceived in 1995, when Mason was listening to the Truth and Reconciliation trials on the radio. The testifying police officer, who had murdered the woman by shooting her in the head, left her with only her private parts covered in plastic. He confessed that he remembered her last request. She had asked to sing "Nkosi Sikelele"/"God Bless Africa" before she was killed. When he faced the commission, he remembered her bravery. At the time of the victim's death, "Nkosi Sikelele" was not a part of the South African National Anthem, but this old hymn was the African National Congress Anthem and an apartheid protest song—yes, "strange fruit" indeed.[18]

Facing her violent death, the woman had the courage to protest, and to call on the name of the Holy Spirit. She did not die in vain or without hope, and her story is not forgotten. Romans 9:25 notes: "I WILL CALL THOSE WHO WERE NOT MY PEOPLE, 'MY PEOPLE,' AND HER WHO WAS NOT BELOVED, 'BELOVED'." "Justice under a tree" gives this woman and the people a voice; the art in the Constitutional Court memorializes her horror story in a beautiful and humane way.

In such powerful art, public theology has answered its call to truth and reconciliation; everyone is welcome to sit under the tree. Thus, Clarkson's theory that law and art do merge towards reconciliation makes some noise— just like hip hop. In 1998, the South African kwaito group, Shaka Boom, wrote and performed a highly controversial, essentially hip hop version of "Nkosi Sikelele" that offended many people. The young group incorporated urban and sexualized dance moves that many felt took away from the reverence of the song, which was originally written as a nineteenth-century Methodist church hymn. Others argued that in the spirit of liberation and artistic interpretation, the young group had given the song new energy and appeal to younger listeners. In a democracy, like it or not, everyone gets the microphone.[19]

Part two of Mason's triptych speaks the loudest. The following words are written in white on the blue dress that Mason sewed out of blue plastic bags, refiguring the ugliness of the small piece of plastic that failed to cover the victim's body. The healing words are as follows:

> Sister, a plastic bag may not be the armour of God but you were wrestling with flesh and blood, and against powers, against the rulers of darkness, against spiritual wickedness in sordid places. Your weapons were your silence and a piece of rubbish. Finding that bag and wearing it until you were disinterred is such a frugal, commonsensical, house-wifely thing to do, an ordinary act . . . At some level you shamed your capturers, and they did not compound their abuse of you by stripping you a second time. Yet they killed you. We only know your story because a sniggering man remembered how brave you were. Memorials to your courage are everywhere; they blow about streets and drift on the tide and cling to thorn-bushes. This dress is made from some of them. Hamba kahle. Umkhonto.[20]

Mason's words acknowledge the power of silence, memory, and memorials. Every human life has value and even plastic can be made into something beautiful. In part one of Mason's triptych, the striking blue dress is surrounded by a fence and a ferocious hyena tearing at the dress. In part three, the final part, the predator is still there, but the dress is surrounded by embers of hope. What stands out is that by writing on the dress, the artist makes the dress perform, or in U.S. black vernacular the dress is "signifyin."[21] The dress speaks the unspeakable: it is beautiful but it is also very sad. In her art, Mason essentially writes the victim a letter of love and compassion.

Speaking of letters, on the day of our group's visit to the Constitutional Court, June 5, 2009, the South African Post Office launched the Art of the Constitutional Court stamps featuring ten stamps bearing the artwork of leading South African artists Marlene Dumas, William Kentridge, Judith Mason, Gerard Sekoto, Albert Adams, Penny Siopis, Dumile Femi, Albert Adams, Andrew Verster, Kagiso, and Pat Mautloa.[22] For a serious letter writer and stamp collector, this was an amazing day. Dr. Ivan May, chairperson of the Constitution Hill Trust, notes, "stamps are regarded as little ambassadors since they travel the world."[23] If these stamps are little ambassadors, what do they say exactly? The artists hope that their works symbolize hope without erasing or forgetting the nation's marred history.

The apostle Paul's letter to the church at Corinth provides insight on the relationship that exists between scripture, public theology, and reconciliation. Paul writes: "Therefore, we are ambassadors for Christ, as though God were making an appeal through us; we beg you on behalf of Christ, be reconciled to God."[24] Christians are called to bring diverse people together, to put aside differences in race, sex, and nationality, and to become united with one another. The *ubuntu* Theology of Desmond Tutu notes that reconciliation does not come from forgiveness or revenge, but from healing relationships.[25] The ultimate reconciliation is with Jesus Christ.

So why are stamps so important? Isn't it the letter that really matters? What do stamps cost us? Why do some of us collect them? First of all, the letter could not get to its destination without the stamp. The letter has to make the journey, but the trip has to be paid for. We keep the stamps because they remind us of the journey which is just as important as the message in the letter. Sometimes, the stamps can tell us more than the contents of the letter because there are not enough words, paint, canvas, or song lyrics to communicate the trip. I recall the character "Stamp Paid" in Toni Morrison's novel, *Beloved* (1987). I always loved this character who was famous for bringing enslaved African Americans to freedom, from

Kentucky into Ohio, by crossing the Ohio River. He would bring verbal messages, written letters, packages, and of course, free people to Ohio. When these freed people tried to pay him back, he remembers his own heartbreaking journey to freedom:

> Born Joshua, he renamed himself when he handed his wife to his master's son. Handed her over in the sense that he did not kill anybody, thereby himself, because his wife demanded he stay alive. Otherwise, she reasoned, where and to whom could she return when the boy was through? With that gift, he decided that he didn't owe anybody anything. Whatever his obligations were, the act paid them off. [. . .] So he extended this debtlessness to other people by helping them pay out and off whatever they owed in misery. Beaten runaways? He ferried them and rendered them paid for; gave them their own bill of sale, so to speak. "You paid it; now life owes you." And the receipt, as it were, was a welcome door that he never had to knock on. . . .[26]

The essence of the Constitutional Court is a welcome door, and it is open to all South African citizens.

Thieves in the Temple

Our group's ideas of the welcome door and human dignity were challenged as we visited an overcrowded refugee mission housed in the Johannesburg Central Methodist Mission (CMM), led by Bishop Paul Verryn.[27] It seemed ironic that the Bishop's name was Paul and that he too struggled with cynical neighbors who, much like the Sadducees and the Pharisees, were concerned with outside appearances versus actually being good neighbors. Our group was absolutely overwhelmed at the situation that Bishop Paul was trying to manage: there were over three thousand Zimbabwean refugees living in the church building. Bishop Paul had a history of being a grassroots activist, and he and his small staff refused to let their Zimbabwean neighbors go hungry or homeless in the streets of Johannesburg. The understaffed and under-resourced church had witnessed two murders, an undocumented amount of rape, and innumerable incidents of fighting and robbery within its walls. While the church protected the refugees, the majority of whom were

Zimbabwean, from the hunger and cold, many times, even with a security team, it could not protect the refugees from each other. The skeptical outside community called this church a "den of iniquity." The bishop laughed at this biblical irony which made a mockery of his life's work, which in reality had made the place a house of prayer and service. Consider Matthew 21:12-13:

> And Jesus entered the temple and drove out all those who were buying and selling in the temple, and overturned the tables of the money changers and the seats of those who were selling doves. And He said to them, "It is written, 'MY HOUSE SHALL BE CALLED A HOUSE OF PRAYER'; but you are making it a ROBBERS' DEN."

In the case of CMM, the judgmental public failed to recognize the work of true theology.

Prince has a song about this disappointing paradox, his 1990 hit, "Thieves in the Temple"—of thugs in the house of God who "don't care where they kick," but only care about bringing hurt. He calls on "Love—if U're there" to bring salvation from such "cold despair."[28] The Scriptures show that Jesus is angered by the thieves in the temples. Anger can be a sin, but Jesus acts out of righteous indignation—he responds to a moral wrong. He overturns the money tables, but he does not leave the scene. He becomes what the hip hop world calls the emcee (mc): master of ceremonies. He instructs the crowds and gives them "the message." He does not just rap, but he teaches. Jesus takes the time to heal the sick and to teach those who are willing to stay behind and listen. The real art of hip hop is getting your audience to stay with you. Usually those who are unheard, suffering, hungry, or physically or spiritually poor don't mind listening. If you read Matthew 21 closely, you will see that the children and the infants were most influenced by Christ's teaching; they were the ones shouting praises in the temple. The young people were Christ's greatest witnesses, and they are today, like it or not, some of hip hop's greatest fans.

In God We Trust

Besides the eleven official languages spoken in South Africa there are numerous African immigrants living in South Africa that speak very little English, but they managed to speak hip hop and engaged me in very brief and casual hip hop conversations. It came as no surprise to me that random young people at Internet cafes, on buses, in street markets, and at malls where familiar with many U.S. rappers, such as the larger-than-life mega-rapper and film star, 50 Cent, formerly known as Curtis Jackson. Amazingly, the people I spoke with pronounced 50 Cent's name better than many English-speaking white Americans, who often failed to capture the black vernacular cadence of his name.

Of course, our group had a very diverse and full agenda, and time simply did not allow for longer interviews. I knew I was losing a lot in translation. For example, during free time, I looked for hip hop CDs. Asking store clerks for help, I was immediately directed to U.S. hip hop artists. When I asked for South African hip hop, the clerks would show me house or funk music. We could not even agree on the definition of hip hop. What they called funk sounded like hip hop to me. It had a beat, I could dance to it, but I could not really understand the lyrics. I noticed that many of the songs were not in English, and I knew that it would be very difficult for me to find someone to translate Xhosa or Zulu once I returned to the U.S. I was tired and running out of time. In a mad dash to return to our bus, I just started buying random CDs that had covers that looked like 1980s and 1990s old school hip hop album covers. Like a kid in a candy store, I purchased the following titles: Jub Jub's *Fresh Air* (because he reminded me of Will Smith in the *Fresh Prince of Bell-Air* television series); Tsekeleke, Fattis & Monis (because they had a song called "Fatty" and reminded me of the one hit wonder 1980s rap group The Fat Boys); and Lebo's *Drama Queen* (because with her long white blond hair and brown skin she looked like both the sexy rapper Eve, who is one of the few successful female hip hop artists, and the Queen of Hip Hop Soul, Mary J. Blige, who sings "No More Drama"). As you can imagine, in just minutes, I spent many South African Rands on music. So I participated in the globalization and internationalization of hip hop culture.

After leaving the store, I could not leave the artist Lebo's CD alone. The album's cover featured the woman's dark face, blond hair, and light brown eyes on the front; the back cover shows Lebo leaving a public restroom with illegible white graffiti on the door and the word WOMEN above her regal platinum blond hair. The whole package screamed at me, "I have something to say that you need to hear." Song titles like "Ditaba," "Awu Dede," "Ae Ye Teng," and "Ngiyakhutanda" (Tsoti language, I think) were completely lost on me, while the English titles "Ma Africa," "Dangerous," "Shake," and "Oh Jehova" intrigued me. As I listened to the song "Oh Jehova," which turned out not necessarily to be a gospel song, I knew I needed to investigate Lebo's biography.

Turns out she was a former member of the controversial group Boom Shaka. It was her dancing and sex appeal that had offended some audiences. Like many U.S. hip hop artists, Lebo had her roots in the black church. In 2001, she was South Africa's most successful female vocal artist, though a few year later, she resisted having her music labeled as either hip hop or kwaito (a South African house music genre), which helped explain my trouble at the music store.[29] Lebo's music translates many different African traditions into popular culture. In 2003, she sang at Nelson Mandela's 85th birthday bash; she also performed at Heritage Day and Youth Day in front of sixteen thousand people.[30] Also in 2003, she gave an interview in which she recognized the power and historical importance of her music:

> [12]The difference was with us, like I say, we were the most controversial group in the country. The first thing is we changed our national anthem, and we put a dance beat in it. No one is allowed to do that but we were able to pull that off so that actually shows you how much power Boom Shaka had behind the music scene itself. We sang in our African languages and when you added a little bit of house to the mix of African melodies and rhythms it became kwaito. It was kwaito because we didn't want to be categorised with the old artists who sang bubblegum music, people like Brenda Fassie, Kamazoo, Senyaka, they were the top people in the music industry before we came up. So the youth wanted to have something totally different from what the others had done before. And kwaito was also different from any international music, so it was something the youth could represent themselves as. Kwaito has been going for as long as I've been in the industry now, it's been more than ten years. If I had to change anything about kwaito music it would be the lyrics in order for the foreign countries as well to be able to understand. They call it

kwaito because it is more of the kasi music, I mean the kasi tongue, we speak in our tsotsitaal, and different languages according to how you grew up. So I would change it into something that everyone would be able to relate to and understand and they would be able to sing and say the words that we are singing.[31]

Lebo died in a tragic accident in 2006, but not without having made an impression on South African youth.

Without the benefit of online lyrics or the music in the inside cover, below is what I was able to transcribe of Lebo's 2004 English song "Oh Jevohah." Sounding very much like contemporary U.S. hip hop artists, Lebo's song begins with male voices rapping:

[Strong bass beat]
Are we recording? This is another beatmatic's production . . .
          holler back!
Come on! What! What! Come on!! What! What! Come on!!
What!
What!! Come on! Yeah! Yeah!
Let's do this shit! Do this shit!
It's double homicide!
When I murder you with these rhymes while I'm killing time
All of ya'll thought I was playing when I kept saying to all of you all
          that this rap game was mine
You'll all pay the price and you will face the consequence of trying to
          downplay my intelligence.
God forgive me cause I can't repent for everything I've said for all I
          said I meant
This is my testament to all of those who believe they can defeat me
          with their rhyme content
I got to make money like 50 Cent.
I gotta gain respect like Jay-Z's *Blueprint*.[32]

After listening to "Oh Jehovah" several times, I finally heard its Christian message. Lebo claims that music has the power to take its listeners to heaven and to free them. She claims she does not need ecstasy and that her music is not a fantasy. In the chorus, Lebo repeatedly sings the following lyrics to her listeners: "Oh Jehovah, can I be your preacher, let the music hold ya." The song has a definite anti-drug message. Given her tragic death in a car accident at a young age, her church background, and her socially conscious history, Lebo's music, or as her song pronounces it letter-by-letter, L–E–B–O's music, preaches a message that places her music in the realm of hip hop(e). It is imperative not to drop the "e" from hip hope.

Lebo's music, like Billie Holiday's, translates many different African traditions into popular culture. Holiday's music is both jazz and blues, but through great performances became the American popular music of the 1930s. Angela Davis argues in *Blues Legacies and Black Feminism*, "Of the various ways Holiday's work remains connected to the blues tradition, one of the most striking is the intimate connection it reveals between love, sexuality, individuality and freedom."[33] Davis, like many other critics of hip hop, takes exception with the image of the African queen in hip hop culture. She observes: "In hip hop culture, black women are often portrayed as 'African queens,' to be accorded respect by their men. What is frequently implied by the evocation of 'queens,' however, is that the ultimate authority rests with the 'kings.'"[34] While I agree with Davis, I make the distinction that the term "drama queen" implies that the woman is the director of the performance of her identity. As Lebo's pose on the back cover of her CD suggests, the casting and stage direction make all the difference. The drama queen directs her own show.

On the surface, what I would call the 50 Cent side of the hip hop coin, young people are encouraged to pursue wealth, purchase expensive clothing, perform vulgar dances, and perpetuate unhealthy sexual behaviors. But underneath the hype—the positive side of the hip hop coin and the core tradition of hip hop culture—youth are empowered to be their own advocates for justice and change, to tell their own stories in their own languages, to hear good news spoken in a language that values their humanity, and to have something tangible to get excited about. If you examine the gangster autobiography of 50 Cent, in the 2004 hip hop film *Get Rich or Die Tryin'*, the hope of the story is that hip hop is the key to Curtis Jackson's freedom and it helps him get out of the ghetto. Unfortunately, 50 Cent can't reconcile his past with his future—and mental escape appears impossible. In one popular song, he tries to reconcile himself to God. In "God Gave Me Style" (2005), one of the few 50 Cent songs that directly glorifies God, he raps:

> Listen you can call me what you want, black and ugly
> But you can't convince me the Lord don't love me
> When my CDs drop, they sell the best
> You call it luck, why can't it just be I'm blessed
>
> I'm a trackstar, runnin' through life, chasin' my dream
> Best deal I made was tradin' the mic for that triple beam.
> I zone off thinkin' is there really heaven or hell
> So what happens to a changed man who dies in a cell
> I need no answers to these questions, cuz time will tell
> Got a date with destiny, she's more than a girl
> Don't much good come from me, but my music
> Is a gift given from God so I'ma use it (Yeaaah!)[35]

While the majority of 50 Cent's lyrics do not invoke God, this beautiful song repents and recognizes that "God gave [him] style and grace" and success. He discusses his mic in relationship to the cross, which he refers to as the "triple beam." His use of "triple beam" invokes the presence of the Godhead: God, Jesus, and the Holy Spirit. 50 Cent appears to recognize that he will have to answer to his treatment of women when he raps that he has a date with destiny, not a girl. Indeed, "God Gave Me Style" contrasts with other 50 Cent songs that objectify women and extol violence. Perhaps he is preparing for a judgment day and just hasn't woken up yet.

While this song is repentant, coupled with the rest of 50 Cent's discography, it illustrates that 50 Cent is little more than Kentridge's "Sleeper," or the man in Prince's "1999" dream who doesn't care. During one of our many discussions on the tour bus, one of my white North American colleagues surprised me by informing me that some of 50 Cent's lyrics for "God Gave Me Style" were stolen from the socially conscious British alternative rock group, Cold Play, who wrote and performed their version years before 50 Cent's multi-platinum album was released—talk about a *thief in the temple*. While 50 Cent only borrowed a few lines from the songs (God gave me style/God gave me grace/God put this smile upon my face) and completely changed the rock melody to a rap sound, Cold Play never received any credit for the song lyrics or even a "shout out."[36] In the case of 50 Cent, he is a not a very good ambassador for the United States' national motto, "In God We Trust." In his music videos and concerts, young people around the world see hand-grenades, explicit tattoos, bullet wounds, strippers, guns, fancy clothes, and cars, to give a few visuals. They see a man who worships money, not the God that he claims gave him style and grace. It seems odd that Curtis Jackson would give himself so little value by changing his name to 50 Cent. Unlike Morrison's Stamp Paid, Curtis Jackson's name change does not suggest reconciliation or a pay-it-forward attitude. Thus, it appears that money is a two-edged sword capable of both building and destroying precious lives. For many hip hop artists, the love of money becomes a form of idolatry which causes them to hate themselves and others.

I mentioned to a small group of my junior North American colleagues that I grew up not seeing a face like mine on any U.S. currency. Like 50 Cent, how was I supposed to have a healthy respect for something that did not respect me. As I began to think about coins and cultural representation, it was hard to contain my righteous indignation; the last twenty-five years of my life I had been referred to as the "token" black person in almost all competitive settings.

In South Africa, cultural diversity was mandated by the Constitution and went way beyond the bounds of skin color, yet in my country I felt I had to constantly prove I wasn't hired just because I'm black and a woman. I reflected with my very interested colleagues that privilege was indeed "ALL ABOUT THE BENJAMINS." In the 2008 Indian film *Slum Dog Millionaire*, a young uneducated thief, "a slum dog," from Mumbai knows that Benjamin Franklin is the face on the U.S. one hundred dollar bill; this knowledge gives him an advantage in the Indian version of the televised game show "Who Wants to Be a Millionaire?" Recognizing and respecting U.S. money allows the young thief to escape poverty. What do the faces on money teach our children about love and respect?

White privilege is so pervasive in the U.S. that a simple coin without a black face is relatively unnoticed by white Americans, but it makes a difference in how we interpret our shared histories. Here is a snap shot of the faces on American small change. The penny and the five-dollar bill feature Abe Lincoln, whose face replaced the wheat penny that for many years featured a Native American face, and the same Lincoln who entertained the idea of sending African Americans back to Africa. The nickel showcases Thomas Jefferson, the author of the U.S. Constitution, who was a slave owner who fathered enslaved children. The dime shrinks the great historical figure of Franklin Delano Roosevelt, whose contributions to the U.S. surely warranted more than a place on a dime, which is physically smaller than a penny. Neither last nor least, but rather first, the quarter and the dollar bill present one of our founding fathers and the first president of the United States of America, George Washington, a slave owner who is believed to have fathered a child with an enslaved woman.[37] The wise and very witty Benjamin Franklin, was once a slave owner, but over his life time he drastically changed his views on the institution of slavery, finally concluding that slavery was morally wrong.[38] To me, it does not make "sense" that the words "In God We Trust" appear on all these white patriarchal symbols of privilege and power.[39] These economic symbols matter; they have the power to represent "change."

In the 1990s, the South African currency was changed to feature the country's Big Five animals instead of the nation's white patriarchs. The African elephant, black rhinoceros, lion, cape buffalo, and leopard represent the most challenging animals encountered on South African terrain. South Africans both fear and respect these national treasures. Interestingly, if you examine South African money, you will note there are no references to God, only the South African Reserve Bank. You will also notice that the different bills have English and two other African languages printed on them. For example, the green and purple one hundred Rand note has Xhosa, English, and another African language I did not recognize printed on it, and the ten Rand note has English, Afrikaans, and another African language I did not understand on it. Besides the African languages, each bill has scenic images of South Africa. I wish I had spent more time trying to interpret those images versus spending the multi-colored notes. The South Africans wisely decided to leave the money to the animals, so to speak. Many argue that "animal money" exploits the South African wild game industry, but I would argue that the government found a very creative approach to a very difficult problem of cultural representation. If we change the way money looks, we can change the way people react. Obviously our brothers and sisters in South Africa thought about the face of money after Nelson Mandela was released in 1990, and although changing the faces does not change the value of the bills or the economic stability of the country, it can change how citizens think about themselves and their shared history. As my colleagues and I learned on the trip to South Africa, it is not always about how much something is worth, but it is the symbolism of the token. Faces do matter!

Hip Hope

South African writer Alan Paton, in his best selling 1948 novel, *Cry, The Beloved Country*, writes:

> I was born on a farm, brought up by honourable parents, given all that a child could need or desire. They were upright and kind and law abiding; they taught me prayers and took me regularly to church; they had no trouble with servants and my father was never short of labour. From them I learned all that a child should learn of honour and charity and generosity. But of South Africa I learned nothing at all.[40]

Paton's fictional portrayal of the contrasts between English speaking South Africans, Afrikaners, Colored, and Zulus mirrors the challenge of public theology in South Africa and the challenge of our diverse group on this shared journey. We were Africans and North Americans; additionally, many of us were parents, some of us were clergy, and all of us were educators. In one way or another, each of us experienced a level of privilege in our lives. How could we use our knowledge of South Africa and our faith to make a difference? I see public theology in South Africa through images of purple rain, diverse paintings, theatrical performances, animal money, commemorative stamps, music, dance, film, and novels. As a student and teacher of popular culture, I see endless possibilities for self-reflection, truth and reconciliation, and change, through art. When I think of the power of public theology in the United States, I recall Dr. Martin Luther King Jr.'s April 1963 *Letter from A Birmingham Jail*, and how he spoke to moderate Southern Christians about being tired of waiting. He cites the apostle Paul's journey to the far corners of the Greco-Roman world to carry the gospel of freedom. At the end of his letter, King apologizes for writing such a long letter, "but what else can one do when he is alone in a narrow cell other than write long letters, think long thoughts, and pray long prayers?"[41] In 1970, in one of Angela Davis' infamous "Dear George" love letters that were intercepted by prison guards and called violent, she writes: "The American oppressor has revealed to us what we must do if we are serious about our commitment. If I am serious about you, my love for black people, I should be ready to go all the way. I am." The letter was signed *"Hasta la Victoria* (Until the victory)! I love you. Angela."[42] Today, this controversial figure of historical resistance continues to be an educator, activist, and person of letters, using her magnificent artistic voice to speak for all oppressed people regardless of race, gender, sexuality, or legal conviction.

Nelson Mandela's release after twenty-seven years of imprisonment was an answer to many prayers, and a moment of international anticipation. The 2009 film, *Invictus*, starring Morgan Freeman and Matt Damon, gives us Hollywood's interpretation of a reconciliatory moment in South African history. The film shows the struggle of the all-white Rugby team, the Springboks, and its one black player, Chester Williams, to win the 1995 World Cup title.

The team faced a new democratic nation, new flag, new national anthem, and new black African president—and the world was its audience. The only thing that remained the same was the team's name. At the time, rugby was essentially a white sport, a privilege that white South Africans had taken for granted, but eventually the sport became a national pastime. As host for the 1995 World Cup event, South Africa became ambassador for the world, and as the film shows, how the country met the challenge. In the film, Morgan, playing Mandela, gives the team captain, Francois Pienaar, played by Matt Damon, the nineteenth-century British poem, "Invictus," by William Henley. This is the poem that Mandela kept in jail on a scrap of paper for over twenty-seven years. It reads as follows:

Out of the night that covers me,
Black as the pit from pole to pole,
I thank whatever gods may be
For my unconquerable soul.

In the fell clutch of circumstance
I have not winced nor cried aloud.
Under the bludgeonings of chance
My head is bloody, but unbowed.

Beyond this place of wrath and tears
Looms but the Horror of the shade,
And yet the menace of the years
Finds and shall find me unafraid.

It matters not how strait the gate,
How charged with punishments the scroll,
I am the master of my fate:
I am the captain of my soul.[43]

In the film, upon receiving the poem, Francois explains to his wife: "He wants us to win." As team captain, Francois becomes dedicated to leading the Springboks to victory and embracing the new nation. As the poem suggests, neither Mandela nor Pienaar is surrounded by doubt, shame, or guilt. They are brave and grateful for the opportunity to represent a new South Africa. When I first read the poem, the line "to whatever gods may be" appeared a bit irreverent. But considering the politics of religion in South Africa and the distrust that Mandela might have experienced, I see the line as questioning the tradition that gives authority to laws that contradict what is morally right. According to South Africans, Pienaar was also an extremely religious man and was inspired to play for all South Africans. He honored all forty-three million South Africans in his victory speech. Moreover, the poem's reference to straight gates and scrolls of punishment imply that the speaker is reconciled to himself and the judgment day. The poem's speaker decides how he will react to the circumstances of his situation in life, and he chooses to be the captain of his fate. In other words, he does not give up hope.

In actuality, Mandela gave Pienaar an excerpt from Theodore Roosevelt's 1910 essay, "The Man in the Arena," not the poem "Invictus":

> It is not the critic who counts; not the man who points out how the strong man stumbles, or where the doer of deeds could have done them better. The credit belongs to the man who is actually in the arena, whose face is marred by dust and sweat and blood; who strives valiantly; who errs, who comes short again and again, because there is no effort without error and shortcoming; but who does actually strive to do the deeds; who knows great enthusiasms, the great devotions; who spends himself in a worthy cause; who at the best knows in the end the triumph of high achievement, and who at the worst, if he fails, at least fails while daring greatly, so that his place shall never be with those cold and timid souls who neither know victory nor defeat.[44]

During our time in South Africa, our group met many people in the arena. At times, I wanted to cry as I saw so many people fighting big battles with futile forks instead of powerful swords. Bishop Paul remains in my prayers as he continues to struggle with the legal protection of the children under his care, and his own fight with his church and community. I also remember the Reverend Dr. Spiwo Xapile at the J.L. Zwane Memorial Church in Guguletu, called the AIDS church, who bowed his head as he explained the daily challenges of continuing the work of the church in a community of impoverished grandmothers, orphans, and members fighting with AIDS. When I reflect on these men in the arena of South African public theology and hope, I hear Prince sing that the "Thieves in the Temple" are "kicking me in my heart" and "tearing me all apart," but he holds on, praying for Love's help to "be the better man."

The afflicted congregation we saw in Guguletu is deeply wounded and oppressed, yet, like Mandela, they are not defeated. The children are learning. They are singing in choirs, learning to read, and performing scripturally based skits in the sanctuary. J. L. Zwane even has a sports ministry. When we visited J. L. Zwane, as in our visit to the Constitutional Court, we were welcomed. Although we did not understand everything that was said or sung,

we understood that we belonged—we were beloved. As I observed the color-
ful walls of the church and the beautiful people both young and old, I felt at
home—I was learning about South Africa's hope and hospitality. I left with
my souvenirs: a gospel CD, a J. L. Zwane t-shirt, a lapel pin with the church
logo, and a few pictures with members.

I tried to I pay attention to the interior of the church, and as one of our
host brothers had pointed out, I noticed a stained glass window of a woman
carrying a bucket of blood on her head that looked like a cross—the blood
was splashing out on both sides as she carried the bucket. While the woman
carried the bucket, Jesus carried her. It was an amazing image that was very
healing for me. Many times Christ is portrayed with European traits, but
this image, featuring black stained glass contrasted with red stained glass,
highlighted the blood versus Christ's facial features. Additionally, this work
of art featured a woman carrying water, an image that not only recalls the
Samaritan woman at the well and her cross-cultural encounter with Jesus,
but places women at the center of the work in the church. In traditional
churches, men are often at the pulpit or "holding the mic," while women
are drawing the water and feeding the masses. This window seemed to say
to me, as a black woman of faith, "I see you and you are not invisible to
Christ." In contrast to the "African queen" impression, the black woman
is an equal member of a community working for Christ. She is a woman
in the arena.

Many critics accuse the pop star Prince of trying to be a black Christ, and
it seems that his lyrics would convict him. Is this an insult or a compliment? If
being a black Christ means asking people to love one another and to change,
then being a black Christ could be translated simply to "being Christ-like."
Do we dare walk with the prophetic Prince? Or are we afraid that we will be
misunderstood? U.S. hip hop artist Kanye West, who like 50 Cent is a disappointing study in contradictions, in his 2004 Grammy award winning song,
"Jesus Walks," argues that rap music needs to speak up for Jesus. Hip hop
culture must risk defeat for the greater cause of humanity:

They say you can rap about anything except for Jesus
That means guns, sex, lies, video tapes

But if I talk about God my record won't get played Huh?
Well let this take away from my spins
Which will probably take away from my ends
Then I hope it take away from my sins.[46]

Minus his troubled biography, West's lyrics express the hope of hip hop. Hip hop language calls for audiences to "holla back." We show our enthusiasm for the message by participating in the dance, by shouting with the crowd, and by spreading the good news. When we can, we encourage the person in the arena. Like the children in the temple, we stay because we really don't care what Jesus looks like. We only care about how he makes us feel. We don't owe Jesus anything because he's already paid for our lives. However, we do owe each other a chance to become better people, which is what positive hip hop calls for. In *Cry, The Beloved Country*, Paton expresses his hope for the diverse people of South Africa:

> Yes, God save Africa, the beloved country. God save us from the deep depths of our sins. God save us from the fear that is afraid of justice. God save us from the fear that is afraid of men. God save us all.[47]

Paton's hope still inspires readers years after the end of apartheid. It is a hope that says regardless of what your eyes see, you must not be afraid to believe in God, to call on God, to cry for help, and to dance for deliverance. We must trust our new rhythms and make them our own. We do not abandon scripture, tradition, reason, or experience, but we navigate our interpretation of their meaning. A careful dance establishes the parameters of a new healing relationship.

Notes to Chapter Three

[1] I remembered the song and the lyrics on the tour bus, but reading Matthew Carcieri's *Prince: A Life in Music: A Playlist History* (New York. iUniverse, 2004), 2300, confirmed my instincts about the meaning of "purple rain." Carcieri does not connect Prince's song to events in South Africa or apartheid. My research indicates that no one else has made this connection since the song was written years before the event occurred—not even the artist Prince.

[2] Prince, "1999," single release, Warner Brothers, December 18, 1982.

[3] Dene Smuts, et al., *The Purple Shall Govern: A South African A to Z of Nonviolent Action,* (Cape Town: Oxford University Press, 1991), 11, 14.

[4] Hip Hop is an umbrella term that embraces rap music, hip hop dance (which includes locking, popping, and break dancing), emceeing (which comes from a politically conscious rapper who more than rapping actually teaches a message), deejaying (performed by a person concerned with the techniques of scratching and mixing music to produce the hip hop sound), and graffiti (which is the urban artistic visual expression of hip hop culture and resistance). I will use the terms rap and hip hop interchangeably, but it should be noted that in many circles, not all rap is hip hop. Many critics argue that "real" hip hop is politically conscious.

[5] Brian Morton, *Prince: A Thief in the Temple* (New York: Canon Gate, 2007), is the best available account, but it has not fully separated fact from legend; see p. 17.

[6] Prince, "Purple Rain," single release, Warner Brothers, September 26, 1984.

[7] Ibid.

[8] "Strange Fruit" was originally published under Meeropol's pen name, Lewis Allen, in 1937 as the poem "Bitter Fruit." Its protest meaning was common knowledge to many African Americans, but Angel Davis also documents it in *Blues Legacies and Black Feminism: Gertrude "Ma" Rainey, Bessie Smith, and Billie Holiday* (New York: Vintage Books, 1998), 181, 390.

[9] See an essay on the design of the Constitutional Court: Carrol Clarkson, "Drawing the Line: Justice and the Art of Reconciliation," in François DuBois and Antje du Bois-Pedain, eds., *Justice and Reconciliation in Post Apartheid South Africa* (Cambridge, U.K.: Cambridge University Press, 2008), 267–288. Clarkson does not discuss the art collection of the Constitutional Court, but rather the history of the location of the Constitutional Court, plus relevant poems, autobiographies, speeches, and even a mural called *Abamfusa Lawula-The Purple Shall Govern*. Clarkson's work deals with philosophical questions of language, interpretation, reception, and reconciliation. This chapter offers remarkable insights on the relationship between art and reconciliation.

[10] Clarkson, "Drawing the Line," 269, 274, and 275.

[11] Ibid., 267.

[12] Stackhouse, *Public Theology and Political Economy: Christian Stewardship in Modern Society* (Grand Rapids, MI.: Eerdmans, 1987), 4.

[13] The Constitutional Court website discusses the French version of the play. http://concourt.artvault.co.za/collection.php. Upon further research, I found that the French play had been adapted into absurd puppet theatre by the South African playwright, Jane Taylor. The Constitutional Court website did not mention that Kentridge, who is also a South African film director, was the South African play's director.

[14] William Kentridge, "Director's Note," in "Ubu and the Truth Commission," posted on the website of the Hanspring Puppet Company. http://www.handspringpuppet.co.za/html/ubu.html

[15] The italic is my emphasis. While Archbishop Tutu is known for his rhetoric of "rainbow people," art and history constantly cast him in the role of a purple person. Purple is, of course, the signifying color for archbishops. Desmond M. Tutu, *The Rainbow People of God: The Making of a Peaceful Revolution*, ed. John Allen (New York: Doubleday, 1994), 188. Main quoted text taken from Kentridge, "Director's Note."

[16] This is my summary of Clarkston's argument, based on the conversation between Angela Breidbach and William Kentridge in *William Kentridge, Thinking Aloud: Conversations with Angela Breidbach* (Cape Town and Johannesburg: David Krut, 2006), 70. See Clarkson, 267.

[17] Constitutional Court Website http://concourt.artvault.co.za/collection.php

[18] Tinyiko Maluleke, "Of Collapsible Coffins and Ways of Dying: The Search for Catholic Contextuality in African Perspective," *The Ecumenical Review* 54:3 (2002): 313-331. Maluleke reacts to the September 11, 2001 tragedy and the use of "God Bless America" as a healing song. He poses the new South African national anthem as a ritual designed to give "birth to a new people." Maluleke reminds us of the power of old songs in new contexts.

[19] Sonjah Stanley-Niaah, "Mapping of Black Atlantic Performance Geographies: From Slave Ship to Ghetto," in *Black Geographies and the Politics of Place*, ed. Katherine McKittrick and Clyde Woods (Cambridge, MA: South End Press, 2007), 193-217.

[20] Constitutional Court Website. http://concourt.artvault.co.za/collection.php

[21] The term "signifyin(g)," well-known in the African American community, is coded speech-double-talk. During slavery and Jim Crow, African Americans had to develop a language that they could understand for speaking the unspeakable. This language could save one's life. Henry Louis Gates in his canonical work, *The Signifying Monkey: A Theory of African American Literary Criticism* (New York: Oxford University Press, 1988), discusses how signifyin' was a key aspect of the African experience in the Americas, and the development of the black vernacular speech in the United States.

[22] The stamps are a part of four set stamp series. The first set features the architecture, the second set the art work, the third set the history of the hill, and the final set the constitution. See them on the City of Johannesburg website: www. joburg.org.za/content/view/3899/245/

[23] Ibid.

[24] 2 Corinthians 2:20

[25] Michael Battle, *Reconciliation: The Ubuntu Theology of Desmond Tutu* (Cleveland, OH: Pilgrim Press, 1997), 95.

[26] Morrison, *Beloved*, 185.

[27] This mission and the refugees' situation are discussed at more length in section two of this book.

[28] "Thieves in the Temple" lyrics found at http://www.lyricstime.com/ princethieves- in-the-temple-lyrics.html

[29] Patrick Neate *Where You're At: Globalization of Hip Hop Notes from the Frontline of a Hip Hop Planet* (New York: Riverhead Trade, 2004) discusses the confusion of genres and the controversial nature of Boom Shaka and Lebo Mathosa's performances and lyrics.

[30] Notes from an online musical biography in memory of Lebo Mathosa. http:// www.aboutentertainment.co.za/database/lebo_m.htm

[31] "Interview with Lebo Mathosa," *Kagablog*, October 26, 2006. Original interview 2003. http://kaganof.com/kagablog/2006/10/25/ an-interview-with-lebo-mathosa/

[32] My transcription from Lebo, *Drama Queen*. Lyrics by Lebo Mathosa and Angelo Colling. CCP Record Co, South Africa, 2004. Note references to U.S. hip hop artists in the song.

[33] Angela Y. Davis, *Blues Legacies and Black Feminism: Gertrude "Ma" Rainey, Bessie Smith, and Billie Holiday* (New York: Pantheon Books, 1998), 162.

[34] Ibid., 122.

[35] http://www.azlyrics.com/lyrics/50cent/godgavemestyle.html

[36] U.S. slang for recognition, literally shouting out to your peers.

[37] I realize that this is a disputed position. See, e.g., Linda Allen Bryant, *I Cannot Tell a Lie: The True Story of George Washington's African American Descendants* (Lincoln, NE: iUniverse Star, 2004) which makes the case from family oral history; but see also Henry Wiencek, *An Imperfect God: George Washington, His Slaves and the Creation of America* (New York: Farrar, Straus and Giroux, 2003), which argues that the claim is plausible but not yet proved. After weighing the evidence, I am convinced that Washington had a son by the slave of one of his relatives.

[38] In 1847, Benjamin Franklin was the first face to be featured on the first U.S. postal stamp valued at five cents.

[39] U.S. Secretary of Treasury originated the phrase "In God We Trust" on U.S. currency to boost morale during the Civil War, and it was first printed on the two cent coin.

[40] Alan Paton, Cry, The Beloved Country; A Story of Comfort in Desolation (New York: C. Scribner's Sons, 1948), 207.

[41] Martin Luther King Jr., "Letter from A Birmingham Jail," found at the website of the African Studies Center, University of Pennsylvania: http://www. africa. upenn.edu/Articles_Gen/Letter_Birmingham.html

[42] Aptheker,Bettina, The Morning Breaks: The Trial of Angela Davis (New York: Cornell UP,1999), 215.

[43] Louis Untermeyer, ed, Modern British Poetry (New York: Harcourt, Brace, 1920), 10.

[44] Roosevelt, "Citizenship in a Republic," Speech at the Sorbonne, Paris, April 23, 1910, in The Works of Theodore Roosevelt, Vol. XIII (New York: C. Scribner's Sons, 1926), 506-529.

[45] Prince, "Thieves in the Temple." lyrics found at http://www.lyricstime.com/ prince-thieves-in-the-temple-lyrics.html

[46] Kanye West, "Jesus Walks." lyrics found at http://www.lyricsmode.com/ lyrics/k/kanye_west/jesus_walks.html

[47] Payton, 259.

CHAPTER FOUR

A STRANGER IN MY OWN COUNTRY

Alienation and Public Theology

Godwin Iornenge Akper

The Context

There is a debate going on in South Africa, about for whom is South Africa home, and who is an alien there, who is indigenous to South Africa and who is not, who is a visitor and who is the "host" in the South African context. This debate grinds on, even in South African theological discourse. Perhaps it is natural for this argument to erupt in many sectors, given South Africa's historic layers of migration and settlement, the apartheid regime's relentless sorting and classifying of citizens and sub-citizens. Now too there are debates in the current regime, under new pressure from refugees and migrants from African states to the North, as to whose claims and interests have priority. Looking at all these areas of the debate as a theologian who was once a foreign student in South Africa, I am reminded of a deeper, more spiritual question: where and how does the Christian find home in South Africa? Finding a theological answer to this question will help us to better examine our views and attitudes towards the "other," the alien or stranger in our midst.

District Six

These thoughts came to mind during a visit to an area in Cape Town called District Six, which in 1867 had been named the sixth municipal district of the city. The District Six community was made up of people of different races. Some of the inhabitants were migrants from Asia and the Middle East, but others arrived earlier as slaves, artisans, and merchants who were brought to South Africa by the Dutch East India Company. District Six was a cosmopolitan place in the early days, after the 1948 coming to power of the Afrikaners' National Party.

This government regime introduced the infamous policy of separate development commonly known in the South African circles and beyond as apartheid. The system was based on the conviction that people can best utilize their inherent potential if they are allowed to develop separately without interference from any other race. Therefore, this ideology stated, it was necessary, perhaps even the will of God, that different races should develop separately. The apartheid policies, most notably the Group Areas Act, were put in place to enforce a policy of racial segregation, and this law was enforced by the compulsory removal of over sixty thousand inhabitants of District Six. The forced removals started in 1968, and by 1982 more than sixty thousand inhabitants of the District had been displaced. The removals were controversial, and did not begin en masse until long after the Group Areas Act became law in 1950. The government felt compelled to add particular reasons for the removals of the District's African, Indian, Colored, and White inhabitants. It was alleged that the interracial contacts there caused conflicts, that the place was a slum that needed to be cleared, and that it was full of crime and vice. Therefore the apartheid government felt justified in what was by many accounts a brutal removal of its inhabitants.[1]

The inhabitants, however, painted a radically different picture of their neighborhood. District Six Museum curator, Noor Ebrahim, believes that District Six was a wonderful intercultural and multi-religious society that was cherished by all. During our visit to District Six Museum, Noor spoke of the community in terms quite close to the biblical description of the early church (see Acts, chapter 2). According to Noor, the inhabitants of District Six—up until they were forcefully removed and their building demolished—were each other's "keepers," no matter what.[2] They had lived together for several decades as a family, yet the apartheid administration characterized their *ubuntu* community as a "den" of criminals and criminality, a description that fits a community completely alien to the inhabitants of District Six of Noor Ebrahim.[3]

This stark contrast in views raises some unavoidable questions. For a start, were the inhabitants of District Six so ignorant of their own society that it was in fact as problem-ridden as it was portrayed by the apartheid administration? Did they ask for help to "clean up" their community? What did the forced removal of residents of the District show about whether the residents were or were not the rightful owners of their community? Those of us who heard Noor describe his sorrow when he helplessly stood to watch his parents' house being demolished by security agents, could not help but come to the conclusion that the apartheid administration considered inhabitants of District Six to be aliens. But can one be an alien in one's own house, community, *ubuntu* community, and country to the extent that she or he could be treated the way Noor and his community were treated? Evidently so, by law, under the apartheid regime.

These questions of home, citizenship, and identity are at the heart of the discourse in South African theological circles about Africans being aliens in their own countries.[4] The next section will explore some of the different directions that conversation has taken.

Alienation in South African Theology

The debate on alienation is put on the table in a sophisticated way by two South African theologians, Sarojini Nadar and Tinyikyo Sam Maluleke, in what they call "the agency of the oppressed discourse."[5] The discourse covers a wide range of issues—alienation, consciousness, liberation and survival—in theological perspective, many of them addressed in a special issue of the *Journal of Theology for Southern Africa*.[6] It is clear from these essays that alienation in the South African context is understood in diverse ways. While male and white South African academics may have thought it wise and legitimate to participate in the discourse on African agency,[7] some black African and South African female academics criticize the involvement of whites in the discourse.[8] These criticisms are based on the conviction that involving whites in the conversation, given their legacy of intellectual domination, can put the black discussants into the position of using "rented" power, made available for their use by the whites. Under those terms, the blacks participate in the discourse as aliens even though the discourse is about black peoples and Africa.[9] So the whites are called aliens in the discourse instead. The blacks in the discourse believe that whites are not poor, neither are they "Africans" in the original, black African sense of the term. Therefore, when they discuss issues concerning black Africans, they do so as "foreigners," not as people from whose experience the discourse arose. There are, therefore, black South African theologians who question the sincerity of the white academics who write "about" black abilities, oppression, liberation, and agency.[10] So here is an intense debate about who is at home in the scholarly conversation: who is its host and guest, and who gets to write and speak about whom.

How about the whites in South Africa? Are they at home? Not quite! There are white South Africans who claim to feel more alienated in the present-day South Africa than the blacks. Gerry Snyman, a biblical scholar from the University of South Africa, has taken some pains to prove that even in the days of apartheid, when whites in South Africa occupied privileged position, there were still white families that never enjoyed such privileges. Snyman thinks his parents earned everything they got through hard work, not by privilege or exploiting others. They were, he insists, also alienated from the privileges that whites supposedly enjoyed in the apartheid days. Snyman is upset with the present perception of himself and other white scholars in South Africa as perpetrators of injustice who enjoyed every privilege in the apartheid system and are still hijacking the little resources available to blacks in the present South African academy by claiming "Africanity" in their research work. This implies that Snyman sees himself as alienated in the present South African scholarship, especially in discourses about South Africa and blacks.

To engage African women's perspectives, Mercy Amba Oduyoye, the initiator of the Circle of Concerned African Women Theologians (The Circle) voiced out the alienation of African women (black or white) in both specifically African and broader Black theological discourses. Black theology claims to be a liberating theology, but according to Oduyoye, it does not readily address the concerns of African women. African theology too, which preoccupies itself with Christianity's African inculturation and acculturation, according to the Circle, also intensifies the sufferings of African women.[11]

To extend this point further, the South African theologian Sarojini Nadar has shown how alienated and vulnerable women are in Africa today.[12] This concern has less to do with apartheid legacies and policies than it has to do with the attitudes and "miss-interpretation" of biblical narratives by African men. These perspectives victimize and alienate women in their marital homes across South Africa. Nadar argues this point persuasively by referring to her own life experiences in an Indian "Bible believing" church.[13] These experiences make Nadar say that she is "afraid" of "Bible believing" churches, which she claims made her into a foreigner, not just in her church, but in her own family home as well. Nadar evidently lived with her mother and brother, who was an evangelist in a "Bible believing" church, while she was unmarried. The belief in the Church as well as in their home was that the Bible forbids the wearing of male garments by women and vice versa (Deut. 22:5).[14] As Bible believing Christians, it was sinful for Nadar to wear jeans, both at home and outside. Nadar would wear jeans at home when her brother evangelist was away, but would quickly be reminded by her mum of her brother's return. She would rush into her room and pull the jeans off in order not to "offend Christ and the evangelist" in the home. Until Nadar rebelled, with a more accurate and sound interpretation of the Bible that liberated her from her "Bible believing" home and church, she was alien or even imprisoned (because she had no rights to choose what to wear) in her own family house.

Another example of this alienation given by Nadar is of Kerina, who is married to Peter. Kerina works in a shoe factory, but Peter is an alcoholic. He beats Kerina periodically, although Kerina has to foot all the medical bills of their epileptic child. The last beating that Kerina received from Peter was severe. Results of an x-ray indicated that her skull was cracked.[15] Kerina was tired of the marriage and wanted to separate from Peter, but her "pastor told her that she should return to her husband, pray for him and submit to his will. She did, and the following week he punched her in the face again"![16] According to the "Bible believing" pastor, a woman must submit to her husband in all things. Therefore, Kerina must continue to live with an abusive and "life denying husband." So she lives with Peter as an alien, in a deeply dehumanizing situation because the Bible says so, according to her "Bible believing" church.

Recently, Rothney Tshaka, a theologian at the University of South Africa, asked whether Africans are at home in the Reformed tradition. He argues that African culture and pre-Christian experiences are not addressed in contemporary Reformed theological scholarship in South Africa. More worrisome to Tshaka is that even African Reformed theologians have been assimilated into Western values and tradition to such an extent that they do not take their Africanity into account when doing theology. To him, there is nothing wrong in being Reformed and yet seriously utilizing African resources in theological discourses. Tshaka argues that if black South African Reformed theologians do not take their Africanity seriously, there is no one to assist them in addressing the aspirations and problems of the African peoples. The African is not home in South African Reformed theological scholarship. Thus, Tshaka declares, "African, you are on your own."[17] So here is another major case of alienation within South African theology.

Making Sense of Notions of Alienation in the South African Context

The story of District Six provides an accessible demonstration of how alienation in the South African context is a racial issue. One cannot be at home in his or her country, community, or environment due to racially based oppression from white settlers.[18] The story of District Six implies your skin color alone can be enough to make you a perpetual alien virtually everywhere you go, and we might extend that idea to include your thoughts and scholarship.[19] But how about the abusive treatment that makes Kerina's experience a life worse than geographic aliens elsewhere? How about the life-denying "Bible believing" church that supports abusive practices in homes? Was Nadar denied the right to wear her jeans because she is Indian? But her brother/evangelist, and her whole congregation, are also Indians. So alienation is not necessarily a racial thing, even though in the South African context, apartheid's alienating force was indeed pervasive and had many-dimensioned effects, because its root cause was sin.[20]

How about the testimony of Gerry Snyman, that he is now made to suffer the consequences of participation in apartheid oppression, although he and his family never benefited from the privileges of apartheid? Snyman is not at home in the present-day South Africa; neither is he at home, as a biblical scholar, within the corridors of the South African Old Testament Society. As a white man, he is perceived and treated as an oppressor by the people of color who were oppressed during the apartheid era. Snyman, a South African and a biblical scholar, is considered an alien within the society of biblical scholarship in South Africa. He sees South Africa as his place of origin and home,[21] yet in the African agency discourse, he is not welcome.[22] It is clear from Snyman's experience that not only are the people of color aliens in their own country, whites too are aliens, not only in South Africa, but also to African scholarship. So who is at home in South Africa?

Who Is Not an Alien?

Looking at samples of notions of alienation in the South African context, one would be on legitimate ground in coming to a preliminary conclusion that everyone is an alien in the South African context.[23] The historical situation at District Six and elsewhere indicates that the people of color were aliens in South Africa before 1994 when apartheid actually came to an end, at least politically. But Snyman is an alien in the present day South Africa, simply because he is white and therefore a "colonial residual" in Africa.[24] Does this means that the scale is now tilted in favor of blacks in the present day South Africa? Nadar and Maluleke are saying this is not the case! Blacks are aliens in contemporary South Africa, not any less than they were during apartheid, as long as they do not fully own the African agency discourse. Because of South African history, even what should legitimately belong to blacks in African theological scholarship is taken over by the same white people who "had it all" during the apartheid. The participation of blacks in the discourse on Africa is at the "mercy" of the whites. Blacks then, in effect, rent power from whites to discuss issues that arise from their own context. Tshaka has again raised the issue of South Africans being aliens within the Reformed tradition in their own country. Kerina is alien in her home. Nadar is afraid of her "Bible believing" church. Scenarios like these make me wonder whether anyone is really at home in South Africa. So where is home?

Trying to Find a Home

From a public theological point of view, all the notions of alienation presented above provide an opportunity for theological engagement. If by public theology we mean the theological engagement of the church, society, and the academy, the scenarios about alienation in this essay are all subjects of public theological engagement. Moreover, a public theology does not look at a situation in despair. It sees hope, opportunity for engagement, and attempts to chart a way toward changing the situation. In this last part of the chapter, therefore, I present one of the ways a public theological engagement would suggest moving forward. [25]

My encounter with District Six, the place where these thoughts first came to mind, raised a number of interrelated questions: What types of churches existed there and elsewhere in the city at that time: were they prophetic enough to offer a critique of this situation? Did they take any proactive stance to change or at least improve on the situation? On the part of the academia, did theologians engage the situation? What was God saying to the people of District Six in their changing and challenging circumstances? What is the message of District Six to the broader church community facing similar or more difficult situations?

A public theological engagement would try to reveal how a civil disturbance such as the clearing of District Six destroys community, of the interdependence and commonality, which is so cherished in the African context and expressed in the African philosophy of *ubuntu*. In responding redemptively to a devastating situation such as that, we begin to see an answer to the question, "Where is home?" A church, a prophetic church, would serve as a home to the displaced people while it seeks to confront authorities responsible for such an action. We see this kind of ministry at work in the forthcoming chapters on the Central Methodist Church in Johannesburg. This church serves as a home for the homeless Zimbabweans and other Africans who migrated to South Africa, while criticizing the situation responsible for the migration of these Africans. What are the churches all over Africa doing for the refugees? Are they prophetic enough? If they are, what proactive measures are being put in place to improve on the present situation and to prevent future occurrences?

How about African agency discourse and the refusal of blacks in South African theology to accept white South Africans as legitimate discussants? How about Snyman's rejection of the charge of perpetrator and benefactor of apartheid ideologies? The contention of a public theological enterprise is that the broader society, the church, and the theologians should engage each other to address issues that arise from any or all of them. This is the idea behind the concept of the three publics. A public theologian would want to see black, colored, and white theologians (and with the latter, particularly those like Snyman) engaging each other to address more deeply the issues of white privilege and injustice done to groups of South African populations. Such an engagement will have a goal of creating an environment conducive for people across racial demographics in South Africa to address societal issues together. Direct engagement, honestly facing the issues of power and alienation within scholarship, but then proceeding together, determined to counteract those dividing and diminishing forces, would counteract the mutual alienation and perpetuation of separatism. The scholars will also come to appreciate more of each other's work. Would this not be a safe place, a home, which enfolds both black and white South African theologians?

There is a factual story narrated by Anthony Balcomb at the University of KwaZulu Natal that is helpful here. It is about a poor middle-aged black woman who gave alms to a white alcoholic in a dignified and respectful manner.[26] Balcomb raised the question as to what value judgment informed the action of this black woman that she could give alms to a white man, a symbol of her oppressor, in such a respectful manner. Balcomb believes that if we could find an answer to this question, we may perhaps have gone a long way in our efforts to create a morally upright society in South Africa and indeed in greater Africa. What is clear from Balcomb's story is that a theological engagement of the relationship between blacks and whites on the African continent could help create a better society for all who live there. Supposing that the black discussants in the African agency debate passionately offer to educate their white discussants on the need to participate with blacks as equal partners, and not as superior or alien discussants, addressing a common problem that affects them—what impact would this have on both the discourse and the South African theological community?[27] Public theology would not reject the participation of any group in a public theological discourse like the one on African agency. Snyman's own feeling of white alienation in the present South Africa is also somewhat self-imposed. With some deeper understanding of white privilege, he could gain insights and opportunities to learn beyond what is now possible. For example, Gerald West, the white biblical scholar at the

University of KwaZulu Natal, although he has been criticized by many, has never regretted admitting that he was privileged by the apartheid arrangement. He thinks his interaction with the poor and oppressed black communities in South Africa has been deepened thereby, to his great benefit.[28]

Looking at the situation of women's oppression in Africa in the essay by Nadar, a public theological engagement promises a safe space and therefore a home for both oppressive husbands and oppressed wives in Africa. How about a female biblical scholar engaging both oppressive men and marginalized women in a Bible study program aimed at averting the oppression of women in a "Bible believing church"? Rather than become afraid of a "Bible believing church," a public theologian will seek ways of overcoming oppression in church and society by engaging the theologian, the church community, and the society in a dialogue that could hopefully cause a change for better. West's reading of the Bible with ordinary, untrained poor communities has provided healing for the poor and a better working relationship between the oppressor and the oppressed. Such an engagement could be helpful in dealing with the problem of women's oppression in "Bible believing" churches and others. The churches where such engagements would take place might become a home for both the oppressor and the oppressed in whichever color: black, white, or brown.

Conclusion

The experience of visiting District Six and the District Six Museum brought to mind how broadly experienced an emotion—and indeed for many a concrete social condition—alienation is in South Africa. Focusing on the community there that I know best, the South African Christian theological community, I have seen such widespread expressions of alienation that it is difficult to know who, if anyone, truly feels at home in it. Rather than counseling despair about ever being able to truly feel at home, I have tried to show how a public theological engagement of these situations, featuring open expression, *ubuntu* values, and the promise of safety, might help community members find their way home once more. I know that in each of these instances, alienation runs deep, and the issues are not easily addressed and acquitted. I hope that my brevity in addressing them here is not mistaken for naivety or a lack of depth. Indeed, we know that in an ultimate sense, we are all sojourners and strangers here, and our true home yet awaits us. But living in that hope should free us to address the estrangement that besieges us in so many forms today. By God's grace, we can build some safe if provisional outposts of that coming home, here and now.

Notes to Chapter Four

[1] John C. Western, *Outcast Cape Town* (Berkeley: University of California Press, paperback ed., 1996), 142–159.

[2] Noor Ebrahaim, *Noor's Story: My Life in District Six* (Cape Town: District Six Museum, 1999).

[3] The South African Archbishop emeritus Desmond Tutu defines *ubuntu* as a person through other persons in contradistinction to the Cartesian philosophy of *cogito ego sum* (I think therefore I am). See the following resources for more discussions on *ubuntu*: Desmond Tutu, *No Future without Forgiveness* (New South Wales: Random House, 1999); *God has a Dream: A Vision of Hope for our Time* (Johannesburg: Rider 2004); G. I. Akper, "The Role of The 'Ordinary Reader' in Gerald O. West's Hermeneutics," *Scriptura* 88:1 (2005): 1-13; Nico Koopman, "Trinitarian Anthropology, *Ubuntu* and Human Rights," in Russell Botman & Karin Sporre, eds., *Building a Human Rights Culture: South African and Swedish Perspectives* (Falun: Stralins, 2003), 194–205.

[4] One prime example is Rothney Tshaka, a black South African theologian has done an in-depth analysis of who is qualified to be and who is considered to be an African in the present-day South Africa. See R. S. Tshaka, "African, You Are on Your Own! The Need for African Reformed Christians to Seriously Engage their Africanity in their Reformed Theological Reflections," *Scriptura* 96 (2007): 533–548.

[5] See Tinyikyo Maluleke and Sarojini Nadar, "The Agency of the Oppressed Discourse: Consciousness, Liberation and Survival in Theological Perspective," *Journal of Theology for Southern Africa* (hereinafter, *JTSA*), 120 (2004): 2–4.

[6] *JTSA* 120 (2004).

[7] For definition and a detailed discussion on African agency discourse, see G. I. Akper, "From Multiculturality to Interculturality? Locating the Ongoing African Agency Discourse in the Debate," *Scriptura* 89:2 (2005): 1–11.

[8] The designation "African" itself is contentious. Some South Africans, black or white, do not see white South Africans as Africans. See more on this in the following essays: Madipoane Masenya, "Is White South African Biblical Scholarship African?" *Bulletin for Old Testament Studies in Africa* 12 (2002): 3–8; G. Snyman, "Playing the Role of Perpetrator in the World of Academia in South Africa," *Bulletin for Old Testament Studies in Africa* 12 (2002): 8–20; and G. Snyman, "Constructing and Deconstructing Identities in Post-Apartheid South Africa: A Case of Hybridity versus Africanity?" *Old Testament Essays* 2 (2005): 323–344.

[9] See the comments of Nadar and Maluleke, "The Agency of the Oppressed Discourse," 3. See also Nadar and Maluleke, "Alien Fraudsters in White Academy: Agency in Gendered-Color," *JTSA* 120 (2004): 5–17.

[10] See Akper, "The Role of the 'Ordinary Reader,'" 1-13.

[11] See Mercy Amba Oduyoye, *Introducing African Women's Theology* (Sheffield: Sheffield Academic Books, 2001).

[12] Sarojini Nadar, "'The Bible Says!' Feminism, Hermeneutics and Neo-Pentecostal Challenges," *JTSA* 134 (2009): 131–146.

[13] The apartheid system Balkanized South African populations into whites, Coloreds, Indians, and Blacks (Africans) hierarchically in that order. Under this arrangement, the Indians occupied the third position and blacks (African) were placed at the bottom of the ladder. The point here is that no superior race was involved in what Nadar refers to as "life denying biblical interpretations" in her home.

[14] Nadar, "The Bible Says!," 134.

[15] Ibid., 135.

[16] Ibid.

[17] Tshaka, "African, You Are on Your Own!," 535–542.

[18] Ibid., 540–541

[19] See Nadar and Maluleke, "Alien Fraudster in the Academy."

[20] The "Accompanying Letter to the Belhar Confession, the Confession of the Uniting Reformed Church in Southern Africa," describes racial segregation of people as sin. See C. J. Pauw, *Anti-Apartheid Theology in the Dutch Reformed Family of Churches: A Depth Hermeneutical Analysis* (Dissertation, Vrije Universiteit of Amsterdam, 2007), 195.

[21] G. Snyman, "Playing the Role of a Perpetrator," 9.

[22] M. Masenya, "Is White South Africa Old Testament Scholarship African?" 8.

[23] District Six's inhabitants were from different racial and religious backgrounds. This was actually the reason District Six was destroyed: the presence of the people of all races living together, especially whites living with the people of color.

[24] G.Snyman, "Playing the Role of a Perpetrator," 9

[25] On the meaning and role of public theology in South Africa today, see Nico Koopman, "Public Theology as Prophetic Theology: More than Utopianism and Criticism," *Journal of Theology for Southern Africa* 133 (March 2009): 117-130.

[26] I tell this story and engage the ensuing reflection in more detail in Akper, "From Multiculturality to Interculturality," 1-11.

[27] For a more detailed discussion of the need for an inclusive public theological discussion on African agency discourse, see G. I. Akper, "We the Poor Must Abandon Our Wheelchairs and Begin to Walk Unaided: On African Agency Discourse," *Scriptura* 100:1 (2009): 108–120.

[28] See West's *The Academy of the Poor: Towards a Dialogical Reading of the Bible in the South African context* (Sheffield: Sheffield Academic Press, 1999).

CHURCHES AND SOCIAL PROBLEMS

CHAPTER FIVE

OF PENGUINS AND IMMIGRANTS

Bernard Boyo

Introduction

The South African seminar on public theology exposed us participants to a number of key South African issues that shed light on how the country has grappled with the challenges of the new post-apartheid democracy. One of the primary challenges is the issue of immigrants. They are flocking to South Africa, particularly from politically unstable countries to the North, especially now Zimbabwe, where high levels of inflation, political violence, and abject poverty have left millions of people reeling with hunger and hopelessness. While most of these immigrants have fled in search of a livelihood and better working conditions for survival, others are seeking political asylum. This is a situation that is very often repeated in many countries around the world, including the United States and my native Kenya.

The immigrant issue has elicited diverse responses by the South African hosts, ranging from harassment and rejection (including xenophobic reprisals), torture and extortion by local police, and refusal by South African legislative bodies to enact laws that define refugee status and protect the basic human rights of immigrants. The Church has, in general, made few positive responses, to the detriment of its own biblical mission and calling. There are, however, cases where exceptional acceptance and reception has been extended to immigrant communities, as in the case of Bishop Verryn's Central Methodist Mission church in downtown Johannesburg.

In a contrasting experience to that of human immigrants in South Africa, though, our team of scholars was exposed to the humane protection and preservation of rights extended to an immigrant colony of penguins situated at Boulders Beach, near Simon's Town in the Western Cape. When our team, after many days of intensive meetings, spent a relaxing day sight-seeing, we got off the bus near the shore to take in one of the rare sights of the Western Cape: penguins in Africa! The more I reflected and learned about these birds, the more I found myself thinking about the plight and treatment of immigrants in South Africa.

The Immigrant Penguins

The African penguin (*Spheniscus demersus*), also known as the black-footed penguin, is found on the south-western coast of Africa. Previously they were named jackass penguins because of their donkey-like braying call. However, other species of South American penguins produce the same sound, and thus those in South Africa are now named the African penguin, as they are the only penguin species that breeds in Africa. These penguins include two colonies that migrated in the 1980s from islands in the stormy South Atlantic to the mainland near Cape Town at Boulders Beach of Simon's Town, and to Stony Point at Betty's Bay. The penguin goes through a cycle of life that the right environment can extend up to forty years. The potential dangers exposed to this breed have given rise to the enactment of protection regulations by the South African government to curb uncontrolled harvesting of penguin eggs for food, as well as the disruption of habitat by guano scraping, which threatens to drive the species to extinction. The major threat initially focused on the harvesting of penguin eggs for food, but lately the challenge is compounded by "commercial fisheries, . . . oil pollution . . . competition with Cape Fur Seals for space at breeding colonies and for food resources, as well as predation by seals on penguins . . . predation of eggs and chicks by avian predators such as Kelp Gulls and Sacred Ibises, . . . [and by] mongoose, genets and leopard[s]."[1]

Among the tragedies that greatly threatened the penguin species in South Africa in the recent past are "the two most recent major incidents in June 1994, when the Apollo Sea oil spill resulted in 10,000 African penguins ... being oiled ... and in June 2000, when the Treasure oil spill resulted in 19,000 penguins being oiled."[2] The government took immediate measures to cleanse the environment, and through the Southern African Foundation for the Conservation of Coastal Birds (SANCCOB) has continued to care for the affected penguins.[3] Appropriate structures and procedures were put in place to make sure that the lives of the birds are preserved at all costs. The efforts made to rescue and facilitate the rehabilitation of the immigrant birds is normally carried out with much care and due diligence. Once admitted to SANCCOB, penguins are treated, like human patients, with proper identification details that indicate the government's level of commitment to these immigrants. As Parsons and Underhill indicate: "Penguins admitted ... were individually marked with hospital identity bands around each flipper. ... A card was completed for each bird, on which was recorded details of species, admission information, daily fluids given and fish fed, results of weekly blood tests, weekly weights, weekly grading of the plumage, veterinary evaluations and treatments and the outcome details. ... More effort was placed into establishing the cause of death ... when more post mortems were attempted."[4]

As a vulnerable species, the African penguin is protected under the International Union for the Conservation of Nature and Natural Resources (IUCN), which is the world's main authority on the conservation status of endangered species. This international law ensures that the bird receives all the necessary protection rights for its breeding and preservation. The preservation measures taken protect the birds from any form of human interference, even as they are sheltered at Boulders Beach located in the cape peninsular near Cape Town, which forms part of the Table Mountain National Park, where tourists visit and are able to observe the breeding nests of the birds at close range.

The penguins have, by human enactment of law, been given rights that safeguard their survival, protection, and nurturing. They have been accorded every "penguin right," at least by human standards, to live in a safe haven and secure environment that helps them to breed and "enjoy" their penguin life though being migrants and aliens—strangers par excellence. Although still a human attraction like any other wildlife, these African penguins are entitled to specially provided freedoms, with harsh penalties meted on any person who interferes with the well-being of these foreigners. This thought leads us to the other type of immigrants who have found their "homes" in South Africa.

The Immigrants at Central Methodist Mission

The phenomenon of immigration across countries and continents is as old as the beginning of human existence. The term *migration* refers to the movement of people from one place, region, or country to another with the intention of finding a safe haven. Among the key reasons behind migration is a search for social, political, or economic stability. Immigrants often find themselves in vulnerable situations occasioned by their unstable legal status, and their lack of supportive local networks linking them to protection and opportunity. The rich and well-to-do members of any community are often ignorant of the misery of the immigrants, a situation that generates multiple problems. Their plight is witnessed in virtually all parts of the world and especially in the African continent, where political and economic instabilities have driven millions of people to seek refuge in neighboring countries. There are also victims of internal displacements such as is the case in Kenya, where thousands of poor families were displaced from their homes following disputes of the 2007 elections that resulted into skirmishes that led to the loss of many lives.

The immigrant situation in Johannesburg is replete with a forlorn scenario that hits those who visit the Central Methodist Mission church in downtown Johannesburg where Bishop Paul Verryn provides shelter and food to homeless immigrants. The church has transcended all manner of criticism and challenges to become a beacon of hope for refugees, predominantly from neighboring Zimbabwe, while being a target of wrath and condemnation from the government and businesses. Bishop Verryn says that the church has seen an increase in the number of immigrants from Zimbabwe arriving to seek shelter in South Africa on a daily basis.[5] It is estimated that the church accommodates more than three thousand Zimbabwean refugees and asylum-seekers, with an estimated average of of one hundred to two hundred new new arrivals per week. According to a report of the United Nations High Commissioner for Refugees, "Zimbabweans have sought asylum in South Africa in growing numbers since the disputed March 2008 elections in their country. They join the very large community of Zimbabweans already living in South Africa, many of whom have no legal status and suffer great hardship."[6]

The CMM has become a place of refuge. Journalist Michael Deibert, reporting for InterPress Service, observed that:

> "On every spare inch of space on the floors and narrow staircase of the mission—and on the pavement outside—the destitute curl up to find shelter as best they can from the chill wind that moves between the tall buildings in this city. Mixed in among them every night are hundreds of refugees from South Africa's northern neighbour, Zimbabwe, who have fled their country's slow-motion economic and political implosion."[7]

This response of the church to the plight of the immigrants has not gone well with the authorities and has resulted in a number of threats and, worse still, invasions of the church by armed police. Deibert observes:

> On the evening of Jan. 30 around 23.00 local time, the mission was raided by dozens of officers from the South African Police Service (SAPS) who were allegedly looking for weapons, ammunition and drugs—local merchants having complained that the Byzantine passageways of the multi-storied structure had become a hideout for criminals. According to some who were there that night, the police beat several people severely, destroyed property and looted residents' belongings; some 300 people were summarily hauled off to jail.[8]

This attack did not just target the immigrants but also Bishop Verryn himself, who was a veteran of South Africa's anti-apartheid movement. He was roughed up during the raid and saw people bleeding after being beaten by police. Verryn views the incident as a blow against the kind of society that post-apartheid South Africa is trying to build. "We have had the police in here on occasions when they really have been spectacular in the way in which they've handled tricky situations, in the way in which they've resolved conflicts: they've been immediate and they've been focused," he said. "But there's another side of the police, and it's fascist, it's unbending, it's cynical, it will not listen and it's dictatorial. It's everything you would not want."[9]

It is apparent that Verryn is making, through his actions, a very strong public statement that the mainstream Church is wrong to maintain distance from social problems; the Church must re-think, again, how it engages society. This position raises a cardinal ecclesiological question pertaining to the identity and social responsibility of the Church, particularly with regard to the dispossessed.[10] Verryn demonstrates, by his public stance, that the voice of the Church must be heard clearly in all the "arenas in which definitions of what it means to be human and be a society are at stake," as the American mission theologian, George Hunsberger, puts it. These arenas "are where the Christian community lives its daily presence."[11] In this regard, however, the Church has failed miserably. Indeed, we can argue that the Church's silence in the face of consistent denial, harassment, and torture of immigrants leads to a double cruelty—the immigrants already are being denied their basic rights, but the Church's failure to intercede means they are dispossessing the already dispossessed, denying them the security and defense that churches should provide.

Verryn's actions, to the contrary, are therefore giving the Church an identity that reflects the presence of Christ. As Hunsburger puts it: "By the character of our verbal and personal presence, by walking and standing and speaking in a new way, with new accents, we will make clear that way the reign of God in Jesus Christ presents itself to today's world."[12] Hunsberger brings out the need for the Church to become demonstrably Christian rather than maintaining the "country club" mentality of exclusivism It needs to regain its public voice and identity in its theologizing. As he postulates, "how the church can know, what the church must do, and who the church must be seeks the church's re-entry into its mission to be witnesses to the very public announcement of God's reign and Christ's Lordship."[13]

One of the key propositions that Hunsberger makes is "Courage in Public Action," which clearly is evident in what Verryn is doing. Such action implies that "The Christian community doesn't wait until it can convince the [authorities concerned] that a particular practice would be good for society and it becomes formally instituted.... [The church must be] a 'theocratic community' that lives the practices of God whether or not the society as a whole adopts them or legislates them."[14] It is against such a backdrop that we ask whether or not the Church has clearly understood the practical responsibility of its presence within the community.

Certain questions come to mind as we reflect on what CMM is doing with the immigrants, for instance. Does a congregation only open its doors for worship on Sunday morning to give pew comfort to the well-to-do, who need pastoral endorsement as a ritual to satisfy their own sense of divine duty? Does Verryn have any moral or ethical duty to turn the church halls into lodging to accommodate foreigners who are not even members of CMM?[15] While we may not venture into the ethical aspects of the issue, it is evident that the rights of the immigrants to access basic human needs such as food and shelter are yet to be met even with the numerous enactments of refugee protection rights by international bodies. We have to wonder how seriously the human race values its own kind in comparison to its regard for other creatures, notably the penguins.

Christian Responsibility for Immigrants

So what obligations does the Church have to the dispossessed? The Bible is rife with illustrations and admonitions regarding aliens and strangers and the kind of treatment to be accorded them. The Israelites were constantly reminded of their responsibility with regard to the laws governing the aliens. Exodus 22:21 records a clear command: "Do not mistreat or oppress a foreigner, for you were foreigners in Egypt." This law worked to safeguard the rights and privileges of the aliens in face of exclusion from access to human necessities. Every law pertaining to the religious observances by the Jews applied equally to the aliens, which implies that the Lord regarded them, though outsiders, as his own. Those most vulnerable to oppression are the poor and the aliens, being strangers and having no possessions in a foreign land. They are prone to exposure and exploitation of all sorts. In today's context, refugees and immigrants are absolutely among those the Bible would talk of as in need due to their dispossession.

A Reflection on Matthew 25:35–36

In his teaching, Jesus gives central concern to the needs of the weak and vulnerable. In the Gospel of Matthew, chapter 25, Jesus says, "For I was hungry and you gave me something to eat, I was thirsty and you gave me something to drink, I was a stranger and you invited me in, I needed clothes and you clothed me, I was sick and you looked after me, I was in prison and you came to visit me." Jesus is talking here of what will transpire at the time of final judgment and sets forth the kindnesses that characterize those who will enter into the eternal happiness. Such generosity reflects the character of the people who are eventually ushered into the eternal kingdom based on their acts of feeding, clothing, and visiting the poor. We note here that the issue of forgiveness of sin, which has been the traditional evangelical teaching regarding entry into eternal kingdom, is not featured in this account of the day of judgment. Christ's only focus here is good works, which should be characteristic of Christians. These works of mercy and compassion are more worthy of recognition than acts of piety or "correct" doctrinal theology, more than miracles or deliverance. As one commentator put it, "The sick and imprisoned are visited, not healed and set free."[16]

The prophecy here focuses on the eschatological judgment, where Jesus is seen as judge at the end of age (vv. 41–46), giving rewards to those who have lived well and pronouncing condemnation to those who have lived poorly. Because of potential misinterpretation, it is imperative here that the mark or sign of inner transformation is not measured by piety or accession to a given set of creed, or signs and wonders. Those identified eventually as the "blessed of my father" are not the ones who display their religiosity publicly but rather those who perform acts of mercy even without their own knowledge or record keeping. According to Matthew, therefore, "the word of the kingdom and cross restores the heart to understanding, which in turn produces ethical fruit."[17] The righteous are those who identify with and are concerned about the needs of fellow human beings. The Lord exercises his authority to pronounce just judgment, since he is "no harsh judge devoid of sympathy, but one who has been touched with the feelings of our infirmities."[18] The works of mercy that the individual members of the Church perform reflect the character of Christ himself.

Several observations can be made here:

1. On the Day of Judgment, each individual's sentence will be pronounced according to his or her works.
2. Works of mercy done out of love to Christ will be rewarded.

3. The criterion of award will be not how one has heard the gospel, prayed, or preached, but how one has fed, clothed, and visited the dispossessed.

4. Whatever good or evil is done to the poor, Christ reckons it as done to himself.

In this case, then, we can argue that our concern for the needy should include both authentic human pity and a recognition of the divine in the downtrodden, as Christ's substantive and meritorious representatives. How then can we relate this passage to the involvement of the Church in the case of South African immigrants?

Lessons for the Church's Public Theology

It is imperative that the Church becomes more proactive in the affairs of the world and more specifically, in identification with the needs of the poor. The manner in which the immigrants at CMM have constantly been harassed and mistreated, denied basic rights as any other human being—while the Church at large has not stood in support of Bishop Verryn—leaves a lot to be desired. If indeed the Church is the body of Christ and thus serves in his place on earth, then the needs of the immigrants must be at the forefront in its public engagement. The Church must suffer in identification with its master in the suffering of those for whom he suffered. James Cone argues that "Christians are called to suffer with God in the fight against evil in the present age.... This vocation is not a passive endurance of injustice but, rather, a political and social praxis of liberation in the world, relieving the suffering of the little ones and proclaiming that God has freed them to struggle for the fulfillment of humanity."[19]

Mark Kramer cautions, however, that this calling is quite costly, because

> Suffering is unattractive, difficult, and painful, ... and yet real compassion enjoins us to identify with others' suffering as much as possible. It asks us to go where it hurts, to enter into places of pain, to share in brokenness, fear, confusion, and anguish.... Compassion requires us to be weak with weak, vulnerable with the vulnerable, and powerless with the powerless....[20]

If the Church is to live true to its calling, then it has no option but to get involved in the plight of the dispossessed immigrants. CMM has indeed given the Church food for thought in the manner in which we need to be Church in the face of the poor, the suffering, and specifically the immigrants. The church building is not a mansion for the comforted and wealthy but rather a haven for those who are seeking comfort, a shelter for the dispossessed and a home for the homeless.

It is ironic that as human beings we are able to nurture and provide for the well-being of non-human creatures such as penguins, and even go to extra lengths in enacting laws and legislating protection rights. This we have done diligently and yet have abdicated our role and responsibility to be "our brother's keeper" by way of making provisions for those in need. The plight of the immigrants at CMM and indeed many other parts of the globe, not the least my own native Kenya, is a classic illustration of how the people have failed the world. If indeed the gauge of our approval and the measurement of our righteousness will be on the basis of how we make provisions for the needy, it is only proper that we as a Church develop a theology that parallels our shared interest in the protection of immigrant penguin rights in dealing with the immigrants at CMM. The laws enacted by the South African government criminalize any form of interference with the peace and tranquility enjoyed by the immigrant penguins. The millions of taxpayers' money and the efforts put by non-governmental and charitable organizations on their behalf all show the power of human compassion and initiative. If the penguins can receive such care and attention, it behooves the Church therefore to learn from these programs how far they need to go in taking care of the immigrants and refugees.

Conclusion

The theology of the Church must draw lessons from its contextual realities as it seeks to be relevant. In so doing, we can postulate a "penguin theology" that informs the Church on how to treat the immigrants. The penguins have been embraced and "empowered" in their fragility while the human immigrants at CMM have suffered numerous blows through incessant oppression and denial. Suffering hunger, thirst, homelessness, and sometimes even imprisonment, these immigrants have been excluded from society. Theologian Miroslav Volf observes: "Exclusion takes place when the violence of expulsion, assimilation, or subjugation and the indifference of abandonment replace the dynamics of taking in and keeping out as well as the mutuality of giving and receiving."[21] The Church must create structures that help meet the basic human needs of the immigrants in the same way the penguin immigrant's needs have been met.

Notes to Chapter Five

[1] "African Penguin," International Penguin Conservation Work Group, accessed August 27, 2011, http://www.penguins.cl/african-penguins.htm.

[2] N. J. Parsons and L. G. Underhill, "Oiled and injured African penguins spheniscus dermesus and other seabirds admitted for rehabilitation in the Western Cape, South Africa, 2001 and 2002," *African Journal of Marine Science* 27.1 (January 2005): 289.

[3] This is an internationally recognized rehabilitation organization whose core function is to rehabilitate oiled, injured, ill, and artificially rearing orphaned seabirds on a daily basis; prepare for and manage the rehabilitation of seabirds during a major oil spill; raise awareness about conservation through environmental education; and collaborate on research projects.

[4] Parson and Underhill, 289.

[5] Interview with Paul Verryn, June 4, 2009.

[6] "Southern Africa," UNHCR Global Appeal 2009 Update, the UN Refugee Agency, December 1, 2008, http://www.unhcr.org/4922d41c11.pdf. The report points out, "Refugees and asylum-seekers in South Africa enjoy freedom of movement. But the challenges they face when trying to integrate into local communities were highlighted by the xenophobic attacks on foreigners in May 2008. These resulted in the deaths of more than 60 people and the displacement of some 46,000 others in Cape Town, Durban, Johannesburg and Pretoria."

[7] Michael Deibert, "In South Africa, Zimbabwean Refugees Find Sanctuary and Contempt," Inter-Press Service, May 4, 2008, http://ipsnews.net/news.asp?idnews=42225.

[8] Ibid.

[9] Ibid.

[10] See especially Mark Kramer, *Dispossessed: Life in Our World's Urban Slums,* Maryknoll: Orbis Books, 2006). Kramer analyses the life of the poor in informal settlements in five urban centers. I contend that the immigrants are not only dispossessed but dehumanized.

[11] George R. Hunsberger, "The Missional Voice and Posture of Public Theologizing," in *Missiology: An International Review,* 34:1 (2006): 18.

[12] Hunsberger, 19.

[13] Hunsberger, 20. There are five features that Hunsberger discusses as a guide to the Church's public theologizing, which are: A Spirit of Companionship, Humility in Truth-Telling, Particularity in Discourse, Courage in Public Action, and An Eye on the Horizon.

[14] Hunsberger, 25.

[15] It is worth noting the intrigues that this action by Verryn has brought within the Methodist Church of South Africa leading to his suspension and the ongoing differences both with the church as well as the political leadership.

[16] W. D. Davies and Dale C. Allison, *A Critical Commentary on the Gospel According to Saint Matthew*, vol. 3 (Edinburgh: T&T Clark, 1997), 427.

[17] R. V. G. Tasker, ed., "The Gospel According to Matthew: An Introduction and Commentary," in *The Tyndale New Testament Commentaries* (Grand Rapids: Eerdmans, 1961), 238.

[18] Davies and Allison, 427.

[19] James H. Cone, *God of the Oppressed* (Maryknoll: Orbis Books, 1997), 163.

[20] Kramer, *Dispossessed*, 186. He quotes Henri Nouwen, who says that "Compassion means full immersion in the condition of being human." Henri Nouwen, Donald P. McNeill, and Douglas A. Morrison, *Compassion: A Reflection on the Christian Life* (New York: Doubleday, 1983).

[21] Miroslav Volf, *Exclusion and Embrace: A Theological Exploration of Identity, Otherness, and Reconciliation* (Nashville: Abingdon Press, 1996), 67, 100. Volf argues that the concept of embrace is encapsulated in the acts of ""repentance," "forgiveness," "making space in oneself for the other," and "healing of memory" as essential moments in the movement from exclusion to embrace."

IN SEARCH OF A SANCTUARY

Zimbabwean Migrants in South Africa

Sophia Chirongoma

Introduction

Leaving the comfort of your home, being uprooted from all your loved ones and from all that is familiar, and venturing into the unknown: such an experience can only be adequately fathomed by one who has traveled that path. I left my beloved and deeply troubled motherland, Zimbabwe, in 2004, relocating to South Africa. Fortunately for me, I was moving into an academic institution for further studies and had the privilege of enjoying support from the university community and from other Zimbabwean friends. What we saw in June 2009 among the refugees at the Central Methodist Mission in downtown Johannesburg was the result of very different and extremely difficult circumstances. I know that the refugees' sense of uprootedness, homelessness, and despair appears to be a permanent phenomenon, and I can only but glimpse into their experience. I do not claim to have "walked in their shoes," but I write as an "insider-outsider," one who lives in the Diaspora and witnesses the pain, stress, and trauma suffered by those who have not been as fortunate as I have.

This chapter will explore the struggles that Zimbabwean immigrants encounter in a foreign land, challenge the Zimbabwean churches to address the causes of this current humanitarian crisis, and urge the South African churches to embrace the immigrant community and be involved in works of healing, restoring, nurturing, and caring for life—as reflected in the struggles of the Central Methodist Mission. And the churches of the immigrants themselves need to answer Bernard Boyo's call in the prior chapter for a theology of immigration—one that urges believers at the point of departure to press for justice, those who receive the refugees to practice radical hospitality, and those who are the church in exile to walk together with those who suffer.

Things Fall Apart: The Exodus of Zimbabweans

These refugees' and exiles' pain comes, first off, from the conditions back home that uprooted them. Once regarded as the emerging star of post-colonial Africa, Zimbabwe is now a nation teetering on the brink of economic and political collapse.[1] When the Republic of Zimbabwe, known in colonial times as Southern Rhodesia, entered independence in 1980 with promises of peace and prosperity, enlightened by Robert Mugabe's policy of reconciliation, several underlying and unresolved issues laid the foundation for circumstances that led to disastrous political and economic policies. Throughout the first decade of independence, Zimbabwe's economy was highly regarded in the Western circles. The economy grew at an average of 4 percent per year, and substantial gains were made in education and health. Between 1985 and 1989, Zimbabwe managed to cut its debt service ratio in half. However, in the 1990s, the combined effects of HIV and AIDS, drought, poor economic performance, and high levels of poverty led to a stagnation or reversal of some of these gains.[2] Since then, the country has continued to suffer from a large fiscal deficit, low economic performance, high unemployment, price controls, and a lack of foreign currency.

The country's health service, once among the best in the region, has been laid low by the deep socioeconomic crisis, which has robbed it of adequate funding and experienced personnel.[3] For years now, Zimbabwean public hospitals have suffered from chronic shortages of almost anything—drugs, syringes, blood, gloves, and all other essentials—due to repeating budget cuts. Eroding conditions in other fields as well have driven hordes of professionals—nurses and doctors, pharmacists, teachers, engineers, and lawyers—to migrate to neighboring countries that offer better working conditions, especially to Botswana, South Africa, and Mozambique. Others have gone as far as Canada, the United States, and the United Kingdom.

The escalation of political tensions, poverty, disease, and starvation has also intensified the suffering of the rural population such that thousands of rural people are desperately trying to escape by fleeing to the towns and eventually skipping across the border. On the outside, they hope to live free from harassment, torture, and possible death. Plastic shelters and appalling deprivations of food, water, and sanitation are all preferable to life in rural Zimbabwe.

The political crisis intensified when Morgan Tsvangirai, the presidential candidate of the main opposition party, Movement for Democratic Change (MDC), emerged victorious in the 29 March 2008 national election. This result was rejected by the ruling party (ZANU-PF). There was a re-run of the poll, during which ZANU-PF embarked on a reign of terror, torturing and intimidating mainly rural communities to vote for their eighty-two-year-old presidential candidate, who has been ruling for the past thirty years. Through the intervention of the Southern African Development Community, a transitional inclusive government was formed between the Mugabe regime and the MDC in February 2009. However, since then, there has been continual tension that still threatens a complete breakdown of government, with MDC calling for new elections.[4]

The migrations have continued, and one problem they exacerbate has been the spread in HIV infections and HIV-related deaths. About 34 percent of the adult population is infected, and there are about 3,000 deaths per week; these facts aggravate the already slow economic growth and social development. Home-based care for HIV-related ailments has been disrupted due to the departure of trained staff, volunteers, and clients alike.[5]

In sum, millions of Zimbabweans have been fleeing to neighboring countries to escape from poverty, starvation, government-supported raids, political persecution, or violent land seizures. Millions of people have become homeless, tens of thousands violently killed. These migratory patterns also lead to increased vulnerability among the migrants, including risky sexual practices and gender-based violence, as we shall see in our case study of one refugee site, the Central Methodist Mission (CMM), in downtown Johannesburg. As Bernard Boyo has made clear in the prior chapter, the intent at CMM is to be a safe haven for the homeless. Unfortunately, many of the troubles accompanying the refugees follow them into the church.

A Troubled Sanctuary

Zimbabwean immigrants arriving in South Africa are often given a reception that is less than welcoming. Many are subject to xenophobic attacks by South Africans, who are themselves struggling to survive.[6] Most of the people interviewed at the CMM indicated that they had experienced more hostility than hospitality after they crossed the border. They commonly face alienation, homesickness, bitterness, resentment, depression, fear, frustration, low self-esteem, and paranoia. Nhamodzenyika put it succinctly, "Most of the people are xenophobic. They look down at us. They don't recognize us as black. They don't recognize us as southern African people."[7] Adds Tambudzai, a twenty-nine-year-old lady who worked as a data entry clerk and MDC volunteer before leaving Zimbabwe in 2005, "They don't treat us well. They take us not as their neighbors, but as animals. . . . When you go and say you are looking for a job, they treat you as if you are not an African, and you deserve to suffer. But we don't deserve that."[8]

Out of desperation, most trained and experienced personnel left the country without proper travel documents such as a work permit or residence permit. Upon arrival in South Africa, they joined other skilled and unskilled workers in grabbing any employment opportunities available. Desperate to secure employment as a "general hand," many professionals would safely hide their certificates, diplomas, or degree transcripts and completely strip themselves of their true identities.[9] As Lilian Dube aptly puts it, "Their academic and professional qualifications become redundant as they find themselves at the mercy of some employers who are all too willing to absorb the illegal immigrants as wage slaves."[10] Some will be employed as security guards, gardeners, maids, retail assistants, construction workers, or any other menial task that is readily available. With such employment, they will be earning very little (under two hundred dollars per month) leaving them with very little hope of saving up money to send back home.[11] Says Dambudzo,[12] a twenty-three-year-old secondary school teacher from Harare: "We sleep outside in the streets. Sometimes we spend days without eating anything; we spend weeks without working. . . . It's better to sleep on the streets, where my life is somewhat safe, than to sleep in a house when my life is in danger."[13]

Since they cannot afford decent accommodation, the migrants often live in informal settlements such as Alexandra in Johannesburg, and approximately three thousand have found their way to the CMM, a church complex in the inner city of Johannesburg under the headship of the controversial Methodist bishop of Johannesburg, Paul Verryn.[14] Since only a small percentage of refugees applying for asylum are granted legal status, the rest live in "an indeterminate state, waiting for the right time to return home safely to Zimbabwe. Central Methodist Mission is their place of refuge."[15]

This congregation and ministry center, Verryn explains, "has been involved in social justice issues ever since the apartheid era . . . when this church took the decision that it was no longer a church but a mission, and that its focus was not only on the community that gathered here week by week, but that its very specific focus was on the world." Responding to the migrants' plight in 2007, the church began "to shelter refugees not only from the cold but also from crime and state repression," and the number being sheltered each night began to grow.[16] The ministry of CMM to the migrants has raised a controversy, both local and international. While some sympathize and support the work, others respond with utter contempt and disregard to this "den of robbers." On numerous occasions, CMM has been raided and residents—Verryn included—have been brutalized by either the police or private vigilantes.

One can hardly ascertain the exact number of people staying in and around the church. The last headcount, according to a person who resides there and also works there as the head of security officers, yielded 3,700 people.[17] The majority of the people are from Zimbabwe (approximately 75 percent), but there are others from at least eight other foreign nations—Mozambique, the Democratic Republic of Congo, Sudan, Nigeria, Tanzania, Kenya, Swaziland, Ethiopia—and approximately 16 percent are South Africans who come from other provinces to seek employment in Johannesburg. Among these people, there were at one counting more than 1,600 single men and about 900 women, plus 68 mothers with babies, 211 unaccompanied minors, and approximately 60 couples.[18]

The church's open-door policy attracts "'the tired, the poor, the huddled masses yearning to breathe free,' but it is hardly a comfortable refuge."[19] One writer aptly depicts the scenario:

> Circumstances have transformed the six-story, inner-city church into a village. . . . The offices, classrooms and social service spaces where the church's regular programs operate during the day are given over to the refugees in the evening. . . . The sheer numbers can be overwhelming—both for the church staff and the physical plant itself. Central Methodist, for example, has six toilets available for approximately 700 people staying there at any one time. The conditions are exceedingly difficult.[20]

Residents are only allowed to enter the building from six in the evening to sleep and they must all leave early the following morning at six, regardless of the weather conditions, be it hot, cold, rainy, or thundering. They are encouraged to go out either for school or work, or to look for jobs.[21] Several of the bigger rooms upstairs are allotted to women and children and to married couples. One can only imagine how dehumanizing it is for married couples who have to share sleeping space with other couples, without any privacy. The largest number of overnight guests are single men. According to Tongai, one of the security officers, "At night they cram in on every spare inch of space wherever they can, literally sleeping all over the floors, the narrow stairways, in the pews, outside the elevators—and on the pavement outside . . . to find shelter as best they can from the chill wind that moves between the tall buildings in this city. . . ."[22] Verryn also explained that people used to squat on the street outside, but due to persistent and aggressive police raids, following complaints from local businesses, the church facility had to take in a further three hundred people.[23]

In addition to providing a place to live, the mission, via the "Ray of Hope" comprehensive ministry to refugees, has managed to provide one substantial meal per day, infant care and supplies, a medical clinic staffed by Doctors Without Borders, a preschool, and primary and secondary schooling at Albert Street Refugee School in Johannesburg. Formerly the Albert Street School offered education to black children who were barred from white schools, but it was closed by the apartheid government in 1958. In July 2008, the school reopened to serve refugee children.[24] Many of the refugees from Zimbabwe are teachers or other professional staff. An American visitor observed that "they're bright, often highly educated people . . . who might help move their own country but are coming here to suffer."[25]

The CMM ministers to its guests' spirits as well, with church services everyday at 7:00 P.M. and everyone in the building encouraged to attend. It is open to people of other faiths who are also welcome to partake of the Holy Communion. These services do not always feature preaching, but they are a time of fellowship for residents to share their daily experiences, hopes, fears, and frustrations. It is also a time for making important announcements, such as employment or educational opportunities. Wednesday sessions are set apart as "healing, nurturing and transformation sessions," whereby refugees share words of encouragement through testimonies.[26]

Challenges Faced by Refugees—at CMM and Beyond

Although the CMM offers a sanctuary, there are many challenges faced by the refugees living there. First, the conditions at Central Methodist Mission are very difficult because of overcrowding, though it is for many the only alternative to living on the streets. Upon entering the mission, one suddenly realizes that this is another territory, a place that is swamped with people whose faces register numerous expressions varying from hope, resilience, poverty, despair, and resignation. The environment is littered and densely populated. One writer noted that "the first thing that hit me was the pungent smell of stale sweat and urine. The lobby was dingy with paint peeling off the walls, cracked floor tiles and old bags piled in a corner."[27] I will forever remember the faces of children on the stairway that one Thursday afternoon when we visited the mission. These children evidently had not bathed for several days but they were look-ing happy and contented. Some were busy playing and others were diligently looking after their siblings whilst their parents were out there seeking a living.

Other problems abound at CMM. Despite a volunteer security squad on site, women and children still suffer harassment. Police raids and private vigi-lante invasions of CMM have happened. Refugees found in the vicinity of the

CMM have been arrested for loitering. Many of the belongings of those sleeping outside the Church—including their few items of clothing and blankets, identity documents, passports, work papers, and asylum-seeker permits—have been destroyed during raids and arrests.[28] In some instances, police solicited bribes from refugees, threatening to tear up their asylum papers, and terrorizing and possibly imprisoning those without papers.[29] Verryn recalls: "On the evening of 30 January 2008, around 11 o'clock at night, the mission was raided by dozens of officers from the South African Police Service (SAPS) who were allegedly looking for weapons, ammunition and drugs." They were responding, they said, to local merchants who complained that "the Byzantine passageways of the multi-storied structure had become a hideout for criminals." Verryn himself was arrested. No drugs or contraband were found.[30]

There is very little recourse for the refugees during such raids because the very people who are supposed to be protecting them are actually manipulating and abusing them. While applying for refugee status, Zimbabweans are regularly detained by South African police, and often beaten. Like other foreigners in Johannesburg, they are vulnerable to the growing levels of anti-foreign violence.[31] Local communities take advantage of their foreigners' uncertain status and commit all sorts of crimes against them. For instance, in June 2009, residents of the CMM were attacked by a band of local vigilantes in the middle of the night and were sprayed with sewerage waste. Verryn bitterly points out the motives he sees behind these attacks:

> Johannesburg is currently rebranding itself as a "world class city." But foreigners without money are not always so welcome. . . . The World Cup [is] next year . . . everybody wants the city to be clean and beautiful and spick and span. We need to get rid of the cockroaches, who are the poor, and shove them into some corner because that's not what a world-class city really looks like. . . . If they could smudge us into oblivion it probably would be the happiest day of the bureaucrats' life.[32]

At CMM and on the streets, immigrant women are at the "bottom of the pile"; they suffer triple oppression because of their gender, their nationality, and their problematic immigration status. Women and children are easy targets and fall prey to all sorts of abuses. According to Interpol, South Africa has the highest rate of rape in the world, as well as the highest incidence of HIV. The One-in-Nine Campaign[33] concurs that South Africa ranks top in the world when it comes to violence against women.[34] Lacking decent accommodation and being deprived of adequate legal protection, repeated rape cases of the vulnerable immigrant women with no resident papers go unreported to the police for obvious reasons, leaving them doubly exposed to danger. Some girls too young to look after themselves are sexually abused, fall pregnant, and then have to learn to care for themselves and their babies.[35]

Perhaps a bit of background on refugee women's situation would help explain their plight. Entering the country illegally limits one's chances to travel back home and visit family. These forced and extended absences have destroyed the country's social fabric—especially the family—and have fueled the flame of the HIV epidemic.[36] Many young married men are forced to cross the croc-odile-infested Limpopo River to secure employment, buy basic provisions for their families, and send these with some money back home via cross-border traders. Living and working under very harsh conditions, these family men will gradually start feeling lonely and eventually succumb to the alluring ladies of the night who may end up exhausting all the men's hard-earned cash, forcing them to abandon family back home.[37]

These migratory patterns pose an enormous strain on marital relation-ships; creating a huge economic burden on the wives to ensure the family's survival.[38] A low social status, economic vulnerability, and limited livelihood opportunities increase the likelihood that some women have been forced to commercialize sex in order to obtain work, food, money, consumable goods, or a warm place to stay.[39] Survival sex compromises the women's dignity and exacerbates their vulnerability to HIV infection. Survival/transactional sex therefore ranks top among the major sources of spreading HIV.[40]

There is also alcohol and drug abuse among immigrants, even though both are banned at CMM. The sale of drugs, especially dagga/marijuana, happens, and fighting breaks out, particularly because of ethnic tensions between the Ndebeles and the Shona from Zimbabwe. Due to overcrowding and inad-equate sanitation, there are also disease outbreaks. There is one death about every two weeks at the church, with winter months being especially harsh. According to one refugee leader at CMM, there were "six diagnoses of cholera in 2008 but no fatalities thanks to the work of Médecins Sans Frontières. Screenings for HIV and tuberculosis have also gone some way to staving off disaster."[41]

However difficult the conditions at the CMM and elsewhere for the immigrants, there will have to be vast and substantial socioeconomic and political changes before they return to Zimbabwe. A random survey conducted by Verryn in May 2009 reflected that out of the 1,700 people in the building at the time, only 120 said they would go back if they could. This reflects how deeply wounded the people are and how desperate they are, preferring to continue staying under such deplorable circumstances than return home and face the poverty, trauma, and torture from which they escaped.

A Challenge to the Christian Community in Zimbabwe

The suicidal policies orchestrated by ZANU-PF have left most Zimbabweans with very limited alternatives but to join the great trek into the Diaspora, "tearing the Zimbabwean family fabric apart, creating a national havoc at home and abroad."[42] Hence, if these socioeconomic, political, and governance issues are not given adequate attention, we will continue dealing with the symptoms, rather than the fundamental root causes of the problem.[43] "If you see a baby drowning," says social critic Wayne Ellwood, "you jump in to save it; and if you see a second and a third, you do the same. Soon you are so busy saving drowning babies you never look up to see there is someone there throwing these babies in the river."[44] Anyone denied their human rights becomes more vulnerable to poverty, destitution, HIV infection, lack of quality care, and lack of access to medication.[45] So the church must denounce any policies that deny people the right to own land or property; enjoy political and economic freedom and access to information. These matters pertaining to social transformation for social justice form an integral part of missio dei (God's mission).

Since the outbreak of the humanitarian crisis in Zimbabwe around the year 2000, the church's prophetic voice has not been so vocal. Some three years into the crisis, in July 2003, the Zimbabwe Council of Churches (ZCC) produced a statement, appealing for forgiveness for not doing enough to stop political violence, hunger and the economic collapse of the nation. The council confessed that it had watched passively as poverty worsened, leaving children begging on the streets. It also apologized that it "stood by amid the collapse of state health and education services and widening political divisions in the nation."[46] Furthermore, it confessed,

> We have, with our own eyes, watched as violence, rape, intimidation, harassment and various forms of torture have ravaged the nation. Yet some perpetrators have been set free.... We have been witness to and buried our people who have starved to death due to food shortages... while we have continued to pray, we have not been moved to action. We as a council apologize to the people of Zimbabwe for not having done enough at a time when the nation looked to us for guidance....[47]

In a separate statement a week later, the Catholic Bishops Conference, the Zimbabwe Council of Churches, and the Evangelical Fellowship of other Christian groups said they were united in their resolve to pursue "the route of a peaceful, mediated settlement which will bring normalcy to our nation."[48] This was the beginning of a continuous process whereby heads of denominations would unite in speaking out against the unfolding humanitarian crisis.

Unfortunately, the church's prophetic role in denouncing injustices perpetrated upon humanity in Zimbabwe was threatened by the NGO bill, passed by ZANU-PF in 2004. The bill restrains churches from "meddling into politics," confining the church's role to the pulpit and works of charity only. Any political involvement is deemed "out of bounds" for the church.

The church must not be intimidated and silenced by such empty threats; rather it must be a prophetic church, actively engaged in correcting injustices and discrimination of any form, even at the danger of one's life.[49] According to Ackermann (2004:42), "holiness is not withdrawal from the smell of crisis, but engagement, often risky, in situations where God is present."[50] This is exactly what the former Catholic Archbishop of Bulawayo Pius Ncube stood out for in the Zimbabwean society; he openly spoke out against any injustices in government and out.[51] If all Christians were as vocal, probably transformation would have been long realized.

Another major faith-based development was the formation of the Christian Alliance (CA) in September 2006. Speaking about the Save Zimbabwe Campaign, Reverend Patson Netha, one of the founders of CA said:

The Christian Alliance is best placed to lead this campaign because we are non-partisan and not interested in contesting or delegating political power.[52] Our only interest is to see that Zimbabweans can worship and praise their maker in freedom, peace and prosperity as God intended them to. We could no longer sit and watch the people suffer and go to other countries to seek better lives. We will, therefore, never tire or give up until the goal is achieved.[53]

When asked about the relationship between the CA and the formal church umbrella bodies—the Evangelical Fellowship of Zimbabwe, the Zimbabwe Council of Churches and the Zimbabwe Catholic Bishops' Conference—that had recently met with President Mugabe at State House and then gave televised support to the government, the Convener of CA, Bishop Kadenge had this to say:

We are aware that there are other initiatives seeking to solve the Zimbabwe crisis. We welcome these efforts especially if they are by fellow Christians. However, we must not be working at cross purposes or fighting each other. This would not be in the spirit of the gospel which we preach. If we are working towards the same goal of establishing peace and justice in Zimbabwe there should be a time soon when our efforts should converge for the common good. . . . Our message to the President of Zimbabwe is that as a child of God, who professes to be a Christian,[54] we love him. He and the ruling Zanu PF party, which he leads, should now stop treating fellow Zimbabweans, of all colours, as enemies to be destroyed. They need to confess and repent of the past before God and peacefully work together with the rest of Zimbabwe to find a solution to the country's problems. The alternative, which is violent confrontation, is just too ghastly to even contemplate. . . .[55]

Bishop Kadenge's speech reveals several facets of the manner in which Christians responding to the country's humanitarian crisis have been at times so divided such that their common goal becomes difficult to bring to fruition. A statement issued by the Catholic Bishops' Conference in April 2007 succinctly captures the dilemma presented by such diverse divisions:

In Zimbabwe today, there are Christians on all sides of the conflict; and there are many Christians sitting on the fence. . . . Active members of our Parish and Pastoral Councils are prominent officials at all levels of the ruling party. Equally distinguished and committed office-bearers of the opposition parties actively support church activities in every parish and diocese. . . . Outside the church, a few steps away, Christian policemen and soldiers assault and beat peaceful, unarmed demonstrators and torture detainees. . . . We have concluded that the crisis of our Country is, in essence, a crisis of governance and a crisis of leadership apart from being a spiritual and moral crisis.[56]

In contrast to the Catholic Church, African Anglican Bishops issued a pastoral letter which appeared to "broadly toe the government line." The attitude of the Anglican Church's response to the Mugabe regime revolves around Nolbert Kunonga, the Bishop of Harare, who in 2006 became the first Anglican priest in Africa in more than one hundred years to face prosecution by his peers. The charges included preaching racial hatred.[57] Since his appointment in 2001, Kunonga has consistently used his pulpit to "praise Mugabe and decry critics of the regime."[58] As a reward, he was given a farm and a seven-bedroom house overlooking a lake. Any priest who dares to speak out finds himself transferred to a remote parish and intimidated. More than half the Anglican priests from Harare, the largest diocese, have fled the country, protesting that the church has become an extension of the regime. At least ten have sought sanctuary in Britain. "Kunonga has terrorised Christians and turned the diocese into a religious branch of [the ruling] Zanu-PF," said a priest now living in England.[59]

Having noted these divergent responses from the church community in Zimbabwe, we want to call all the Christian denominations to be much more vigilant in their prophetic role, especially with regard to denouncing structural injustices that are costing many thousands of young lives. The church should stand up and be the voice of the voiceless, speaking truth to power,[60] and working to transform "death-dealing practices while strengthening life-enhancing ones."[61]

The Kairos Document, which was framed to theologically expose and denounce apartheid in South Africa, foregrounds the need for prophetic transformation toward justice, heralding an illustrative lesson for Zimbabweans. It insists,

> True justice demands a radical change of structure.... It confronts the evils of the time and speaks out against them in no uncertain terms. Prophetic theology is not afraid to take a stand, clearly and unambiguously.... Despite all the criticisms, condemnations and warnings of doom, prophecy always has a message of hope for the future.... [It will] name the sins and the evils that surround us and the salvation that we are hoping for.[62]

The church in Zimbabwe should be prophetic enough to work toward setting the structures right, structures that keep the whole populace trapped in death-dealing and life-diminishing circumstances. The church must unequivocally demand God's justice for the needy and take a stand against any socioeconomic and judicial practices that disadvantage and victimize those without a voice. The church must confront issues such as the impasse within the inclusive government, which has made it almost impossible for many willing international donors to release aid to the cash-strapped economy. The church must denounce persistent political violence and intimidation that continue to force many out of the country daily. In times of crisis, people look to the church for moral guidance in the midst of this near-collapse socially, economically, and politically; therefore, "the church must make its stand absolutely clear and never tire of explaining and dialoguing about it."[63] The Kairos Document summarizes exactly what is pertinent for the church in Zimbabwe in the face of poverty, gender and social injustice, corruption, and the many dysfunctional institutional structures:

> The church should challenge, inspire and motivate people. It has a message of the cross that inspires us to make sacrifices for justice and liberation. It has a message of hope that challenges us to wake up and to act with hope and confidence. The church must preach this message not only in words and sermons and statements but also through its actions, programmes, campaigns and divine services.[64]

To the Churches of South Africa: Develop a Theology of Migration and Refuge[65]

For the majority of Zimbabweans, migration to South Africa is a desperate search for survival, for *sadza*,[66] "for medication, for dignity and a place to hide" and ultimately "for love and a place to feel at home."[67] The churches in South Africa should borrow a leaf from the CMM, for it is one of the few ministries that have embraced the refugee community and responded practically and holistically to their needs. In addition, there are several related efforts by individual congregations and denominations that respond to the plight of the refugees. During the xenophobic attacks in May 2008, the Rondebosch Uniting Reformed Church in Cape Town played a formidable role in housing and feeding the displaced refugees. Seventh Day Adventist churches also sheltered and cared for many displaced Zimbabwean refugees during the resumed attacks in Cape Town in November 2009. May these commendable efforts spread and multiply.

Even so, it seems as though theological endeavors in present-day South Africa are not much focused on the plight of African migrants. A relevant theology should be able to address the fact that migrants experience a vicious cycle of vulnerability, both socially (xenophobic attacks, exclusion, exploitation) and economically (poverty, unemployment, wage slavery). As Dube puts it, such theology should respond to the questions "people ask and it should flow from the immigrants' experiences and stories, from what it means to be a Christian in a particular time and place (*kairos*). Relevant theologies will offer protection and care for those in flight from death and alienation."[68] Says Zimbabwean theologian Ezra Chitando, "the [immigrant] church must be one with friendly feet, which ministers to every need . . . [and] it must become an all-embracing community."[69]

Article 4 of the Belhar Confession speaks to the Christians' attitude to the immigrant communities since it covers justice for, and protection of the stranger.[70] It states:

> We believe that . . . in a world full of injustice and enmity He is in a special way the God of the destitute, the poor and the wronged and that he calls his Church to follow Him in this, that He brings justice

to the oppressed and gives bread to the hungry . . . supports the down-trodden, protects the stranger, helps orphans and the widows and blocks the path of the ungodly. . . . The church must therefore stand by people in any form of suffering and need . . . the church must witness against and strive against any form of injustice so that justice may roll down like waters, and righteousness like an ever-flowing stream. . . .[71]

This confession provides a valuable tool in fighting xenophobia and injustice towards migrants. It portrays God as the God of justice, the God of the "destitute," "poor," and "wronged." God calls the community of faith to action in protecting the stranger, and in standing in solidarity with people in any form of suffering and need. This is indeed a summary of what the CMM stands for. It is however unfortunate that among many voices that oppose and criticize the CMM ministry to the refugees,[72] there are in fact members of the CMM congregation who complain about the "smelly and dirty" refugees. It is even more unfortunate that so few other congregations and religious social ministries have taken up their care and cause. Overall, the leadership of the Methodist Church of Southern Africa has been proactive and supportive of the refugee ministry, adopting and issuing a statement at a meeting in Kempton Park in early July 2005, urging "all South Africans to appraise themselves of the pain of our neighbours" and imploring "the Christian community to open its doors and hearts to the millions of refugees from Zimbabwe." It urged church leaders "to address publicly and often the scourge of xenophobia."[73]

The South African Council of Churches (SACC) has also unequivocally supported the CMM refugee ministry and openly criticised the Zimbabwean and South African governments as well as the Christian community for inaction with regards the refugees' plight. This statement, issued in November 2009, came in response to the negative publicity that the CMM was receiving after a surprise visit paid by the provincial government's health and social development officials. The SACC charged,

The primary villain is not Bishop Paul Verryn, but government. . . . These people moved into [the church] because it responded to a humanitarian crisis, to which few other people, including the local, provincial and national government responded. . . . The primary villain, first and foremost . . . is government, and not the Central Methodist Church.[74]

The SACC said the committee's visit was "understandable, yet rather late," and the closure of the church would serve to satisfy the interests of those who want the sight of poor and destitute people removed from the centre of "their beloved city—especially now that the 2010 Soccer World Cup was coming."[75] Such statements are commendable; however, it would be very helpful if the SACC and other church bodies would also prompt direct action, in the form of programs that directly address the refugees' plight.

A theology of migration, while not accepting or tolerating injustice, should also be a theology of lamentation. As Musa Dube makes clear, a theology of lament "is not a theology of hopelessness and victimization. . . . Those who lament are making a social protest against conditions of their existence . . . and [for] the need for transformation—the need to let justice roll down into our streets and homes."[76]

A community of believers must fight for a just society that guarantees equal rights for all God's children, and teach fundamental Christian ethics that foster mutual understanding and respect. Where gender discrimination, poverty, and other forms of oppression are perpetuated, the world is laying oppressive foundations for violence and ill-health. We are healthier where justice is not just the privilege of a select few, but is for all and with all members of earth's community.[77] The poverty of Africa, we are learning, is an entanglement, that is, a situation where interconnected systems (including spiritual crisis) result in what Bryant Myers calls a poverty trap.[78] The reality is that you cannot disentangle yourself from one problem without dealing with its interrelationship with the others. "Material poverty, physical weakness, isolation, vulnerability, powerlessness, and spiritual poverty," says Myers, "all work to reinforce the chains of poverty."[79] Since migrants have talents that increase the host country's human capacity for positive development, the absence of sound, just, and creative policies harnessing immigrants' resources could stand in the way of national development.[80] South Africa would be missing a crucial development opportunity if it failed to establish a truly inclusive multicultural ethos.[81]

To the Diaspora Church: Offering Hope, Faith, Love—and Accompaniment[82]

Now we turn to the church that the immigrants bring with them—the Diaspora Church. It must rise to the occasion and engender feelings of hope and solidarity among the immigrant communities who are living away from their families in deplorable, violent conditions. This hope derives from the healing power of the Holy Spirit to transform the most desolate places and hopeless situations. It is inspired by the way Jesus used his body to heal broken, ailing, and lifeless bodies and gave them a touch of life.[83] Writing about faith and hope in a similar desolate situation, a professor of public health argued that faith

> is a crucial adaptive asset when a family or larger scale social entity is faced with an unprecedented challenge or opportunity. Faith makes possible adaptive leaps because it is not surprised by surprise; it anticipates that which may not yet have precedent; it enables action beyond data; imagination not entirely captive to existing technique.[84]

The faith shared by the refugee community at the CMM and beyond is a very important asset that keeps them going, even amidst most trying circumstances.

The spirit of *ubuntu* should also guide the immigrant church in responding to the migrant communities.[85] Hospitality to the stranger must take precedence. The Diaspora church must feel the immigrants' pain and cry the immigrants' tears. The woundedness of the migrant community should be every Christian's concern (1 Cor. 12:1–31). Writing in the context of caring in the HIV era, Ezra Chitando was reminded of the *ubuntu* virtues among the Shona people, where

> visitors are to be treated with utmost courtesy. When visitors announce their departure, hosts are expected to try to persuade them to stay. When visitors leave, hosts are expected to see them out of the homestead. More importantly, they are also expected to travel with them for a good part of the journey. *Kuperekedza* (to accompany) implies identifying with the person undertaking the journey. In effect, they are told, "You are not alone on this journey. I share your struggle."[86]

This is an important reminder to the Diaspora church. It must express solidarity with "strangers and sojourners in their gates." It must engage in *accompaniment* and travel the immigrants' journey of uprootedness, disengagement, hopelessness, and despair. Crucially, it must break down barriers between "us" and "them," ridding itself of stereotyping, selfishness, and ignorance. It must embrace the migrant community, cultivating a feeling of warmth and assurance bound by the same faith and hope. There is hope when women of faith in the Mothers' Union (*Manyano* Movement) join hands in redemptive work within the communities shattered by hate and crime. There is hope when the Central Methodist Church in Johannesburg provides sanctuary to all the immigrants needing shelter and food, when the Pretoria Community Ministry (PCM) provides a safe space and a loving, hospitable community for those who have arrived in South Africa after weeks of travel.[87] There is hope when the PCM hosts several awareness campaigns to sensitize the South African community to the beauty of diversity, when they compose songs such as "Joseph was *Amakwerekwere*."[88] As Ezra Chitando puts it, "a church with friendly feet walks alongside" those who are displaced and are despairing. It courageously proclaims to be a community of pilgrims, bound for the permanent residence for all believers. It refuses to throw stones (John 8:1–11) and recognizes that the gospel compels Christians to love without limits.[89]

Jesus proclaims in John 10:10, "I came that they may have life, and have it abundantly," so Christians should accord fullness of life to all the strangers at their doorstep. Christians should celebrate the gospel as liberation for those oppressed and in bondage (Luke 4:18ff). By bearing faithful witness to God's work in the world and by seeking *shalom* in our communities, we are drawn immediately into a world of suffering, in which people struggle with poverty, homelessness, sickness, violence, lack of education, health care, sanitation, ugliness, powerlessness, hopelessness, and self-denigration. The immigrant church should challenge all these negative forces and be involved in the works of healing, restoring, nurturing and caring for life.[90]

The vision of God's *shalom* should be the guiding principle. It means, the late Steve de Gruchy reminded us, "dwelling at peace in all our relationships at four levels: with God, with creation, with other people and with ourselves … it means to delight in our physical surroundings and to delight in community. . . .

It is clear that at the heart of shalom is the life that God has brought into being, and the desire to ensure that it is respected, nurtured and enjoyed."[91]

Conclusion

This chapter raises a clarion call to the Church to awaken and effectively respond to the challenges confronting immigrants daily. It calls for sensitivity and urgency in dealing with the root causes of migration, the African political and socioeconomic upheaval that have created "pandemonium at home and away."[92] It calls for a theology of migration that is transformative, prophetic, compassionate, and liberative. It appeals to the conscience of our South African brothers and sisters, to spread the welcome mat and stand on the side of the misunderstood, marginalized, and vulnerable. It commends the efforts made by several church agencies in responding to the plight of refugees, but also calls for more coordinated and concerted efforts so that these responses can flow deep and wide from the Christian community and minister to all refuges in need of support throughout the whole country. And it calls for a more profound grasp of this mission on the part of the immigrant churches as well. In closing, we listen to Genevieve James, herself "a fourth generation South African of Indian origin":

> If we are to be the rainbow nation . . . or the poster child for recon-
> ciliation and tolerance, then we must treat immigrants with dignity,
> understanding and respect. We must remember that . . . not too long
> ago we needed refuge, now we are in the position to grant refuge. . . .
> South Africa now seems to be the Joseph, the brother and chief pro-
> vider to the starving and oppressed family on the continent. . . . We can
> take a cue from Joseph and wisely structure policy and laws to build
> up rather than squander local resources, have the heart of compassion
> to feed the hungry, care for the sick and clothe the naked who enter
> our space. After all it is in blessing that we ourselves will be blessed.[93]

Notes to Chapter Six

[1] The story of Zimbabwe's national crisis is well-known; I have learned it best from the context of the crisis in public health. See for example, Andrew T. Price-Smith and John L. Daly, "Downward Spiral: HIV/AIDS, State Capacity, and Political Conflict in Zimbabwe," *Peace Works* 53 (Washington: United States Institute of Peace, 2004).

[2] Ministry of Health and Child Welfare, *National Health Strategy for Zimbabwe, 1997-2007* (Harare: Government Printers, 1997).

[3] "Zimbabwe: Hospitals Hit Hard by Strike," 30 October 2003. Found at web site for IRIN (Integrated Regional Information Networks, U.N. Office for the Coordination of Humanitarian Affairs), www.irinnews.org/report. asp?ReportID=37563.

[4] "REPORT: Zimbabwe—Way forward," *ZimOnline: Zimbabwe's Independent News Agency*, November 5, 2009, http://www.zimonline.co.za/Article. aspx?ArticleId=5344.

[5] These disruptions intensified in 2005 during the infamous clean-up operation dubbed Murambatsvina, translated as restore order/clean up/drive out trash/filth, a campaign to destroy squatter settlements that was launched by the government of Zimbabwe. It was carried out from May 19 to June 12, 2005, leaving about seven hundred thousand people homeless, without access to food, water, sanitation, or health care.

[6] Genevieve James, "Due South: The Challenges and Opportunities of African Migrancy to South Africa," in *From Our Side: Emerging Perspectives on Development and Ethics*, edited by Steve De Gruchy, Sytse Strijbos, and Nico Koopman (Amsterdam: Rozenberg, 2008), 61–74.

[7] Interview at the Central Methodist Mission 4 June 2009. In quoting these interviews, I am changing the names of those who spoke with me.

[8] Interview at the Central Methodist Mission 4 June 2009.

[9] In March 2009, the South African government "opened their border" to Zimbabwean nationals by waiving visa requirements and fees, thus making it easier for Zimbabweans to move legally in and out of South Africa. There are provisions for those who reside illegally to acquire proper status as well, but many remain without official identity. Louise Flanagan, "Zim Nationals Get More Leeway in SA," *The Star*, May 20, 2009, 9.

[10] This section draws some insights from the work of Lilian Dube in her article "HIV and AIDS: Gender and Migration: Towards a Theological Engagement," *Journal of Constructive Theology* 15:2 (December 2009), 71–82, where she reflects on the challenges encountered by African immigrants living abroad.

[11] Surprisingly, some people manage to make ends meet and send a little money back home to their dependents on a monthly basis.

[12] Not real name.

[13] In a briefing to the Nagel-Plowshares team at the Central Methodist Mission on 4 June 2009, Dambudzo revealed that he ran for his life from his home because he and his family had been beaten up by ZANU-PF militias because they were MDC supporters.

[14] During our visit to the CMM (4 June 2009), Bishop Paul Verryn was director of its refugee ministry, "Ray of Hope." In January 2010, Verryn was suspended from the office of Bishop by his denomination, facing allegations of having publicly advocated and engaged in legal action without the Presiding Bishop's permission. During his suspension, he was denied any rights to minister to the refuge community at CMM. Verryn tenaciously contested this suspension and finally, on April 29, 2010, the Methodist Church arbitrator ruled in Verryn's favor and set aside the suspension and the charges. Verryn is allowed to resume direction of the CMM refugee ministry but is retired from the bishop's office and is not allowed to preach or offer Holy Communion. See, Harriet McLea, "Methodist Church Suspends Paul Verryn; Bishop Is to Face Disciplinary Charges," *Times Live*, January 22, 2010, http://www.timeslive.co.za/news/article272226.ece. See also Paul Jeffrey, "Room for Refugees? A Johannesburg Church Opens Its Doors," *Christian Century*, April 20, 2010: 22–25.

[15] Judith Santiago, "Journey to Hope," January 29, 2009, published at website of United Methodist Committee on Relief (UMCOR), http://new.gbgm-umc.org/umcor/newsroom/releases/archives09/journeytohope/.

[16] Paul Verryn, briefing to the Nagel-Plowshares team, CMM, 4 June 2009.

[17] These numbers fluctuate because of the comings in and out of the refugees, but it is an established fact that at any given time, there are usually three thousand or more residents in and around the CMM.

[18] Ambrose, resident and also works as a security guard at the CMM, reported this attendance to us in June 2009

[19] "South African Methodists Offer Hope to Zimbabwe Refugees," *Ekklesia*, July 27, 2007, http://www.ekklesia.co.uk/node/5492.

[20] Ibid.

[21] Paul Verryn, briefing to the Nagel-Plowshares team, CMM, June 4, 2009

[22] Tongai, interview at the Central Methodist Mission, June 4, 2009

[23] Paul Verryn, quoted by David Smith, "Letter from Africa: Johannesburg's Methodist Homeless Mission," *Guardian*, September 1, 2009, http://www.guardian.co.uk/world/2009/sep/01/letter-from-johannesburg-methodist-mission.

[24] Santiago, "Journey to Hope."

[25] Rev. Carleen Gerber, quoted in "South African Methodists Offer Hope to Zimbabwe Refugees."

[26] Verryn, briefing to the Nagel-Plowshares team.

[27] Smith, "Letter from Africa."

[28] Michael Deibert, "In South Africa, Zimbabwean Refugees Find Sanctuary and Contempt," *Inter-Press Service*, 4 May 2008. Found at http://ipsnews.net/news. asp?idnews=42225

[29] Mususa, interview at the Central Methodist Mission, June 4, 2009.

[30] Verryn quoted in Deibert, "In South Africa, Zimbabwean Refugees Find Sanctuary and Contempt."

[31] Tonderai, interview at the Central Methodist Mission, June 4, 2009.

[32] Verryn quoted in Smith, "Letter from Africa."

[33] The One-in-Nine campaign was established by seven women's rights and AIDS organizations in February 2006 to demonstrate support for Khwezi, the woman who laid a charge of rape against Jacob Zuma (currently state president for South Africa). It pledges to support all women who report having been raped, and suffer ongoing abuse and discrimination because they have spoken out about these violations. The Campaign is so named because only one in every nine women who are raped actually reports that rape; it also symbolizes the reality that at least one in every nine women in South Africa is subjected to these violations.

[34] Louise Du Toit, *A Philosophical Investigation of Rape: The Making and Unmaking of the Feminine Self* (New York: Routledge, 2009), documents that South Africa harbours a very high incidence of rape.

[35] Elizabeth, interview at the Central Methodist Mission, June 4, 2009.

[36] Lilian Dube, "HIV and AIDS: Gender and Migration," 75.

[37] Even after South Africa waived the visa for Zimbabweans, the application fees for a passport or a temporary travel document starting from five hundred rand upwards are beyond the reach of many poor Zimbabweans such that some people are still crossing the border illegally.

[38] Karen Jochelson, "Sexually Transmitted Diseases in Nineteenth and Twentieth—Century South Africa," in *Histories of Sexually Transmitted Diseases and HIV/AIDS in Sub-Saharan Africa*, ed. Philip Setel, Milton James Lewis, and Maryinez Lyons (Westport: Greenwood Press, 1999), 217–243.

[39] Elesinah Chauke, "Theological Challenges and Ecclesiological Responses to Women Experiencing HIV/AIDS: A South Eastern Zimbabwe Context," in *African Women, HIV/AIDS and Faith Communities*, ed. Isabel Phiri, Beverley Haddad, and Madipoane Masenya (Pietermaritzburg: Cluster Publications, 2003), 128–148.

[40] Sophie Chirongoma, "Women's and Children's Rights in the Time of HIV and AIDS in Zimbabwe: An Analysis of Gender Inequalities and Its Impact on People's Health," *Journal of Theology for Southern Africa* 126 (November 2006): 48-65. See also Dube, "HIV and AIDS Gender and Migration," 73–74.

[41] Shingirirai (not real name), interview at the Central Methodist Mission, June 4, 2009.

[42] Dube, "HIV and AIDS Gender and Migration . . .", 75.

[43] Steve de Gruchy, "Editorial: Doing Theology in a Time of AIDS," *Journal of Theology for Southern Africa* 125 (July 2006): 2-6; and Girma Mohammed, "Immigrants and the Problem of Integration: A Hermeneutical Approach to Understand the Identity of the Ethiopian Diaspora," in *From Our Side: Emerging Perspectives on Development and Ethics* (Amsterdam: Rozenberg, 2008), 47–60.

[44] Ellwood quoted in David Korten, "From relief to people's movements," *Getting to the 21st Century: Voluntary Action and the Global Agenda* (West Hartford: Kumarian Press, 1990), 120.

[45] Chirongoma, "Women's and Children's Rights," 48–65.

[46] The Zimbabwe Council of Churches (ZCC) includes about a dozen denominations comprising more than half the population of Zimbabwe.

[47] Angus Shaw, "Zimbabwe Churches Apologize for Inaction in Zimbabwe Crisis," Associated Press, July 17, 2003.

[48] Ibid.

[49] Margaret Gecaga, "Women and Political Participation in Kenya," in *Divine Empowerment of Women in Africa's Complex Realities*, edited by Elizabeth Amoah (Accra:Sam-Woode, 2001), 42.

[50] Denise Ackermann, "Tamar's Cry: Re-Reading an Ancient Text in the Midst of an HIV and AIDS Pandemic," in *Grant Me Justice! HIV/AIDS &Gender Readings of the Bible*, edited by Musa W. Dube and Musimbi Kanyoro (Pietermaritzburg: Cluster Publications, 2004), 42.

[51] Ncube openly denounced the evils perpetrated by Robert Mugabe and ZANU-PF members. Unfortunately, he was entrapped in a sex scandal in 2007, silenced, and had to resign from office.

[52] Alarmed by this alliance, the government press started to publish spurious and misleading reports about the formation of a political party. Some leaders of CA were arrested and interrogated in an effort to intimidate them. Bishop Kadenge has also received several threats to his life from unidentified people over the phone.

[53] Pius Wakatama, "Christian Alliance leads the 'Save Zimbabwe Campaign,'" *The Standard*, September 10, 2006, http://www.thestandard.co.zw/opinion/15676.html.

[54] Robert Mugabe is a professed member of the Roman Catholic Church in Zimbabwe. Paradoxically, the Catholic Church, particularly through the Bishops' Conference, speaks unequivocally against the oppressive Mugabe regime. Meanwhile, Anglican Bishop of Harare, Nolbert Kunonga, openly colludes with the Mugabe regime, wrecking havoc in the Anglican Church in Zimbabwe.

[55] Wakatama, "Christian Alliance Leads the 'Save Zimbabwe Campaign.'"

[56] "God Hears the Cry of the Oppressed," *Sokwanele*, April 5, 2007, http://www.sokwanele.com/thisiszimbabwe/archives/category/church/page/3.

[57] In 2005, Kunonga appeared before an ecclesiastical court to face thirty-eight charges arising from scores of complaints: incitement to murder, intimidating critics,

ignoring church law, mishandling church funds and bringing militant ZANU PF politics to the pulpit. For more information, see "Shameful silence on Nolbert Kunonga, Anglican Bishop of Harare," *Sokwanele*, January 5, 2006, http://www. sokwanele.com/articles/sokwanele/nolbertkunonga_05jan2006.html.

[58] Christiana Lamb, "Church of the Flunkey Bolsters Mugabe's grip," *Times Online*, June 11, 2006, http://www.timesonline.co.uk/tol/news/world/article673571.ece.

[59] The priest quoted here requested to remain anonymous as his family still lives in Harare. For more information on this bitterly divided Anglican Church in Zimbabwe, see Christina Lamb, "Church of the Flunkey."

[60] Sophia Chirongoma and Domoka Lucinda Manda, "*Ubuntu* and Women's Health Agency in Contemporary South Africa," in *From Our Side: Emerging Perspectives on Development and Ethics*, 18

[61] Ezra Chitando, *Living in Hope: African Churches and HIV/AIDS 2* (Geneva: WCC Publications, 2007), 1.

[62] Kairos Theologians, *The Kairos Document: Challenge to the Church* (Braamfontein: Skotaville Publishers, 1986), 27.

[63] Ibid., 27.

[64] Ibid., 30.

[65] I am indebted to Lilian Dube for this concept. See Dube, "HIV and AIDS: Gender and Migration," 72 and 76–78.

[66] Sadza is the staple food for Zimbabweans; it is a thick porridge prepared out of maize-meal (corn) and water. It is known as *Phutu* in South Africa.

[67] Dube, "HIV and AIDS Gender and Migration," 71–72.

[68] Ibid., 76.

[69] Chitando, *Living with Hope*, 2–3.

[70] The Belhar Confession is a statement of faith that was drawn up and adopted by the Synod of the Dutch Reformed Mission in South Africa in 1986. For more on this topic, see James, "Due South," 70–71.

[71] "The Belhar Confession," published by the Presbyterian Church USA, September 1986, http://www.pcusa.org/resource/belhar-confession/.

[72] This includes opposition and criticism from among the churches, even from within the Methodist Church members in South Africa.

[73] "Methodist Church Statement on Zimbabwe and Zimbabwean Refugees," posted by the South African Council of Churches, July 2005, http://www.sacc.org. za/news05/methzim.html.

[74] "SACC on the Situation at Central Methodist Church," posted by the South African Council of Churches, November 2, 2009, http://www.sacc.org.za/news09/ CMC.html.

[75] Ibid.

[76] Musa Dube, "In the Circle of Life: African Women Theologians Engagement with HIV & AIDS," paper presented at the Circle-EHAIA Consultation in Johannesburg, July 2–6, 2006, 38.

[77] Ibid.

[78] Bryant Myers, *Working with the Poor: Principles and Practices of Transformational Development* (Maryknoll: Orbis, 1999), 67.

[79] Ibid.

[80] The South African government now may issue at the border a three-month work permit for Zimbabweans wishing to enter and seek employment, but it requires a return for each renewal, which is a hardship for many.

[81] James, "Due South," 70.

[82] I am indebted to Ezra Chitando for the use of the term "Accompaniment" and its implications. See his two volumes, *Living with Hope: African Churches and HIV/AIDS1* (Geneva: WCC Publications, 2007) and *Acting in Hope: African Churches and HIV/AIDS 2* (Geneva: WCC Publications, 2007).

[83] Dube, "HIV and AIDS: Gender and Migration," 78–79.

[84] Gary Gunderson, "What is Worth Knowing about Religious Health Assets in Africa at this Particular Time," unpublished framing paper for International Case Study Colloquium, African Religious Health Assets Program, University of Cape Town, Pretoria, South Africa, July 13–16, 2005, 5.

[85] The word *ubuntu* in simple terms means "humanity," "humanness," or "being human"; it also entails notions of care and interrelatedness, what it is to be human and what is necessary for human beings to grow and find fulfillment. The concept of *ubuntu* is also found in many other African languages, though not necessarily under the same name. See Chirongoma and Manda, "*Ubuntu* and women's health agency."

[86] Chitando, *Living with Hope*, 2.

[87] PCM is composed of interdenominational inner-city churches, NGOs, and other mission organizations. Also, see James, "Due South," 71.

[88] This song suggests that the biblical character Joseph, who was taken as a slave to Egypt was also a foreigner. The song plays on South Africans' knowledge of biblical characters and appeals to their sense of understanding.

[89] Chitando, *Living with Hope*, 2–3.

[90] Steve de Gruchy, "Integrating Mission and Development: Ten Theological Theses," *The International Congregational Journal* 5:1 (Fall 2005): 27–36.

[91] Steve de Gruchy, "A Theological Appreciation of the Sustainable Livelihoods Framework," paper presented at The School of Religion and Theology Doctoral Seminar, University of KwaZulu Natal, Pietermaritzburg, South Africa, July 26–28 2004, 13

[92] Dube, "HIV and AIDS: Gender and Migration," 75.

[93] James, "Due South," 71.

CHAPTER SEVEN

GIVING HOPE

Church-based Social Capital

Charles Awasu

Introduction

Among the many social, cultural, and political institutions we visited in South Africa, the churches were, for me, the most fascinating. The institution of the Church, in classic sociological literature, exists to maintain social cohesion, communal belonging, and traditional social patterns.[1] Churches also tend to emphasize individual worth and personal transformation. This emphasis on personal spiritual change gives hope for a better life to participants, especially to people who are economically and socially vulnerable. Beyond these conserving and supporting functions, however, churches can support the engagement of societal problems by promoting change—both at the individual level and in rebuilding families and communities. Churches also may help society move toward fairness, equality, and justice through the provision of religious, spiritual, and social services to people who might otherwise be left without. Indeed, a growing literature suggests that churches provide members with "social capital," empowering them to accomplish these instrumental goals.[2] Social capital is the norms and networks of social relations that build trust and mutual reciprocity among community residents, social organizations, and civic institutions.[3] Social capital contributes to positive outcomes by: (a) providing values and norms that channel behavior in certain directions and away from others, (b) promoting the circulation of information, and (c) encouraging both exchange relations and long-term investments of time and energy within contexts governed by norms of reciprocity, trust, and mutual obligation.[4]

The Church also can have an important broader role in transforming societies by engaging in political protest and policy advocacy. In South Africa, the black churches in particular played a significant role in the dismantling of the apartheid system. And at the height of that struggle, churches of many kinds and communities were voices of reason and restraint and mediators in the racial and inter-ethnic strife. The transition to majority rule in 1994, however, appeared to end the Church's mission of proclaiming justice and opposing the exploitation by the apartheid system. In spite of attempts to renew the churches' prophetic stance, the new South African political dispensation has left church leaders searching for new relevance.[5]

And lest one think that churches do only progressive, reformist things, we need to recall the simple, functional definition of churches' social role with which we began: to maintain social cohesion, communal belonging, and traditional social patterns. This definition has a fairly conservative, order-and-tradition-maintaining cast to it, and indeed, these roles too have been present in South Africa—not only among the English- and Afrikaans-speaking churches, but among the varied black African church communities as well.

This chapter explores both sides of the functional coin, in the context of how churches in South Africa use their social capital to address the major social problems of refugees and HIV/AIDS. These twin crises arise within the context of the huge political and economic challenges to the post-apartheid state. Churches, however, have unique forms of social capital for addressing these problems, especially at the local level. Yet churches also foster stigma and gender injustice that mitigate their ability to help solve these social problems. As we shall see in brief case studies of the two congregations we visited—an AIDS-sensitive church and a refugee sheltering church—there are exemplary ministries in place that show positive uses of church-based social capital. The chapter concludes by suggesting that in order to effectively combat HIV/

AIDS, social scientists and church leaders alike should study more intently both the benefits of social capital and the impediments to positive social engagement within local church settings.

Post-apartheid South Africa

From the beginnings of the modernizing, capitalist era in South Africa, the racialized hierarchy created there crippled the capacity of Africans to pursue their economic livelihood. Apartheid's social engineering systematically disenfranchised the black majority. Apartheid effectively closed opportunities for the majority of the population to accumulate capital and own land or businesses while reducing access to education and healthcare.[6] Consequently, South Africa is a society where deeply entrenched poverty, illiteracy, unemployment, and loss of human dignity among the majority of the black population co-exist with great economic wealth and a "first world" lifestyle among the white population.[7]

In 1994, political control of the state shifted to the numerically dominant black African community. However, South Africa's vast economic wealth continues to be controlled by white business owners. As a result, the racialized and ethnicized cleaving has generated a power-sharing arrangement between two separate economic and political spheres. Their interaction is charged with opposition.[8] To date, South Africa has achieved a high level of political and economic stability since the transition to democracy. However, despite the classification of South Africa as a middle-income nation with per capita income of $10,100,[9] the entire economy is split, with highly unequal socio-economic conditions along racial, gender, and geographic lines. Approximately 95 percent of the poor are black.[10] Women are particularly affected, with female-headed households having a 50 percent higher poverty rate than male-headed households.[11] Income and asset inequality is severe. Land distribution is one of the most unequal in the world, with 87 percent of the available land owned by a mere 13 percent of the South African population. The landowners are mostly white.[12]

The African National Congress (ANC) came to power in 1994 with a commitment to nationalization, under pressure from the majority of the black population, to end years of white economic privilege and increase state spending on welfare and poverty alleviation. The ANC measures were largely muzzled by concessions made at CODESA (Convention for Democratic South Africa), in response to threats of capital withdrawal, jittery currency markets, and pressure to pursue neo-liberal market policies.[13] In an effort to de-racialize the public and private sectors, the ANC government sought to Africanize the business community through the Black Economic Empowerment (BEE) initiative and other affirmative action programs. Unfortunately, the BEE has profited only a very small minority, while the economic position of the vast majority of black South Africans remain unchanged or worsened.[14]

The Challenge of HIV/AIDS

The problems of poverty in South Africa are compounded by the HIV/AIDS crisis in public health. According to the Joint United Nations Programme on HIV/AIDS (UNAIDS), an estimated number of 5.7 million people are living with HIV in South Africa. Approximately 3.2 million are women and 280,000 are children ages 0–14.[15] The rate of HIV prevalence among women attending antenatal clinics was 29 percent in 2006. Among younger adults (ages 15–49), HIV prevalence was 18.3 percent in 2006.[16] There is significant variation in HIV prevalence by province, ranging from 39.1 percent in Kwazulu-Natal to 15.1 percent in the Western Cape.[17] Life expectancy for a child born in 2007 is less than 50 years, down from 62 years in 1992.[18] Adult mortality is three times as high in South Africa as in the middle-income countries with similar income per capita. Between 1997 and 2004, the death rates for women tripled while it doubled for men.[19]

Poor black South Africans are particularly vulnerable to HIV/AIDS and tuberculosis. These diseases have severely strained the health care system and contributed to a decline in a range of health indicators, notably infant and maternal mortality, as well as overall life expectancy. The stark racial inequities in health outcomes are widely recognized.[20] AIDS is clearly having a significant impact on epidemiological and demographic estimates. The disease also affects the costs, allocation, and efficiency of government services.[21]

The government response has at times been criticized as inconsistent.[22] However, in 2004, the Health Department launched the "Comprehensive Plan for Management, Care and Treatment of HIV and AIDS."[23] In April 2010, the Department of Health launched a nationwide HIV counseling and testing drive.[24] The campaign targets those ages 12 years and older, and hopes to reach 15 million people by 2011.[25] Recently Deputy President Kgalema Motlanthe announced that South Africa has earmarked an amount of $1.1 billion in its 2010–2011 budget for the AIDS response. South Africa has also taken the responsibility of providing antiretroviral treatment from its own budget and aims to provide access to nearly 2.1 million people living with HIV/AIDS. As a result, South Africa now has one of the largest treatment programs in the world.[26]

Despite the tepid response of the church in tackling the magnitude of the social problems, there are examples of church-based activities developed in the field of HIV/AIDS—many of them addressing the needs of orphans.[27] In general, mainline churches including the Anglican, Methodist, and Roman Catholic churches involved themselves in piecemeal responses to the pandemic during the 1990s. Their activities were concentrated on home-based care, counseling work, and caring for orphans. On the other hand, the Pentecostal and Charismatic churches did very little to engage with HIV/AIDS until recently.[28]

More recently, the South African Council of Churches (SACC) has helped to establish a number of home-based AIDS care groups. These relieve overcrowding in hospitals, allow for the dignified treatment of patients and help de-stigmatize the disease. Several other church organizations have programs for those infected with or affected by HIV/AIDS. These organizations include Living Hope (Baptist Church), Fountains of Life and Provision (Mennonite Central Committee),[29] Anglican Aids & Healthcare Trust (Anglican),[30] Siyabhabha Trust (Caritas),[31] and ZAP AIDS (Catholic Welfare and Development).[32] Most of these programs engage in educational activities in public schools, prisons, and churches; collect food for AIDS victims and their families; care for children and AIDS orphans; and provide shelters for street children.

The Social Capital of the Church

Given these mixed responses on the part of churches to the AIDS crisis in South Africa, we need to see what insights arise from the growing scholarly literature on churches and social capital. Religious congregations have long been understood to be places where friendships can be made, support found, comfort and assurance received, and opportunities for service reinforced.[33] Social capital studies in church contexts builds on this idea. Social capital is considered a social resource that generates the kinds of networks, norms, and relationships that help individuals and communities attain important goals.[34] Thus, congregations are increasingly described as sources of social services for the needy, as places for recruiting volunteers, as meeting places for self-help groups, and as administrative mechanisms for faith-based governmental initiatives.[35] Social capital consists of interpersonal networks such as these that help people attain their goals.[36]

Religious involvement has been identified as an important source of social capital. Several researchers have examined the relationship between religious involvement and various measures of social capital, including formal volunteering for religious organizations, civics education, informal caregiving, friendships, participation in small supportive groups, support for families, and inter-organizational networks.[37] Recent governmental interest in the role of faith-based organizations in the United States and elsewhere as providers of social services has further emphasized the potential for religious involvement in social transformation.[38]

According to an American urban ministry leader, Robert Bachelder, the key to revitalizing distressed neighborhoods lies in the amount of social capital available in a community. In addition to the spiritual sustenance they offer, churches generate social capital and invest heavily in the surrounding community. Sustaining viable communities requires places where people can gather together, work together, and learn to trust one another.[39] Through "fellowship" church members come to see themselves as a family, a community of people who care for one another and do things together.[40] This family-like atmosphere provides "spiritual strength" and bonding that generates social capital. As people learn to communicate with each other and trust each other, they create a vital network that holds society together.[41]

In the United States, churches have played a particularly important role in equalizing political participation because they are sites where people of color and low-income people have had the opportunity to learn civic skills.

These skills are translated to politics, through letter-writing, speech-making, and learning how to plan and make decisions in meetings.[42] More broadly, the African American church has supplied the social networks, leadership, and motivation needed to mobilize African Americans for community renewal and political empowerment.[43] European Americans also have relied upon the strong social capital of their communities, especially those centered on the Catholic parish, to shape public policy.[44] By providing opportunities for people to work together, the church provides a place for people to become part of the community and learn civic skills that encourage community development.

In South Africa, the church is widely recognized as an important factor in society. Eighty percent of South Africans claim to be Christians.[45] Throughout South Africa, churches provide a regular sense of hope and community engagement. However, the apartheid-regimented social divisions are reflected in the way that church life has been ordered in South Africa. In many cases, Afrikaans-speaking churches not only submitted to, but also encouraged, racist government policies.[46] Specifically, churches supported the Act 55 of 1949, which prohibited interracial marriages; the Immorality Act of 1950 and the 1957 Consolidation Act on Immorality, which forbade sexual relations between the whites and all other races; and the 1957 Amendment Act on Native Affairs with the so-called "church-article" that prohibited non-whites from attending services in white areas.[47]

On the other hand, many churches and para-church organizations mobilized efforts to confront apartheid. For example, the South African Council of Churches (SACC)[48] was instrumental in framing the liberation struggle on religious and moral grounds. In the 1980s, SACC became a strong factor in the revival of mass action against apartheid and a formidable supporter of the campaign for sanctions against South Africa. Many church leaders like Desmond Tutu and Allan Boesak also used their authority and position to fight for social justice.[49] However, not all churches or clergy conceptualized their calling as one to confront apartheid. There was not a unanimous church position related to the fight against apartheid. Leaders of the Anglican Church spoke out in opposition to apartheid, but church members disagreed over tactics for expressing their views. Some white Anglicans vigorously opposed their church's involvement in politics, while many black Anglicans became leaders in the anti-apartheid movement.[50] The varied network of South African evangelicals, white and black, also took a variety of positions—supporting, opposed, and purportedly apolitical—toward the apartheid regime.[51] The overwhelmingly black Methodist Church openly adopted anti-apartheid positions on many public issues. However, this activism by its leaders led to low support among the membership, who feared public scrutiny on this politically sensitive issue.[52]

Despite the difficult social terrain, the church in South Africa has survived the apartheid ideology, racism, civil strife, political parties, and successive governments. However, since the collapse of apartheid, many churches have suspended their harsh theological characterizations of the state. Furthermore, struggles that were mounted as a matter of faith and principle against the apartheid regime have all but faded away.[53] Yet still, the experiences of the liberation struggle show that many churches utilized their social capital for collective action and played a major role in the defeat of apartheid.

The Church as a Place of Stigma

The legacy of apartheid has demonstrated the effects of negative social capital as manifested in the struggles of the South African churches regarding issues of racism, discrimination, diversity, and intolerance.[54] The racialized and ethnic cleavings were characterized by distrust, fear, racism, and exclusion of outsiders. As a result, the available social capital in the churches was not a homogenous resource equally available to all members of the community.[55] Historically, many churches saw integration of all races and ethnic groups as a threat rather than an opportunity to demonstrate God's love.[56] Often, that threat has been expressed in racial contempt and conflict, exclusion, discrimination, and intolerance. The dangerous theological and spiritual dimensions of racism under apartheid have raised fundamental questions about the oppression and discrimination in the church, and there were churches that remained silent during the anti-apartheid struggle.[57] Other churches justified the theology of segregation and doctrine of purity, believing that God divided all people into collective units and permanently separated them from each other.[58]

In sum, many in South Africa, including the churches, have engaged in a negative "othering" process that involved the exploitation of power imbalances to favor whites over coloreds, Indians, Africans, and now, African immigrants.

All these institutional and structural boundaries constructed between groups during the apartheid days still persist. We see these attitudes in the strong negative views that South Africans hold about immigrants, particularly people from other African countries. African migrants are blamed for taking jobs from needy South Africans, causing crime in the country, and for carrying diseases such as HIV/AIDS.[59]

Churches are paralyzed by the stigma and discrimination that exists in the community and find it difficult to engage with issues of xenophobia and HIV/AIDS in the public arena.[60] The silence that surrounds them is compounded by the fact that xenophobia and HIV/AIDS are considered cultural taboo subjects in public forums and more especially in church. Few churches even speak and teach about the reality of HIV/AIDS. Thus the Church in some cases has become a place of stigma, discrimination, and rejection, using otherness to stigmatize groups by race, immigration status, sexuality, and condition of mental or physical health.[61]

By moralizing sexuality, gender relations, and the body in general, churches contribute to the stigmatization of HIV/AIDS. Historically, the Church has reduced issues of sexuality and morality to personal choice and self-determining agency alone. This has obscured the importance of material and social conditions that shape sexual relations and underlie the spread of the virus, such as poverty and social inequality.[62] Sexual taboos and the lack of analysis of patriarchy and gender injustice within the church and society contribute to the stigmatization and marginalization of refugees and People Living with HIV/AIDS (PLWHA). Purity codes have long been the source of theological framework applied to sufferers of disease and denigration, reinforcing their pain and their exclusion from the social body of salvation.[63] Many in the Church believe that HIV/AIDS is a "punishment from God" and assume that a person is infected because of disobedience or promiscuous behavior.

The role of the Church in producing and policing stigma is profound. According to Gerald West, the dominant theology in the South African church is a theology of retribution.[64] This theology has devastating effects on the peoples of South Africa and in some ways renders the Church leaders impotent. The balance between the sternness of the law and the mercy of the gospel remains a continuing perplexity for many churches.[65] God's holiness and God's love are particularly acute in matters having to do with sexuality. Interestingly, the Church has not been able to rise above the negative social structures. Much of the administrative-political structures developed in implementing apartheid philosophy still persist.

Gender Injustice

The South African churches' response to these critical matters is complicated further by gender roles and relations. According to the new Constitution, South Africa is a non-racist and non-sexist society. However, in practice, the sociopolitical structures continue to perpetuate patriarchal control of women.[66] Sadly, many churches accept prevailing values from society and make selective use of biblical texts to reinforce these values. Religious beliefs support and are complicit in male dominance. Cultural issues reinforce and in some cases are reinforced by evangelical attitudes. Predominant literalist biblical interpretations imposed on existing patriarchal African cultures reinforce the subordinate position of women and perpetuate sexism.

Women face additional burdens during forced migration because of their gender. In most cases, immigration policies are biased towards skills- and wealth-based criteria, which discriminate against women coming from cultures that have denied them both.[67] Rules for granting entry are driven by labor-market needs, advantaging individuals with desirable skills, expertise, resources, and entrepreneurial skills. Women's low level of education, low language skills, and low employable skills limit their ability to be resettled in third countries. Furthermore, during immigration hearings, only the head of family (often a man) is interviewed. When the head of family fulfills the requirements, his benefits are extended to members of his family. When his application is rejected, his whole family is rejected. Furthermore, domestic violence, rape, and other harms particularly committed against women are not dealt with in the processing of asylum applications.

Several researchers have affirmed that gender role norms are among the strongest underlying social factors that influence sexual behaviors.[68] Norms related to masculinity and sexuality place young men and young women at high risk of HIV infection. Practices such as widow inheritance, bride price, "offering" sex with a woman as a sign of hospitality, and child betrothal entrench male dominance.[69] The gendered nature of HIV/AIDS is borne out by practices where men put women and girls at risk of infection. Evangelical attitudes do compound the situation when an incomplete knowledge or biased selection of biblical text leads to unbalanced views. Several Old Testament scriptures are used to justify God's punishment on HIV/AIDS victims. Religious teachings are at times used as the primary source to propagate abuses of women as part of God's will.[70] Narrow biblical interpretations support the belief that God bestowed upon men power and authority over women.

The dramatic disproportion of women living with HIV/AIDS is due to sex and gender inequity. The unequal balance of social power between young men and women, combined with the patterns of risk behaviors among young men, suggests a connection between masculinities and sexual and reproductive outcomes.[71] Women's vulnerability is heightened by their economic dependence on men, lack of access to education, poverty, sexual exploitation, coercion, and rape. Many in the Church believe that sex is to be endured rather than enjoyed as a gift from God. As a result of their subordinate cultural status, women are expected to be passive and innocent in matters related to sex.[72] It is accepted that women's role is to please men sexually, and they have little to say over the kinds of sexual practices they engage in.[73] Such teachings by Christians about sex and gender relationships take away women's control over their bodies.[74] Churches seem unable or unwilling to help equip young women to withstand the social pressures to participate in these dangerous behaviors. The lack of open discussions in churches about healthy sexual activity makes the Christian influence one that indirectly contributes to the spread of HIV.

In our brief sojourn in South Africa, however, we saw some rather different approaches to the crises of xenophobia and HIV/AIDS. At one extraordinary congregation, we saw ministries that overcame the impediments that hinder so many churches in addressing these issues.

Restorative Healing at the J. L. Zwane Church

The J. L. Zwane Memorial Church in Guguletu functions both as a church and a multi-purpose community center that provides a range of services to the residents. The center's major focus is on HIV/AIDS prevention, care, and support programs.[75] According to the pastor, Rev. Xapile, "we came here because we wanted to take a stand against HIV."[76] When most churches slammed the doors on the HIV infected, the J. L. Zwane Center threw its doors wide open. The Center, which is also referred to locally as the "AIDS Church" has been ostracized by other pastors and churches because of their acceptance of victims of HIV/AIDS.

The church acts as an agent of social transformation by providing hope, group motivation, and group solidarity to those who come to the Center. Social trust appears to be quite high among the members of the church. This trust seems to be producing a high level of social capital. The church has developed into a community where people who are infected or otherwise affected by HIV/AIDS are loved and cared for regardless of social status. Thus, the people, services, and other material resources gathered at the church create social capital. J. L. Zwane helps sustain the common good by organizing, inspiring, and equipping township residents to help each other.

Due to the large number of people infected with and affected by HIV/ AIDS in Guguletu, the J. L. Zwane Center has a variety of social services to address the problem, including a health clinic, HIV/AIDS education programs, hospice care, nutrition programs, the donation of food and other material items, support for orphanages, a theatre, and an after-school study program. The church provides coping assistance, including facts about the disease, counseling, advice, and prayer—in short, emotional, physical, and spiritual support. Group participants are also trained in counseling skills to provide care and support to others in the community infected with or affected by HIV/AIDS.

Staff and volunteers from the J. L. Zwane Center visit children who have lost their parents to deliver food, provide companionship, and to talk.[77] The church-supported Rainbow School helps children after school with their homework and provides a positive and interactive environment. One of the major ministries at the J. L. Zwane Center involves the use of music to educate people about HIV/AIDS. Through a highly entertaining collection of songs, a group of young musicians named Siyaya teach the ABCs of AIDS education (Abstain, Be faithful, use Condoms).[78]

The church has been very adept at fostering greater understanding, promoting equity for HIV patients, and providing access to treatments and care. This has encouraged HIV/AIDS patients to openly declare their status and has also encouraged others to go for voluntary counseling and testing for HIV. Further, frequent addresses of the pastor on shame-related HIV stigma enhances the community's capacity to deal with HIV-related issues. Disclosure of HIV status to the pastors and other members of the church have facilitated emotional healing and support. Furthermore, HIV status disclosure to the congregation improves the disease's prognosis by facilitating initiation and adherence to treatment.

At the J. L. Zwane Church, worshippers pack the large sanctuary on Sundays for worship—joyous singing and dancing. They affirm their belief in God and his grace by supporting their solidarity—lifting up one another. Many in the congregation have disclosed their HIV positive status without shame. During each Sunday worship service, there is an HIV/AIDS presentation.[79] Usually, a member of the church who has been infected or affected by HIV/AIDS gives a testimony about the goodness of God. Other times, public health workers, doctors, and other medical personnel present educational information on HIV/AIDS to the congregation. In this atmosphere, the stigma of HIV/AIDS is stripped away and a positive identity is formed.

The J. L. Zwane Center has been able to humanize HIV/AIDS victims. At the Center, participation in Church rituals and scriptural explanations has allowed those impacted by HIV/AIDS to develop a sense of self that is based on the image of God. The faith practices and beliefs engendered at the J. L. Zwane Center provide a sense of peace and hope, which builds and strengthens the community's capacity to cope with HIV/AIDS. Beliefs about God taught at the church help mediate HIV–related shame in several ways and do reduce both shame and the HIV/AIDS stigma. Engagement with the church has reduced the social isolation of the HIV/AIDS population. And through its pastor, the church is supporting advocacy for stronger programs of prevention and treatment.

Conclusion

South Africa's transition to majority rule has been complicated by the life-threatening experiences of millions of its residents who were expecting to benefit from the end of apartheid. The legacies of poverty, illiteracy, unemployment, and stigmatized status have generated significant problems for victims of

HIV/AIDS and African migrants looking for reasons to be hopeful in the new South Africa. The HIV/AIDS crisis in the post-apartheid era has provided the church with manifold challenges and opportunities to use its social capital for community development. The evidence from the South African context demonstrates that the church does have an abundance of social capital that is empowering. The legacy of an apartheid-ordered society and a theology that stigmatizes can combine to marginalize women, refugees, HIV/AIDS victims, the poor, and others who are most in need of the Church's help.

Both the J. L. Zwane Church and Center have been able to use their social capital in more affirmative ways as they provide support, dignity, care, healing, and hope to refugees and those affected by HIV/AIDS. Engagement with these churches has reduced the social isolation of refugees and HIV/AIDS affected people. By breaking the conspiracy of silence about asylum seekers and HIV/AIDS, the church and its leaders have influenced community, society, church, and national leaders. Mainly they have heightened the debate concerning the problems of asylum seekers and the impact of HIV/AIDS. The initiatives championed by these two churches have highlighted the fact that most of South Africa's distressed communities are seeded with churches that have significant social capital that can be tapped in the struggle for social transformation. Policy makers, social workers, and public health practitioners should be encouraged to understand the significance of the social capital generated by churches and how that resource can be used to enhance the wider community. And top-level church leaders should now see that the vision and values they preach, enact into public resolutions and advocated in national media, gain traction when they are embodied and enacted locally in congregations. How can godly and world-saving ideas be given some legs, and the shackles be taken off that may bind them? The answer, now braced by much social theory, is an old one—through the local church.

Notes to Chapter Seven

[1] Ernst Troeltsch, *The Social Teachings of the Christian Churches* (New York: Macmillan, 1931).

[2] For a fuller discussion, see Andrew Greely, "Coleman Revisited: Religious Structures as a Source of Social Capital," *American Behavioral Scientist*, 40 (1997): 481–510; R. Stephen Warner, "Work in Progress Toward a new Paradigm for Sociological Study of Religion in the United States," *American Journal of Sociology* 98 (1993): 1044–1093; Darren E. Sherkat and Christopher G. Ellison, "Recent Developments and Current Controversies in the Sociology of Religion," *Annual Review of Sociology* 25 (1999): 363-394.

[3] Mark Warren, Philip Thompson, and Susan Saegart, "Social Capital and Poor Communities: A Framework for Analysis," paper presented at the conference on Social Capital and Poor Communities: Building and Using Social Assets to Combat Poverty, CUNY Graduate School and University Center, New York, March 1999.

[4] James Coleman, "Social Capital in the Creation of Human Capital," *American Journal of Sociology* 94, supplement (1988): 95–120; Alejandro Portes, "Social Capital: Its Origins and Applications in Modern Sociology," *Annual Sociology* 24 (1988): 1–24.

[5] John De Gruchy and Steve De Gruchy, *The Church Struggle in South Africa* (Minneapolis: Fortress Press, 2005).

[6] Sharon Subreenduth, "Why, Why Are We Not Allowed Even . . . ?: A De/colonizing Narrative of Complicity and Resistance in Post/Apartheid South Africa," *International Journal of Qualitative Studies in Education* 19.5 (2006): 617–638.

[7] Landon Meyer, Rodney Ehrlich, & Ezra Susser, "Social Epidemiology in South Africa," *Epidemiologic Reviews* 26 (2004): 112-123. Accessed October 27, 2011. http://epirev.oxfordjournals.org

[8] Antoinette Handley, *Business and the State in Africa: Economic Policy-Making in the Neo-Liberal Era* (New York: Cambridge University Press, 2008).

[9] "Income and Expenditure of Households, 2005–2006: Statistical Release PO100," South Africa Statistics, South Africa Government, March 4, 2008, http://www.statssa.gov.za/Publications/P0100/P01002005.pdf.

[10] Murray Leibbrandt et al. "Trends in South African Income Distribution and Poverty since the Fall of Apartheid," OECD Social Employment and Migration Working Papers, No. 101, OECD Publishing, 2010. Accessed October 28, 2011. http://dx.doi.org/10.1787/5kmms0t7p1ms-en

[11] Ibid.

[12] Charles Hamilton, et al., *Beyond Racism: Race and Inequality in Brazil, South Africa and the United States* (Boulder: Lynne Rienner Publishers, 2001).

[13] Ibid.

[14] Stefan Andreasson, "The African National Congress and its Critics: 'Predatory Liberalism,' Black Empowerment and Intra-Alliance Tensions in Post-Apartheid South Africa," *Democratization* 13.2 (2006): 303–322.

[15] "Country Progress Report on the Declaration of Commitment on HIV/AIDS: Republic of South Africa," UNAIDS, United Nations, March 31, 2010, http://www.unaids.org/en/dataanalysis/monitoringcountryprogress/2010progressreportssubmittedbycountries/southafrica_2010_country_progress_report_en.pdf.

[16] Ibid.

[17] "South Africa: Country Situation," UNAIDS, United Nations, July 2008, http://data.unaids.org/pub/FactSheet/2008/sa08_soa_en.pdf.

[18] World Health Statistics 2011. Accessed October 28, 2011. http: www.who.int/gho/publications/world_health_statistics/2011/en/index.html

[19] "Country Progress Report," (2010). UNAIDS.

[20] Cathy Campbell, Brian Williams, and Denise Gilgen, "Is Social Capital a Useful Conceptual Tool for Exploring Community Level Influences on HIV Infection? An Exploratory Case Study from South Africa," *Aids Care* 14.1 (2002): 41–54.

[21] One of the key challenges to the global South in expanding the availability of medication is the steep cost of antiretroviral drugs.

[22] In 2000, President Thabo Mbeki publicly questioned the Western scientific orthodoxy that AIDS is caused by the HIV virus. Following international condemnation, Mbeki recanted these views and appointed a new head to lead the government's HIV/AIDS response. In April 2010, the Zuma government, in collaboration with the South African National AIDS Council, the Department of Health, and other stakeholders has stepped up the HIV testing and counseling on a large scale.

[23] See "Comprehensive HIV and AIDS Care, Management and Treatment Plan for South Africa," Department of Health, Republic of South Africa, accessed April 21, 2010, http:www.doh.gov.za/docs/hivaids-progressrep.html.

[24] http://www.infor.gov.za/speech/DynamicAction?pageid=4618&tid=8861

[25] Ibid.

[26] "Country Progress Report," (2010). UNAIDS.

[27] Philippe Denis, "The Church's Impact on HIV/AIDS Prevention and Mitigation in South Africa," *Journal of Theology for Southern Africa* 134 (2009): 66–81.

[28] See also Helen Epstein, *The Invisible Cure: Africa, the West and the Fight Against AIDS* (New York: Farrar, Straus and Giroux, 2007).

[29] Mennonite Central Committee. http://aids.mcc.org/spotlight/southern-africa

[30] "Anglican Aids & Healthcare Trust." Anglican Church of Southern Africa. Accessed August 26, 2011. http://www.anglicanaids.net/.

[31] Caritas, accessed August 27, 2011, http://www.caritas.org/.

[32] Catholic Welfare & Development, accessed April 23, 2010, http:www.cwd.org. za/searchpro/index.asp?.

[33] See for examples, Gerhard E. Lenski, *The Religious Factor: A Sociological Study of Religion's Impact on Politics, Economics, and Family Life* (Garden City: Doubleday, 1961); Charles Glock, Benjamin B. Ringer, and Earl R. Babbie, *To Comfort and to Challenge: A Dilemma of the Contemporary Church* (Berkeley: University of California Press, 1967).

[34] Glenn Loury, "Why Should We Care about Group Inequality?" *Social Philosophy and Policy* 5 (1987): 843-867; James S. Coleman, *Foundations of Social Theory* (Cambridge: Harvard University Press, 1990); Robert Putnam, *Making Democracy Work: Civic Traditions in Modern Italy* (Princeton: Princeton University Press, 1993); and Robert Putnam, *Bowling Alone: The Collapse and Revival of American Community* (New York: Simon & Schuster, 2000).

[35] Nancy T. Ammerman, *Congregations and Community* (New Brunswick: Rutgers University Press, 1997); Jerry Z. Park and Christian Smith, "'To whom much has been given . . .': Religious Capital and Community Voluntarism Among Churchgoing Protestants," *Journal for the Scientific Study of Religion* 39 (2000): 272–286; Penny Edgell Becker and Pawan H. Dhingra, "Religious Involvement and Volunteering: Implications for Civil Society," *Sociology of Religion* 62 (2001): 315–336.

[36] Robert Wuthnow. "Religious Involvement and Status-bridging Social Capital," *Journal for the Scientific Study of Religion* 41 (2002): 669–684.

[37] See for examples, Ammerman, Park and Smith; and Becker and Dhingra.

[38] E. J. Dionne, Jr., ed., *Community Works: The Revival of Civil Society in America* (Washington, D.C.: Brookings Institution Press, 2000).

[39] Robert Bachelder, "Building Communities Inside Out," *The Christian Century*, 117.22, (2000): 802–404. See also Hara Wright-Smith, "The Impact of Inner City Commuter and Community Congregations on Civic Engagement and Social Action (Delaware)," (Dissertation, University of Pennsylvania, 2004); and Putnam, *Making Democracy Work*).

[40] Awasu, C. "Salt and Light: The Social Value of the Church in the Post-Industrial Inner City," *Intégrité Journal*, 7.1 (2008): 48–57.

[41] Ibid.

[42] Sidney Verba, Kay Lehman Schlozman, and Henry E. Brady, *Voice and Equality: Civic Voluntarism in American Politics* (Cambridge: Harvard University Press, 1995).

[43] For a discussion, see Frederick Harris, "Religious Institutions and African American Political Mobilization," in *Classifying by Race*, edited by Paul Peterson (Princeton: Princeton University Press, 1995); C. Eric Lincoln and Lawrence H. Mamiya, *The Black Church in the African-American Experience* (Durham: Duke University Press, 1990).

[44] John McGreevy, *Parish Boundaries: The Catholic Encounter with Race in the Twentieth Century Urban North* (Chicago: University of Chicago Press, 1996). McGreevey shows, however, that the group solidarity fostered by churches does not always favor "welcoming the stranger."

[45] Rita M. Brynes, ed., *South Africa: A Country Study* (Washington, D.C.: U.S. Government Printing Office, 1996).

[46] David Bosch, "Racism and Revolution: Response of the Churches in South Africa," *Occasional Bulletin of Missionary Research* 3.1 (1979): 13–20.

[47] M. John Lamola, "Change is Pain: A Projective Reflection on the Mission of the Church in South Africa and Beyond," *International Review of Mission* 83 (1994): 37–44.

[48] The SACC was in alliance with ANC and other liberation movements during the anti-apartheid struggle. However, in recent times the SACC has adopted a critical engagement stance and has been extremely critical of the ANC—especially for its role in the September 2009 attacks on the Kennedy Road informal settlements. Mmanaledi Matgaboge, "Why ANC Dumped Council of Churches," *Mail & Guardian*, September 18, 2009, http://www.mg.co.za/article/2009-09-18-why-anc-dumped-council-of-churches.

[49] De Gruchy and De Gruchy, *The Church Struggle in South Africa.*

[50] Robert Miller, "A Rock in a Weary Land: Aids, South Africa, and the Church," *Social Work in Public Health* 24 (2009): 22–38.

[51] Anthony Balcomb, "From Apartheid to the New Dispensation: Evangelicals and the Democratization of South Africa," in *Evangelical Christianity and Democracy in Africa*, edited by Terence O. Ranger (New York: Oxford University Press, 2008), 191–223.

[52] Brynes, *South Africa: A Country Study*, 135.

[53] Recently, the ANC created the National Interfaith Conference (NILC)—seen by many as an attempt to reshape the religious landscape. For a fuller discussion, see Tinyiko Sam Maluleke, "Of Power Perfected in Weakness: Challenges Facing the Ecumenical Movement and the People of South Africa Today," address by the president at the SACC Central Committee Meeting, March 9, 2010, http://www.sacc.org.za/docs/CCMAdPrez.pdf.

[54] Alejandro Portes and Patricia Landolt, "The Downside of Social Capital," *The American Prospect* 26 (May 1996): 18–21.

[55] Campbell, Williams, and Gilgen, "Is Social Capital a Useful Conceptual Tool?"

[56] Bosch, "Racism and Revolution."

[57] Ibid.

[58] David Bosch, "Towards a New South Africa: The Role of the Church," paper presented at the ecumenical meeting of the Dutch Reformed Church, Port Elizabeth, March, 1991.

[59] Randsford Danso and David McDonald, "Writing Xenophobia: Immigration and the Print Media in Post-Apartheid South Africa," *Africa Today* 48.3 (2001): 115–137.

[60] Stigmatization is seen by some as a product of prejudicial thoughts and behavior that results from actions of government, communities, employers, health care providers, families, friends, and other social agencies. For a fuller discussion, see Edwin Cameron, "Legal Rights, Human Rights and AIDS: The First Decade," report from South Africa 2, *AIDS Analysis Africa* 3.6 (1993): 3–4.

[61] See G. Petros, G. et al. "HIV/AIDS and 'Othering' in South Africa: The Blame Goes On," *Culture, Health and Sexuality* 8.1 (2006): 67–77; and John De Gruchy, "Christians in Conflict: The Social Reality of the South African Church," *Journal of Theology for Southern Africa* 51 (1985): 16–27.

[62] See Larry Sawers and Eileen Stillwaggon, "Understanding the South African 'Anomaly': Poverty, Endemic Disease and HIV," *Development & Change* 14.2 (2010): 195–224.

[63] James Perkinson, "Breaking the Silence, Bearing the Stigma: The Pastoral and Prophetic Responsibilities of the Church in the Political Economy of HIV/AIDS," *Journal of the Interdenominational Theological Center* 35.1–2 (2007–2008): 161–172.

[64] Gerald West, "Reading Job 'Positively' in the Context of HIV/AIDS in South Africa," *Concilum* 4 (2004): 112–124.

[65] Thomas Oden, *Pastoral Counsel*, Classical Pastoral Care, Volume 3 (Grand Rapids: Baker Books, 2004), 169.

[66] Linda E. Thomas, "What the Mind Forgets the Body Remembers: HIV/AIDS in South Africa—A Theological and Anthropological Issue," *Currents in Theology and Mission* 35.4 (2008): 276–287.

[67] Sara L. Zeigler and Kendra B. Stewart, "Positioning Women's Rights Within Asylum Policy," *Frontiers* 30.4 (2009): 115–142.

[68] See Gary Barker and Christine Ricardo, "Young Men and the Construction of Masculinity in Sub-Sahara Africa," World Bank, Social Development Papers: Conflict Prevention and Reconstruction, paper no. 26, June 2005; Regina Gorgen, Mohamed L Yansane, Michael Marx, and Dominique Millimounou, "Sexual Behaviors and Attitudes among Unmarried Youths in Guinea," *International Family Planning Perspectives* 24.2 (1998): 65–71; Neeru Gupta and Mary Mahy, "Sexual Initiation Among Adolescent Girls and Boys: Trends and Differentials in Sub-Saharan Africa," *Archives of Sexual Behavior* 32.1 (2003): 41–53.

[69] Beverly Haddad, "Reflections on the Church and HIV/AIDS: South Africa," *Theology Today* 62 (2005): 35.

[70] See Tinyiko Sam Maluleke and Sarojini Sadar, "Breaking the Covenant of Violence Against Women," *Journal of Theology in Southern Africa* 114 (November 2002): 14.

[71] Eunice Kamaara, "Stigmatization of Persons Living with HIV/AIDS in Africa: Pastoral Challenges," *African Ecclesial Review* (2004): 38

[72] Kim Rivers and Peter Aggleton, "Men and the HIV Epidemic," HIV and Development Program, United Nations Development Program, 1998, http://www. undp.org/hiv/publications/gender/mene.htm.

[73] Haddad, "Reflections on the Church and HIV/AIDS."

[74] Thomas, "What the Mind Forgets."

[75] J. L. Zwane Church & Center, accessed August 27, 2011, http://www.jlzwane. sun.ac.za/.

[76] Meeting with Pastor Spiwo Xapile, June 9, 2009.

[77] Observations based on field visits with J. L. Zwane staff to AIDS orphans, Guguletu, June 9, 2009.

[78] Sisaya uses African music, dance, and theater to educate people about HIV/ AIDS.

[79] Observations made at Sunday morning church service, June 14, 2009.

CHAPTER EIGHT

THE PERFECT STORM OF 2008

Afrophobia in Present Day South Africa

Rothney Tshaka

Introduction

On the 12th of May 2008, a series of riots erupted in the townships of Alexandra near Johannesburg, where at least twenty-five people were killed and many more injured. African immigrants were targeted by the local black South Africans. Most of these immigrants were Africans from neighboring southern nations Mozambique, Malawi, Zambia, and Zimbabwe. Soon the violence spread to other parts of South Africa, especial the coastal cities of Cape Town, George, and Durban, where immigrants from Somalia (who mostly own small convenient stores in the black townships across South Africa) were also targeted. The degree of violence targeted against these fellow Africans stunned many around the globe, including South Africans themselves.[1] When we visited the Central Methodist Church in downtown Johannesburg only a year later, the anti-immigrant tensions were still very much in evidence.

The xenophobic riots and ongoing tensions raised a number of questions which many South Africans thought were of the past. Once regarded as the racist capital of the world, South Africa stunned the nations when it conducted democratic elections for the first time in 1994, and made a peaceful transition toward a multi-racial democracy. Afterward, South Africa was raised up as the miracle child of the world. Yet the legacy of apartheid endures, made manifest in the racial and ethnic fragmentation that this beautiful and beloved country still encounters.

However, this chapter will make the case that one cannot fully comprehend the May 2008 riots without understanding two underlying causes: an internalized racism that affects many black South Africans, and the daunting social and economic conditions that they still encounter. Many have pointed to enduring poverty and disadvantage as drivers of xenophobia, but this is not the whole answer. Many black South Africans who have escaped poverty still harbor prejudice and resentment toward our black brothers and sisters from other parts of Africa.

While it is unnecessary to repeat the story of apartheid here, it is nonetheless fundamental that we remember the psychic destruction it brought about. Doing this will enable us to better understand the xenophobic attacks, which became known as "the Perfect Storm" by the South African Migrants Project (SAMP).[2] More than usually meets the eye, South Africa is sitting on a racial powder keg which is compounded by the lack of economic opportunity and the failure to deliver basic services to the most vulnerable—the black masses. Unless action is taken soon to address the conditions of the majority of black people in this country, the "Perfect Storm" of 2008 will prove to be nothing in comparison with what is yet to come.

There are numerous elements attached to the issue of xenophobia and these elements are equally important. SAMP rightly concedes that the fundamental elements are historical, material, political and managerial.[3] Without wanting to negate these realities, I wish to probe another element: Afrophobia. If we are going to fully understand the current problem, we must consider the psychic impact that colonialism and apartheid had on black people. The issues of race and racism, white privilege, and internalized oppression make a significant contribution to the "nervous condition" of the many ordinary black people in present day South Africa. Curiously enough, given this nation's legacy, these racial and racist dynamics often go unexamined.

This chapter will draw out these issues, first, by carefully defining the concept of racism and its internalization, and by exploring their nuances and implications, leaning heavily on research done by our North American counterparts. The lack of consensus here about what is meant by racism, for instance, has led many of us to speak wrongly about it. Second, this work will engage the condition of many black South Africans and provide insights as to why such conditions are dangerous and problematic—why these conditions pose significant challenges to the stability of this country and the region in general.

This is a study by a Christian ethicist with a confessional background. As a Christian ethicist I remain encouraged by the theological resources that we have at our disposal to deal with the problems indicated. One such resource is the Belhar Confession of the Uniting Reformed Church in Southern Africa (URCSA). This confession contains clear guidelines of how Christians are to identify with those who are on the margins of society. The Belhar Confession is a clear testimony to the fact that what affects the civil community affects the Christian community.

While the Belhar Confession has been accepted as a gift in other parts of the world, it sadly remains at best an unknown and sometimes controversial document for many black South Africans.[4] The controversy over this document will become clear later in this chapter. It is not the intention of this study to engage in an intense analysis of the history and relevance of this confession, but to affirm it as a prophetic challenger and a teacher, motivating Christians to identify with the most vulnerable in society. Gaining a clear understanding of what this confession teaches can guide black Christians' views of foreign blacks in our communities and their relationships with them.

Afrophobia and Racism

The contemporary Nigerian poet and pan-Africanist, philosopher, Chinweizu, has a very perceptive understanding of the syndrome he calls "Negrophobia." This "fear and dislike of blacks," he said, is "a great disease." He continues: "It has killed more blacks in the last five hundred years than all other diseases combined; more than malaria, more than epidemics and plagues of all sorts, [and] in the coming years, it could kill more than AIDS. It is a psychological disease, a disease of the mind which harvests dead black bodies every day."[5] But since the concept "negro" has had its own evolution, it is perhaps prudent that we speak of Afrophobia instead of Negrophobia.[6]

At the heart of Afrophobia, and indeed the treatment meted out toward blacks, is the black other is the question of power. Power is often thought of as having control over economic or political matters. But power involves the control of values, perception and outlook as well. These dimensions of power are not well understood in South Africa. For many, such talk about racism is considered irrelevant and backward. The reason for this is two-fold. First, it is tempting to wish the past away because of its ugliness. Many people, especially white people, claim that they were not aware of the devastation for which apartheid alone is responsible. Their professions of ignorance are plausible, given the evident separation between black and white in this country.

The second is the fact that racism has not been defined adequately, here in the South African. For many, the most convenient definition of racism is racial prejudice. It makes things simpler if one can classify all human beings in categories under those who are bad and those who are good, with racial prejudice used as a convenient determining yardstick. As long as one does not verbalize his or her racial prejudices, that someone is considered a good person. This attitude leaves an impression that there are people who do not have racial prejudices even though they live in a world in which they are bombarded with stereotypes of the other. South Africa since 1994 has become a rather polite society in which true feelings of the other are not verbalized for fear of being politically incorrect. There is both good and bad in such an approach. The good is that we have been forced to be sensitive and civil toward others, but the bad is that because of this political correctness, we are increasingly becoming a dishonest society, dishonest about how we really feel about the other.

As a result, there is much popular talk in South Africa that we are a country that is striving towards a non-racial society. Embedded in this talk is the assumption that racial prejudice can be quickly eradicated. There is also much talk of a reverse racism in South Africa, as if the effect whites might experience is equivalent to what blacks experience. Such talk is possible because we have confined talk about racism to racial prejudice and have not extended it to systems and structures that discriminate and continue to discriminate against people based on race.

So any useful definition of racism must have this broader scope. Racism therefore should be defined as racial prejudice alongside institutional power. Racism needs to factor in the social and economic privileges that are there for whites because of their whiteness—whether whites ask for them or not. Talk of racism only as personal prejudice does not seem to reckon with the fact that we are all—black and white—affected by racism. My review of North American literature on the subject of racism has let me to conclude that South African deliberations on racism have yet to engage the views of racism's broader scope and deeper power.

Let us consider some of these implications, just briefly. The African American psychologist Beverly Tatum, says that frequently white people do not notice racism's more systemic features:

> There is always someone who hasn't noticed the stereotypical images of people of colour in the media, who hasn't observed the housing discrimination in their community, who hasn't read the newspaper articles about documented racial bias in lending practices among well-known banks, who isn't aware of the racial tracking pattern at the local school, who hasn't seen the reports of rising incidents of racially motivated hate crimes in America. In short, someone who hasn't been paying attention to the existence of racism.[7]

Yet for blacks, there is no way that they can really escape the reality of racism. The impact of racism, argues Tatum, begins very early, even in children's pre-school years. This is so because people are always exposed to misinformation about people different from themselves. Thanks to apartheid, many South Africans grew up in neighborhoods where we had limited chances of interacting with people from different races. Thus, because of the social segregation that is still omnipresent in South Africa, we continue to collect secondhand and therefore distorted information about the other. Assumptions happen because of what we say of the other, but also because of what is not said about the other.

Tatum argues for instance that "the distortion of historical information about people of color leads young people (and older people too) to make assumptions that may go unchallenged for a long time." She tells the story a young white male student who got angry with her and responded by saying "it was not his fault that blacks did not write books." Tatum continues to explain that although this student might not have been taught this at school, the fact that he was not exposed to black writers led him to that conclusion.[8] Tatum concludes that stereotypes by omissions and distortions all contribute to prejudice. She defines prejudice as "a preconceived judgment or opinion, usually based on limited information."[9] Based on this definition, we can then deduce that all human beings are prejudiced by socialization, simply because we are continually exposed to misinformation about others. Another important concept is cultural racism. Power manifests itself in numerous ways and not necessarily politically or economically. Tatum defines cultural racism as "the cultural images and messages that affirm the assumed superiority of whites and the assumed inferiority of blacks."[10] We shall see that this is not confined necessarily to white versus black but that this is evident among blacks and perhaps among whites themselves.

Racism, Tatum argues, is like smog. It is

> sometimes so thick and therefore visible and other times it is less apparent, yet it is always there each day and we are breathing it. The knowledge that smog is out there whether we see it or not, does not lead us to label ourselves "smog-breathers" (and so most of us do not describe ourselves as prejudiced), but if we live in a smoggy place, we cannot avoid breathing the air. By the same token, because we live in an environment in which we are bombarded with stereotypical images in the media, or are frequently exposed to the ethnic jokes of friends and families members, we will certainly develop negative categories of the other.[11]

The smog analogy establishes the fact that both black and white people are affected, whether they know it or choose to ignore it. Members of the stereotypical groups may resent and resist these stereotypes, but often, more than they realize, internalize these oppressive categories. This syndrome has been described by many black leaders. Historian Carter J Woodson describes it as the black person knowing his or her place in society.[12] Malcolm X was thinking of it when he said, "the black person was taught to use only the back door of the house his white master. To such an extent that he [sic] would cut out a back door even when there is no back door to his master house."[13] Harold Cruse speaks of the African as being "a perpetual child."[14]

Black internalized oppression encourages a flight from the black self. The Martiniquen-Algerian philosopher, Frantz Fanon, argues that Africa is a creation of the West. This construct assumes that the better the African is able to imitate the Westerner, the closer he or she is coming to being a human being.[15] Because blackness is characterized as negativity and badness, many blacks are in a rush to flee from such badness. This flight from the self does not only happen among the blacks who become assimilated into the established order, but it is something that is happening even among the masses. There is always an intense need to be a little better than the other.

Woodson saw this phenomenon clearly in an American setting where

this refusal of Negroes to take orders from one another is due largely to the fact that slaveholders taught their bondmen [sic] that they were as good or better as or better than any others and therefore, should not be subjected to any member of their race. If they were to be subordinated to someone it should be to the white man [sic] of superior culture and social position. This keeps the whole race on a lower level, restricted to the atmosphere of trifles which do not concern their traducers.[16]

It is this systematic training that causes many Africans to look at other blacks with disdain. In the South African, one often hears of black foreigners are not welcome because they come and steal our jobs and women. Yet nothing is said of white foreigners. Seen in this light, Andile Mngxitama suggests, it is perhaps best to characterize the May 2008 attacks by South Africans on Africans north of the Limpopo River not as xenophobia but rather as Afrophobia.

We must now add a third element that is often ignored—"colorism." Cedric Herring argues that "'colorism' is the discriminatory treatment of individuals falling within the same 'racial' group on the basis of skin color." He continues to maintain that "it operates both intra-racially and interracially. Intra-racially colorism occurs when members of a racial group make distinctions based upon skin color between members of their own race. Interracially it occurs when distinctions are made upon skin color between members of another race."[17]

What must be remembered, asserts Herring, is that colorism, much like the notion of race, is historically contingent on supremacist assumptions. Thus in the West, preferences are typically measured against putative European (i.e. white) standards. To strengthen his point, Herring reminds us that these preferences have involved physical features including skin color, hair texture, thickness of lips, eye color, nose shape, and other phenotypical features.[18]

Looking at colorism in Latin America, Eduardo Bonilla-Silva argues that pigmentocracy has been central to the maintenance of white power because it fosters (a) divisions among all those in secondary racial strata, (b) divisions within racial strata limiting the likelihood of within-stratum unity, (c) mobility viewed as individual and conditional upon whitening, and (d) white elites being regarded as legitimate representatives of the "nation" even though they do not look like the average member of the nation.[19]

So now, returning to the events of May 2008, perhaps it is best to see the Perfect Storm riots riding the wave of Afrophobia instead of xenophobia. Xenophobia is described as fear and hatred of the stranger. Yet in the case of South Africa, the stranger is clearly the darker African. As author and activist Andile Mngxitama describes it, in the case of South Africa, there are no white foreigners. Indeed, he continues, "we think of these [white foreigners] as benefactors, as tourists, investors and business people who must be protected."[20] So having internalized oppressive racist stereotypes of what it means to be black and African, South African blacks have become Afrophobic.

The Nervous Conditions of Blacks in Democratic South Africa

It is not, however, enough to draw attention to the current frame of mind of the ordinary black South Africans. More importantly, we must ask, what do political and economic conditions in present day South Africa contribute to the South African black population's fearful and barbaric behavior toward his or her fellow Africans? This has been the more common approach to the issue at hand, and while I have argued that it does not provide a sufficient answer, it does contain some necessary ingredients for the explosion that occurred. Indeed, there has been a tension that has been prevalent in South Africa since the dawn of democracy in 1994. This tension has increased dramatically in recent years with the upsurge of public demonstrations for the lack of service delivery. Improving political conditions are bound to create expectation from the masses that have been marginalized for ages that their conditions would improve. These expectations quickly turned into frustration and lingering anxiety when both groups realizes that full citizenship brought them little concrete benefit. While the leaders of the masses managed to secure the political governing of the country, the economy of the country remained largely controlled by the white minority. The economy, people discovered, was not merely a department in government, but a powerful and independent phenomenon that did not seem to be working in favor of the vast majority of black people. There are two sides to these economic tensions in South Africa: frustration for people of color, and anxiety for the whites.

The anxiety of the privileged whites prompts many to find justification for why things must continue as they are. Most know it is best not to use overtly racist language to justify an economic system that continues to privilege them and relatively few people of color. They then employ a different form of talk in which whiteness remains the unexamined norm. Many continue to deny the privileges attached to whiteness. The American expert on racial behavior, Tim Wise argues that white denial manifests itself in four primary ways: minimization, rationalization, deflection, and claims of competing victimization.[21] I refer briefly to Wise's description of these phenomena:

a. *Minimization* refers to the tendency for whites to make molehills out of what may indeed be mountains when it comes to racism and discrimination. Claims that black people "play the race card" or that individual success stories (á la Oprah Winfrey or Barack Obama) signify the demise of racism as a persistent social problem "are among the most common arrows in the quiver of white deniers." He continues to note that these whites are the very people who will claim that humor is taken too seriously, and this is used to minimize the damage that racial subordination can wreak. It must also be pointed out that it is not only the overt racists who are guilty of minimization, but minimization is found amongst the best white liberals as well.

b. *Rationalization*—although related to the first one, rationalization is distinguished from minimization in a fundamental manner. While minimization seek to downplay the struggles of black people due to racism and discrimination, rationalization often acknowledges the fact that racial bias is tangible even within themselves, but then seeks to justify its existence by claiming that prejudice flows from logical and understandable thought processes, informed by personal experiences. These whites will claim that their experiences with certain racial groups justify the biases that they have toward them.

c. *Deflection* relates to the way that whites will often seek to change the subject when racism is brought up. They will insist that the focus should be on cultural defects within the black community and the need for black people to "take personal responsibility" for their lives instead of worrying about discrimination.

d. *Competing victimization.* While black people are often accused of "playing the race card," it is clear that many white people sometimes act as victims of racism. In the case of South Africa, the phrase reverse racism is quickly gaining popularity.

At the heart of systemic and institutions racism is the question of power. The South African black power pioneer, Steve Biko, insisted that whites were quite conscious of the fact that apartheid institutions and systems afforded them privileges, and were quick to defend them: "[T]he South African white community . . . is a community of people who sit to enjoy a privileged position that they do not deserve, are aware of this, and therefore spend their time trying to justify why they are doing so."[22]

With regard to the frustration felt by those of color who thought the new dispensation would bring economic advantages along with citizenry, we need to understand why the "black other" is a convenient scapegoat. One frequently heard South African blacks on various social levels argue that blacks from other African counties are not welcome in this land. Basing their research partially on a SAMP report of 1997–1998, Ransford Danso and David McDonald illustrated how the South African media has helped perpetuate the stereotype that black foreigners are largely responsible for the upsurge of crime in South Africa.[23] By focusing on this example, we hope to understand Biko's condemnation of South African blacks: "[T]he black man has become a shell, a shadow of man, completely defeated, drowning in his own misery, a slave, an ox bearing the yoke of oppression with sheepish timidity."[24] So let us pursue this syndrome of frustration, which renders the black person a perpetual child in his own country.

Africa, it is agreed, is a fragmented world, broken up as it is It is fragmented not only by the diversity of traditional black societies, but also by the desires of the colonial powers. This fragmentation goes back to the time when Otto von Bismarck invited the major European powers to Berlin to "carve up" Africa in the "scramble" for territory.[25] West African writer and social critic Francis Nyamnjoh reminds us that "combing the world for opportunities has historically been the privileges of whites, who have been encouraged by their imperial governments to settle foreign territories, and who have always benefited from fellow whites on the ground, from colonial officers to missionaries through business, journalists and scholars."[26] He continues: "without necessarily being a homogenous collectivity, whites have always managed to tame their differences in the interest of the economic, cultural and political hegemonies of the West vis-à-vis the rest."[27]

The African, it seems, has yet to learn that his or her struggle is the same struggle as his or her brothers or sisters whose origin is elsewhere in Africa. The result of this fragmentation has raised brother against brother and sister against sister. In response to the question, what is wrong with the African, Jessie Kabwila Kapasula argued that, "there is nothing is wrong with the African; he [sic] is simply a good student. He [sic] does what he or she was taught to do."[28]

Such compliance is the "racial smog" phenomenon of which Tatum spoke. It affects us all, whether we are able to see the fog or not. In this way, all exhibit racial prejudice. Since we live in a world where we are inundated with misinformation about the other, then we are bound to internalize such views. Some internalize white privilege, while others internalize oppression. Since blackness, in as far as it is associated with the bad and the ugly, is a product of whiteness, which is associated with goodness and purity, there has always been an intense need for blacks to flee from themselves. Such blacks have often sought ways of distinguishing themselves from other blacks, so that they appear better than the rest. This flight from the black self is responsible for the sectional politics among blacks both in Africa and in South Africa in particular.

Biko pioneered an understanding of this flight from the black self and suggested black consciousness as a means of interrupting it, and countering the fragmentation of Africa and Africans.[29] To substantiate the claim that Africa is fragmented, Fanon reminds us of the division of Africa into white and black Africa—that is Africa south of the Sahara and Africa north of the Sahara.[30] Inherent in this division, says Fanon, is the belief that white Africa is better off than black Africa because of the way that it is able to imitate the West.

In like manner, black African foreigners, with whom most South Africans have little contact, are perceived very negatively by most South Africans, black and white. Part of the reason for this can be located in what Fanon calls the luck of where some Africans are located. Fanon observes that "the nationals who live in the more prosperous regions realize their good luck, and show a primary and profound reaction in refusing to feed other nationals."[31] As we have seen, many South Africans are located in black frustration and white anxiety.

The "racial smog" is once again called to light by Antoine Bouillon, who studied the ill-treatment meted out against black foreigners by indigenous Africans in South Africa:

> to demonstrate that these "illegals" clearly have little to offer, South African blacks, perhaps reminiscent of the Boers who named the local black communities "hottentots" to denote "stutterers," deny black African migrants an intelligible language. All they claim to hear is "gibberish"—a "barbaric" form of "stuttering"—hence the tendency to classify them as *Makwerekwere*, among other onomatopoeic references to the strange ways they speak.[32]

The problem is compounded by the media that portrays "illegals" as criminals.

Andile Mngxitama maintains that there is everyday public harassment of these immigrants by the police and the homeland affairs department. "These are part of the undeclared war against black Africans. There are no white

Kwerekweres in our country."[33]The concept *Makwerekwere* when used to refer to black foreigners means different things in different situations.[34] When used by a black South African, it refers to a black person who cannot demonstrate mastery of local South African languages. More importantly, it refers to someone who originates from a country that is assumed to be economically and culturally backward when compared to South Africa.[35] This is an aspect that is always ignored by those who insist that we characterize the May 2008 events as xenophobia instead of Afrophobia.[36]

Nyamnjoh insists that "colorism" is always applied to foreign blacks in South Africa. He writes that, "in terms of skin pigmentation, the racial hierarchy of humanity under apartheid comes into play, since the *Makwerekwere* are usually believed to be the darkest of the dark-skinned, and to be less educated even when more educated than the light-skinned South African blacks."[37] These assumptions about being economically and culturally backward, coupled with colorism, are all used in determining the other and therefore justifying their discriminatory treatment. Sometimes being perceived to be economically and culturally backward is used to justify abuse, as is the case with the violence directed against Somalia's and other groups, which necessarily does not meet the criteria of colorism.

It is often forgotten that South Africa has become the so-called economic hub because it is significantly dependent on cheap black labor. One such form of cheap black labor has been provided by the black foreigner who has no right to claim citizenship while in this country. Nyamnjoh argues that

> citizenship has been defined narrowly around the rights, entitlements and interests of nationals, and although it might be celebrated by those who have traditionally benefitted since the days of apartheid, it is a disappointment to most *Makwerekwere* from beyond the borders whose labour reserves were exploited with impunity and ingratitude by the architects of apartheid in the quest for racialized citizenship and modernity.[38]

South Africa is one of the leading economies on the continent. It is also by far one of the most industrialized countries in Africa, yet it has a much-skewed distribution of wealth. It is ranked as one of the countries with the most liberal constitutions in the world, having opted for a liberal economic and political model. This liberal constitution guarantees individual right of private ownership and control even of what was acquired illegally under the apartheid rule. Nyamnjoh has argued that this option of "equality without justice" has made the post-apartheid context very tense, as ordinary underprivileged South Africans realize that their constitutional rights are slow at delivering the material benefit of citizenship.[39]

The skewed distribution of wealth remains conspicuous in present-day South Africa. In an article titled "We Are Not All Like That: The Monster Bares Its Fangs," Mngxitama reminds us that,

> it is convenient for some to see the outbreak of black violence as some atavistic unexplained black lashing out at black. . . . To think of this violence as a consequence of the relatively comfortable lives we lead would be too much, but if we look at the wealth enjoyed by our white counterparts, if you follow the money trail, historically you will see that the creation of Sandton (that super rich suburb) was made possible by the creation of the sprawling Alexandra. Alexandra is the direct product of Sandton.[40]

While a few black elites have graduated from the slams created by the apartheid regime for various reasons and purposes, the townships are still homes of the majority of South Africans. Biko writes,

> "to anyone living in the black world, the hidden anger and turmoil could always be seen shining through the faces and actions of these voiceless masses but it was never verbalised. Even the active phase, thuggery and vandalism—was directed to one's kind—a clear manifestation of frustration."[41]

Biko speaks of the "black world" simply because there are many South Africas in the one South Africa. This was the case during apartheid; it remains the case even today in democratic South Africa.

This was the plan during apartheid; it remains the case even today in democratic South Africa, where the new government, from time to time, must concede that the economy is not changing the situation of its citizens who live in the black world. Fanon reminds us of a fundamental aspect that is often ignored when a political situation has undergone some change. He argues that "colonial domination has marked certain regions out for privilege." He continues to add that "the colony's economy is not integrated into that of the nation as a whole. It is still organized in order to complete the economy of the different mother countries."[42] Talk about the transformation of the "Second Economy" of this country is therefore not by chance.

Thabo Mbeki rightly asserted that,

the Second Economy emerged during the long period of colonialism and apartheid. That process of impoverishment included ensuring that the white economy had access to unlimited supplies of cheap unskilled black labour, and that this economy did not waste any money on the development of the localities in which the black workers lived. This did not even allow for the possibility of improving the lives of the oppressed majority through the "trickle-down effect."

He continues to point out that, "the Second Economy is caught in a 'poverty trap.'" It cannot "generate the internal savings that would enable it to achieve the high rates of investment it needs. Accordingly, on its own, it is unable to attain rates of growth that would ultimately end its condition of underdevelopment."[43]

When comparing these two worlds of the settler and the native, Fanon noted that "the zone where the native live is not complementary to the zone inhabited by the settlers." The settlers' town, he continues, "is a strong-built town, all made of stone and steel. It is a brightly lit town; the streets are covered with asphalt and the garbage cans swallow all the leavings, unseen, unknown and hardly thought about. The settler's feet are never visible, except perhaps in the sea; but there you are never close enough to see them."[44]

On the other hand, argues Fanon,

the town belonging to the colonized people, the Negro village . . . the reservation, is a place of ill fame, peopled by men of evil repute. They are born there, it matters little where or how; they die there it matters not where nor how. It is a world without spaciousness; men live there

on top of each other, and their huts are built one on top of the other.
The native town is a hungry town, starved of bread, of meat, of shoes,
of coal, of light.[45]

This description given by Fanon about the native village closely resembles the
description of South African black townships by the exiled South African
writer and activist Ezekiel Mphahlele. Although both of them wrote from different perspectives about this condition, the living conditions for most blacks
in South Africa in particular has remained the same. He remembered them as
"an organized rubble of tin cans. The streets were straight; but the houses stood
cheek by jowl, rusty as ever on the outside, as if they thought they might as
well crumble in straight rows if that was to be their fate."[46] In such conditions,
Biko argued that "township life alone makes it a miracle for anyone to live up
to adulthood. There we see a situation of absolute want in which black will kill
black to be able to survive."[47] It is in such a societal nervous condition that the
South African black sees the black immigrant.

Even so, black South Africans must begin to see their inter-connectedness
with blacks living north of the Limpopo River. We must begin to understand
how dangerous such nervous conditions are, not only for the stability of the
country and therefore of the region, but for the stability of the world at large.
Economic journalist Sebastian Mallaby noted that "once a nation descends into
violence, its people focus on immediate survival rather than on the long term.
Savings, investment and wealth creation taper off; government officials seek
spoils for their cronies rather than design policies that might build long term
prosperity. A cycle of poverty, instability and violence emerges." Mallaby thus
argues that nationwide poverty is dangerous and may cause repercussions that
upset international security.[48]

Christian communities are not immune to these nervous conditions. It is
sad, however, to note that Christian communities especially within the townships have neglected to respond to the foul treatment of the black migrants.
They face a reality where people do desperate things every day, as Biko poi-
gnantly pointed out. As daunting as the task may be, Christian communities have a special mandate, from Scriptures, to identify themselves with the
stranger and the marginalized in society. They cannot speak justly in these

situations, however, unless they challenge the structural powers that contribute to the nervous condition of the majority of blacks in South Africa. They must speak truth to power, especially in difficult times. Christian leaders will have to analyze and reveal the truth about these nervous situations instead of being content with the kind of ambulance service that responds to the victims of these hegemonic systems. This is a rather difficult task given the resources at these communities' disposal. These communities are generally still very much dependent and as such have developed an ambivalent personality, which Biko has pointed out.

Conclusion: The Belhar Confession in the Struggle against Afrophobia

Black Christian communities must begin to seriously deal with the question of the black other. For this to happen, we need a strong and determined black leadership in the church. One significant question is whether one can really speak of a black church in the mainline Protestant church tradition in the real sense of the word, given the dependence of the so called daughter churches on the mother churches.[49] Concepts such as "church" or "Christian communities" are still reserved for the exclusive use of the so-called mainline churches. Of course this idea is not stated, but it is clearly implied. With a huge Christian constituency, South Africa has a variety of Christian traditions, but Christianity has proven to be very ambivalent since its first appearance on South African soil. While some Christian leaders and churches taught that the faith justified and gave theological legitimacy to apartheid, the same religion also instilled courage in some to struggle against apartheid.

The Black Theology of Liberation in South Africa was a project undertaken by black Christians within the confessional church traditions—á la Manas Buthelezi, Simon Maimela, Takatso Mofokeng, Itumeleng Mosala, Bonganjalo Goba, Buti Tlhagale, Allan Boesak, Mokgethi Motlhabi, among others. While this approach was successful in mobilizing black Christians to adopt a black hermeneutical approach toward the apartheid ideology, it failed nonetheless to integrate African cultures with the Christian faith. The struggle, the Liberation theologians insisted, was about political economy more than about culture. It did not sufficiently challenge the belief held by many that South Africa is better off thinking of itself as South African instead of as African.

Additionally, this failure was brought about by these advocates' inability to overcome the confessional hurdles in their way. It was important for them to wrestle with their blackness in relation to their confessional traditions, hence talk about Black and Reformed and the like,[50] yet that blackness did not take the "Black Consciousness" question of Africanness seriously.[51] The Christian experience in South Africa is thus one of struggle against marginality on a number of levels.

It is no secret that the fragmentation of the African happens on many fronts, chief among these his or her culture. The refusal of some black Christians to be totally assimilated into this faith clothed in Western cultures contributed to the rise of African Initiated Churches—which are still frowned upon by African Christians in confessional church traditions. From a very early age, the African Christian within the confessional Christian tradition had to learn to negotiate his or her being African and Christian at the same time.[52] Once again in this exercise we can hear Steve Biko's indictment: "When will the African grow up?" In order to survive, the African had to learn to put on *personas* in the country of his or her birth.

It was this obsession to survive that rendered the African leaders in the confessional churches dependent on the "mother church." They learned very quickly to have one sermon when one of the elders of the "mother church" comes to visit and a different one for the local church alone. At the time, the perception that Africans in the mainline churches are better off than those who cling to an African expression of being church has created huge cleavings, even between children of the same parents.

The cardinal question of this section sheds light on how black Christian people can talk about justice, reconciliation, and unity, both with whites and amongst themselves. One possible yardstick could be the Belhar Confession of the Uniting Reformed Church in Southern Africa of 1986.

The Belhar Confession[53] was created by the Uniting Reformed Church in Southern Africa (URCSA). It originated as a theological reaction against the biblical and theological legitimacy given to apartheid by the Dutch Reformed Church in South Africa. It argues that apartheid is a sin and a heresy.[54]

Cardinal to this confession are the issues of justice, reconciliation, and unity. While the stimulus for this confession was the apartheid regime, many have failed to see its relevance when applied to matters where the church still has a responsibility to align with the marginalized. It is true that a number of Christian organizations have felt compelled to make statements opposing such acts. As an example, Nel and Makofane refer to the URCSA statement on the matter titled, "Xenophobic attacks on Refugees." In this statement, the URCSA reminded Christians that Christ himself was a refugee and therefore they should have compassion on refugees.[55]

Many evoke the Belhar Confession when talking about justice and reconciliation with whites, yet no one seems to be referring to this fundamental confession when dealing with the tensions that exist between black South Africans and Africans from neighboring countries. The reason for this, as the SAMP report has established, is that whites are always presumed to be the benefactors while blacks are always presumed to be the beneficiaries. Blacks South Africans fail to see themselves as significant actors in other social arenas while black–white relations are the near-exclusive preoccupation. Once again, here is a devastating legacy of our very painful past. The Belhar Confession remains one essential tool in this regard, because it can help us to see the African stranger as the one who is on the margins of society. In her chapter, our Zimbabwean colleague, Sophia Chirongoma, refers specifically to the fourth article of this confession as she attempts to challenge the negative attitudes displayed to immigrants:[56]

> We believe that . . . in a world full of injustice and enmity He is in a special way the God of the destitute, the poor and the wronged and that he calls his Church to follow Him in this, that He brings justice to the oppressed and gives bread to the hungry . . . supports the downtrodden, protects the stranger, helps orphans and the widows and blocks the path of the ungodly. . . . The church must therefore stand by people in any form of suffering and need . . . the church must witness against and strive against any form of injustice so that justice may roll down like waters, and righteousness like an ever-flowing stream. . . .

What could be more relevant to the immigration crisis we face?

While the Belhar Confession is unyielding in encouraging reconciliation, justice, and unity, curiously enough, it has not been widely addressed to how black South Africans deal with Afrophobia. Until now, there has been no literature that deals specifically with these issues within black communities. Blacks' relative inability to deal with these issues may well be tied to the flight from the black self, as pointed out in this chapter. Black Christian communities need to begin to look at the Belhar Confession, therefore, as something more than simply dealing with segregation between black and white. They need to see its relevance with regard to the segregation between blacks that was engineered under apartheid and remains entrenched in their communities today.

Such fresh approaches to the problem of black self-flight could help us confront the evils that continue to plague our societies. We need to do much more than simply provide "ambulance service" to our communities by critically engaging the systems that create this mess instead. We need to realize that all Christian communities as well as the government must confront the severity of the matter. And most pointedly, black Christian communities need to challenge their own internalized dependency.

Notes to Chapter Eight

[1] Cf. S. Hassim, T. Kupe, et. al. eds., *Go Home or Die here: Violence, Xenophobia and the Reinvention of Difference in South Africa* (Johannesburg: Wits University Press, 2008).

[2] The South African Migration Project (SAMP) provides an in-depth account of Xenophobia in present day South Africa. It locates the origin of the May 2008 events directly after the 1994 democratic elections. It also details the degrees of tolerance, especially against black foreigners among the four racial groups of South Africa. It notes rather sadly that South Africa has become one of the most intolerant countries to the foreigner, especially the black foreigner. J. Crush, ed., *The Perfect Storm: The Realities of Xenophobia in Contemporary South Africa*. South African Migration Project, Southern Africa Research Center (Kingston: Queen's University, 2008). For a visual overview of the destruction materially and spiritually caused by the mentioned events, see also S. Hassim, T. Kupe, et. al. eds., *Go Home or Die Here*.

[3] Crush, *The Perfect Storm*, 1–11.

[4] As part of my community engagement, I volunteer at the Northern Theological Seminary, based in Pretoria. This is a seminary of the Uniting Reformed Church in Southern Africa and my responsibilities include teaching reformed theology. The history of the Dutch Reformed Church family reveals the so-called black "daughter churches" have been heavily dependent on the white Dutch Reformed Church. Not much of that has changed in this current context since the economy of South Africa remains largely white-controlled. The Belhar Confession is seen in a negative light also by students whose local congregations continue to depend on the white DRC for survival; thus it is simplistically associated with black liberation theology, which is seen as problematic in some circles in South Africa. One of my resolutions of popularizing and embodying the Belhar Confession is to allow it to play a bigger role in the liturgy.

[5] A. Mngxitama, "We are not all like that: the monster bares its fangs," Abahlali baseMjondolo, June 12, 2008, http://abahlali.org/node/3645.

[6] "Negritude," for example, was popularized in the 1930s by the likes of founding Senegalese President Léopold Sédar Senghor, Aimé Césaire, and Leon Damas. Its objective was to unite Africans across the globe, a move which was primarily seen as a formidable tool in challenging the French political and intellectual hegemony. But today, "negro" seems to echo centuries of European (mis)characterizations of African people. So this chapter will use "Afro" instead. B. Tatum, *'Why are All the Black Kids Sitting Together in the Cafeteria?' And Other Conversations about Race* (New York: Basic Books, 2003), 3.

[7] Tatum, *Why Are All the Black Kids Sitting Together in the Cafeteria?*, 5.

[8] Ibid., 5.

[9] Ibid.

[10] Ibid., 6.

[11] Ibid.

[12] C. Woodson, *The Mis-Education of the Negro*, New York: Classic House Books, 2008.

[13] Malcolm X, "The Ballot or the Bullet," *All Time Greatest Speeches* (Audio mp3), Vol. 2.11, 2008.

[14] See H. Cruse, *The Crises of the Negro Intellectual: A Historical Analysis of the Failure of Black Leadership* (New York: New York Review of Books, 2005).

[15] F. Fanon, *Black Skin, White Masks* (Grove Press: New York, 2008), 2.

[16] Woodson, *The Mis-Education of the Negro*, 86.

[17] C. Herring, "Skin Deep: Race and Complexion in a Color-Blind Era," in C. Herring, V. Keith, et al, eds., *Skin Deep: How Race and Complexion Matter in the Color-Blind Era* (Chicago: University of Illinois Press, 2004), 3.

[18] Herring, "Skin Deep," 3.

[19] E. Bonilla-Silva and D. Dietrich, "The Latin Americanization of U.S Race Relations," in E. Glenn, ed., *Shades of difference: Why Skin Color Matters* (Palo Alto: Stanford University Press, 2009), 44.

[20] Mngxitama, "We are not all like that."

[21] Cf. T. Wise, *Speaking Treason Fluently: Anti-Racist Reflections from an Angry White Male* (Brooklyn: Soft Skull Press, 2008), 11.

[22] Cf. S. Biko, *I Write What I Like: Selected Writings* (Chicago: Chicago University Press, 2002), 19.

[23] R. Danso and D. Mcdonald, "Writing Xenophobia: Immigration and the Print Media in Post Apartheid South Africa," *Africa Today* 48.3 (Fall 2011): 115-137. The fact that the emphasis of this essay is on the foul treatment of South African blacks against blacks from other African countries does not suggest that white people in this country are more tolerable toward black foreigners, as the SAMP 2008 report indicates (see especially the executive summary to the report). See also Crush, *The Perfect Storm*, 1–11. It is my opinion that the intolerance of whites against black foreigners is underpinned by their anxiety that the presence of blacks will cost them their privileges.

[24] Biko. *I Write What I Like*, 29

[25] K. von Hippel, "Old Concepts and New Challenges: African Nationalism in the Post-Cold War Era," in *Africa in the Post-Cold War International System*, edited by S. Akinrinade and A. Sesayeds (New York: Continuum, 1998), 28.

[26] F. Nyamnjoh, *Insiders and Outsiders: Citizenship and Xenophobia in Contemporary Southern Africa* (Dakar: Codesria Books, 2006), 28.

[27] Ibid., 28

[28] J. Kabwila Kapasula, "Patriarchy and the Oppression of African Women in the 21st Century: a Conversation with Adichie and Dangarembga," unpublished paper read at the Africa Speaks Forum, University of South Africa, July 17, 2009.

[29] Biko, *I Write What I Like*, 36.

[30] F. Fanon, *The Wretched of the Earth* (London: Penguin Books, 2001), 129.

[31] Ibid., 128.

[32] A. Bouillon in Nyamnjoh, *Insiders and Outsiders*, 39.

[33] Mngxitama, "We are not all like that."

[34] This foul treatment of Africans against each other is in no way unique to South Africa. While it is true that many African countries provided shelter for black South Africans who were fleeing South Africa because of the struggle against apartheid, some South Africans were referred to in the Swahili word *Mkimbizi*, which means refugee in Tanzania. While the word in itself had no ill intent and was perhaps corrupted, Nyerere believed that it would be ideal not to use it. This was undergirded by his belief that no African should be a refugee in another African country. By mentioning this, we simply wish to illustrate the point that sectional politics have been pervasive across Africa and were especially enforced when the other was seen to be encroaching on the so-called turf of the other. See Paul Kagame, "To Late President Julius Nyerere Kabarage," posted at Rwanda Kwibohora, July 4, 2009, http://www.gov.rw/liberation15/index.php?option=com_content&view=article&id=47%3Aarmed-struggle-vs-diplomacy&catid=36%3Aarmed-struggle&Itemid=54&showall=1.

[35] Nyamnjoh, *Insiders and Outsiders*, 39

[36] Cf. L. Landau, "Echoing Exclusion: Xenophobia, Law, and the Future of South Africa's Demonic Society," paper presented to the seminar series of the School for Graduate Studies of UNISA, September 9, 2009.

[37] Nyamnjoh, *Insiders and Outsiders*, 39.

[38] Ibid., 40.

[39] Ibid., 5.

[40] Mngxitama, "We are not all like that."

[41] Biko, *I Write What I Like*, 34.

[42] Fanon, *The Wretched of the Earth*, 127.

[43] T. M. Mbeki, "Approaches to Poverty Eradication and Economic Development VII: Transform the Second Economy," *ANC Today* 4.47 (2006).

[44] Fanon, *The Wretched of the Earth*, 30.

[45] Ibid.

[46] Ezekiel Mphahlele, cited in T. Maluleke, "Urban Black Townships: A Challenge to Christian Mission," *Missionalia* 23.2 (1995): 165–183.

[47] Biko, *I Write What I Like*, 75.

[48] S. Mallaby, "The Reluctant Imperialist: Terrorism, Failed States and the Case for American Empire," *Foreign Affairs* 81.2 (2002): 2–7.

[49] The concepts "daughter" and "mother" churches have their origin in the establishment of separate churches for blacks, colored, and Indian Christian communities in South Africa. Since the apartheid regime insisted on the separation of organizations for the different races in SA, Christian communities where organized along racial lines, which of course happened with the justification of the white Dutch Reformed Church. Thus the Dutch Reformed Church in Africa became a church for blacks; the Dutch Reformed Mission church became a church for coloreds; and the Reformed Church in Africa became a church for Indians. Collectively, they were referred to as the daughter churches, because they originated in the white Dutch Reformed Church, which is considered the mother church. These daughter churches were very much dependent, economically, politically, and ecclesiastically, on the mother church. This dependence varies from church to church. The most dependent of them all was and still is the black church.

[50] A Boesak, *Black and Reformed: Apartheid, liberation and the Calvinist tradition* (Maryknoll: Orbis Books, 1984).

[51] I have written more at length about this problem in R. S. Tshaka, "'African you are on your own!'—The need for African Reformed Christians to seriously engage their Africanity in their Reformed theological reflections," in: *Scriptura* 96.3 (2007): 533–548. It is important to remember that as we critique the short-sightedness of Black Liberation Theology for not extending Liberation to the integration of African culture with the Christian faith, we recognize the volatile situation of Black Liberation Theology then. Those who come after always have the luxury of criticism without an appreciation of the situation, yet because we are faced with new challenges, we must ask difficult and uncomfortable questions to see where we might have gone wrong and how to correct this for the future.

[52] Tshaka, "African you are on your own!," 533–548.

[53] An easily accessible English translation of this confession, which was published originally in Afrikaans, can be found at http://www.pcusa.org/media/uploads/theologyandworship/pdfs/belhar.pdf

[54] D. J. Smit and G. D. Cloete, eds., *A Moment of Truth: The Confession of the Dutch Reformed Mission Church, 1982* (Grand Rapids: Eerdmans, 1984). This is a confession brought about by a "confessional" church, which fundamentally believes in documenting its faith. It is by no means the only such Christian statement of its kind; South Africa has seen numerous documents opposing the ideology of apartheid. See for example "The *Kairos* Document: Challenge to the Church: A Theological Comment on the Political Crisis in South Africa," *Journal of Theology for Southern Africa* 51 (1985): 165ff.

[55] R. W. Nel and K. M. Makofane, "The Black African Other, Oikos and Inclusivity: Reflections on the Response of URCSA to SA's Xenophobic Crisis," *Theologia Viatorum* 33.3 (2009): 374–399. See also "Xenophobic Attacks on

Refugees," Uniting Reformed Church in S.A., press release, May 20, 2008, http://www.ngkerk.org.za/documents/Xenophobia.pdf.

[56] Cf. R. S. Tshaka, *Confessional Theology? A critical analysis of the theology of Karl Barth and its significance for the Belhar Confession* (New Castle: Cambridge Scholars Publishing, 2010), 247.

Part III

CHRISTIANITY AND POLITICS

CHAPTER NINE

POWER AND PUBLIC POLICY

James Nkansah-Obrempong

Power is like holding an egg in your hand. It breaks if you hold it tightly, and if you hold it loosely, it falls and breaks.
—Akan Proverb

Introduction

For some time now, I have been concerned about how power is exercised by those appointed by God to rule and lead nations and people. Most African leaders in the political realm as well as in the Church abuse power, exercising it contrary to God's purposes. Our seminar on public theology in South Africa in June–July 2009 provided the ground for this theological and biblical reflection on power and public policy. One relevant experience was at the Voortrekker (pioneer) Monument, which shows the great trek—the Boers fleeing from British brutalities and making a covenant with God, that if he helps them defeat Dingaan and his Zulu warriors, they will serve him as a nation forever. Their victory over the Zulu king and his warriors was interpreted as God's affirmation of white supremacy and dominance over the black people, which influenced the policies of the apartheid regime in South Africa. The abuse of power by the apartheid government was clearly depicted at the

Hector Peterson Museum, memorializing where a thirteen-year-old schoolboy was brutally shot by police at a protest against the government's introduction of Afrikaans as a medium for instruction in Bantu-speaking schools.

Our visit to District Six highlighted again the abuse of power by the apartheid regime in South Africa. District Six is a stretch of prime land at the foot of Cape Town's Table Mountain, dilapidated and overgrown by weeds, except for the remnants of streets, a modicum of places of worship and a few newly erected houses. District Six was a vibrant, multicultural community that apartheid's construction of purity of races could not allow to exist. From the mid-1960s to the 1980s, over sixty thousand people were forcefully removed from that urban space, as the government razed homes and shops and forcibly relocated the community to the dusty sand dunes of the Cape Flats. Experiencing places like this during our visit to South Africa, and confronting the power struggles in many African states, gave birth to biblical and theological reflection on power and public policy. What is power? The word carries a grand mystique, but it can be defined quite simply as "the ability to do or act; vigor, force, strength, authority or influence."[1] When it is used for a person, it denotes that person having force, influence, or authority.

As I reflected on this issue of power, the Akan proverb (set as this chapter's epigraph) came to mind. The proverb shows the delicate nature of exercising power. When it is exercised in the right way, it can build up and transform peoples' destinies. When it is abused, it can be destructive. People exercise power in all spheres of human activity. However, due to their conception of power, we see great abuse and misuse of power by those who have the privilege to exercise it. African leaders notoriously misuse and abuse power to promote their own selfish agendas and goals rather than use power for the good of their people. This pernicious pattern can be attributed to African traditional sociopolitical systems, colonial legacy, and the authoritarian tendencies in African conceptions of solidarity. Power in the African sociopolitical life can be best understood in these contexts.

The abuse and misuse of power is not only the characteristic of political and civic leaders. The problem is widely spread on the African continent. Religious leaders, parents, families, employers, teachers—to mention some few examples—are found to abuse power in their areas of jurisdiction or influence.

Leaders use power to disenfranchise, disempower, and even harm people out-right. In doing so, many Africans are disadvantaged, resulting in the margin-alization of the weak and the destitute by the powerful. Although Africa is endowed with many natural resources, it is the poorest continent in the world to a large extent because of the widespread abuse of power by the continent's leaders and the bad policies resulting from these abuses.

God intends for those who rule to use their power to establish a just soci-ety in order to bring shalom to the people they rule by providing their fun-damental needs and defending the poor and the powerless in society.[2] This chapter is a biblical and theological reflection on the right use of power in the social and political sphere. It will attempt to provide theological and biblical grounds for the right use of power as foundation for enacting good public policies that enhance the dignity of the person and serve the good of society.

In advancing the thesis for this chapter, I will examine African notions of power and the idea of power from biblical and theological perspectives. I will use some biblical examples to illustrate the wrong use of power, and show how this can affect public policies. I will suggest some biblical and theological models of right use of power. These models see power as a tool not for exploi-tation and oppression but for responsible use by stewards of God's power, to serve people and to develop good public policies for the good of all. I will then draw out some implications for right use of power for leaders today to enact policies to enhance the welfare of society. To begin our discussion, let us pose the question, what is power and how is it understood in contemporary societies?

Power in Africa: The Colonial Legacy

The African colonial legacy played a seminal role in shaping the concept and use of power by African political and civic leaders. African leaders' use of power today indeed reflects this inheritance. The political structures of many African countries were modeled after the political and administrative structures of the colonial powers that ruled over them. Most of these structures were put in place to curtail the power of nationals, compelling them to submit to the brutal rule of their masters. What we see today in African sociopolitical life is a replica of what went on during the colonial rule in Africa.

The colonial governments' model of ruling featured coercion. It was intolerant towards those who questioned the regime's activities, and it used state power and machinery to subdue opponents through excessive use of force. This pattern became the norm for African leaders who took over leadership from the colonial administration immediately after independence. The colonial administrators used power to dominate and exploit and amass great wealth for themselves. They took the best lands for themselves and built economic empires for themselves. The colonial ruling class mostly benefited from policies they made; African leaders copied their style. The lasting effects of this trend are most evident in countries like Kenya and Zimbabwe, which had large settler populations, but it shows in other places in Africa, as well. The use of power by the colonial rulers to exploit and acquire national resources for themselves and their friends laid the foundation for political leaders in Africa to loot the resources of their countries and stash them in other countries around the world. These Western banks and host nations know that the money is ill-gotten, yet they welcome these leaders to stash their funds in protected banking accounts.[3]

The apartheid administration in South Africa offers a classic abuse of power. Its public policies discriminated against the indigenous majority and favored the colonial settler minority. The ruling elite intimidated blacks and other people of color. The government in power used the state apparatus and law enforcement agencies to harass and subject black South Africans especially to torture, forced imprisonment, and abuse of their fundamental human rights and dignity. Apartheid, with its clear-cut racism, was visibly evil, but this pattern of the state abusing its power is a common practice in many other African countries, as well. A more current incident is the coup d'etat in Guinea led by Captain Dadis Camara in 2008, where the military government in Guinea used the military to slaughter citizens who were demonstrating against an illegitimate government.[4]

The colonial political elite enjoyed the unaccountable exercise of power; most of these leaders were accountable only to their distant overseers in Europe. So long as they pleased their patrons, they ran away with their evil deeds. They put in place patronage systems that handsomely reward people who are loyal to the leader or power broker. This was common practice both in the colonial administration and in post-independence leadership. Leaders also used state institutions like the police and the military to suppress and oppress opponents who did not patronize the leader's political agenda.

False arrests, intimidation, and torture became the lot of many who stood up against such abuse of power. The State uses its machinery to declare such people traitors, people who must be punished or even killed. Those in power develop propaganda machinery and policies that control national media and freedom of expression and association, in this way cramping all dissident voices within the society. An example is Hastings Kamazu Banda of Malawi, who became the President of Malawi just after independence. He used his power to build political machinery that revolved around his personal authority, and he built for himself an economic power base. His autocratic style of leadership was a reflection of the colonial administrators' style of leadership. He started using his power to clamp down on his opponents and even killed some, through "road accidents." Banda's abuse of power is captured by Paul Zeleza:

> Banda's Malawi, a thirty-year contraption of totalitarian power, was a land of pervasive fear where words were constantly monitored, manipulated, and mutilated, a country stalked by silence and suspicion ... a state of dull uniformity that criminalized difference, ambiguity, creativity, an omniscient regime with a divine right to nationalize time and thought, history and the popular will. And so it censored memories, stories, and words that contested and mocked its singular authority, banishing and imprisoning numerous opponents, real and imaginary, hunting and murdering exiled rebels. . . . *All was contaminated by this naked arbitrary power.*[5]

Banda's case is common in many African nations. Leaders in their quest to hold on to power have changed constitutions and laws of the land so they can stay in power for life. This sense of long-term rule often is rooted in African traditional cultures, where kings sit on thrones for life, and after their demise, power is passed on to their sons, making governance into a family dynasty.

African political and civic leaders exercise power in absolute terms. They love power and often power gets into their head, and they find it difficult to give it up. Lord Acton's old adage that "power corrupts, and absolute power corrupts absolutely" is very true of many African leaders. A case in point is what is going on in Zimbabwe, where President Mugabe has entrenched his political rule by using the state machinery to intimidate and harass his political opponents. Many examples can be cited, from all over Africa.

The unfortunate thing is that in most cases, the Christian church has stood behind these despotic governments and praised the leaders for their dynamic leadership and the stable and peaceful conditions that the leadership has created. In many places where this has happened, there were torture camps and police brutality against citizens, grand corruptions of all shapes, depleted resources, and public policies that did not benefit the masses of the nation. Yet the Church sang the praises of these leaders, and received favors from these leaders as well, material provisions such as land, money, and so forth.[6]

Power in Africa: The Traditional Legacy

The African perception of power involves religion in more cases than these, however. The African religious and cultural legacy itself has also shaped the Africans' conception of power. The African's understanding of power relates to some aspects of African religio-cultural traditions and worldviews that show an inherent tendency toward authoritarian rule as well as sacralized authority in the political office. Dr. Kofi Abrefa Busia, an anthropologist who served briefly as Prime Minister of Ghana, observed that traditional understandings of solidarity had an inherent tendency towards authoritarianism.[7] African leaders insist on solidarity to the point that any dissenting voice is considered unacceptable. People who disagree with leaders find themselves on the wrong side and are labeled as enemies of the government. Such people receive the full fury of the government's power. Busia certainly understood this truth on a personal basis. As an opposition party leader in Ghana, he had to run away to Great Britain to avoid threats from Nkrumah's government.[8]

The late Ghanaian theologian Kwame Bediako makes a similar observation, that the issue of authoritarian governments in Africa's post-independence era should be understood in religious terms. The problem of authoritarianism, he argues, has to "do with the legacy of certain important religious aspects of the African traditional world-view as they relate to authority, power, and political governance, particularly the tendency of traditional society to sacralize authority and political office."[9] Bediako argues that an African ruler can enforce his will on his subjects because he is "the axis of their political relations," in his very person a symbol of their unity and the embodiment of their values.[10]

Bediako's assertion that authoritarian governments reflect the legacy of religious aspects of African traditional worldview has another dimension as well. In many African societies, he argues, "the ruler fulfills an important function as the intermediary between the living and the ancestors." Africans believe "royal ancestors are not dead; they have simply joined their grandsires in the realm of the spirit-fathers, from where they continue to manifest interest in the affairs of the society through the channels of mystical intervention by the appropriate rituals."[11] This spiritual dimension of power is not often appreciated by the West, but there is a spiritual dimension to power. Westerners might agree in the abstract that God is power, but they have little concrete sense of how the whole spiritual realm affects the exercise of power here on earth. Its influence may be good or evil. African rulers believe this, and some of the most notorious autocrats have, like King Saul in the Old Testament, practiced magic arts in the attempt to maintain their hold on power and defeat their political enemies.[12]

These traditional African views of authority help explain why some leaders exercise power as if they are demigods. This particular understanding is rooted in the conception of the ancestors and the sacral role they play in the lives of the living. If African leaders will exercise power in a more appropriate way, then human power has to be desacralized.

But, is the African use of power as sacred, even for domination, unique to Africa or is this a popular notion of power in other cultures as well? The notion of power as domination is, of course, universally practiced around the world. To put the African situation in context, let us look at how Western cultures understand and use power.

Power in Contemporary Western Societies

The concept of power in Western cultures may have developed in different ways from that in Africa, but it is not as radically different as one might think. Western theologians and ethicists are gaining some important insights worth examining here. American theologian Walter Wink thinks Western conceptions of power are drawn basically from its materialistic worldview.[13] If this is true, then the West's use of power will move toward accumulation of material possession. Power will be used to dominate so people can exploit the resources of the world for their benefit. While Western cultures understand power primarily in material terms, Wink observes that many ancient cultures understood power as a "confluence of both spiritual and material factors."[14] It is good that Wink recognizes the spiritual aspect of power and points out how these dimensions affect the use of power in the physical dimension of human existence as we have mentioned earlier, because it is important to note the spiritual dimension of power that often eludes modern scholars of our day.

Like Africans, Westerners expect power to result in domination. The American Christian ethicist Christine Hinze calls this understanding of power "super-ordination" or "domination," or "power-over."[15] Western scholarship and journalism commonly express this "dominion over" view of power. We see it in many practical ways, such as when the so-called superpowers of the world are imposing their will and controlling many foreign policies around the world. These policies serve to enrich rich nations through dubious trade treaties and economic policies that benefit them and not the citizens of the nations with which they deal.

Many times, global bodies such as the World Bank and the International Monetary Fund (IMF) have used their economic power to influence national policies of other countries, inducing "structural adjustment" economic policies that have brought hardships to many countries in the developing world. At the national level, leaders in many African countries use their power to suppress and loot their countries' resources by engaging in trade policies and entering into fake contracts with multi-national companies abroad to siphon the resources of the country to foreign banks.[16]

However, Hinze sees a second model of power. This she calls "transformative" power or "power-to" model. The basic notion of power here is one that brings transformation and builds capacity for people to experience good life.[17] This model is not widely used, but it is recognized. Here power is used not as force or coercion but as a means to bring about social transformation that builds society to experience God's shalom. Hinze argues that these theories or models, "power-over" and "power-to," are grounded upon certain "sociological and anthropological presuppositions" that inform the judgments and choices people make.[18] While contemporary social theories may affirm "power over" models, such forces must be challenged by Christian presuppositions. How do we then confront the predominant notion of power in contemporary societies with the "enabling" notion of power?

Hinze proposes a three-fold task for a comprehensive approach to socio-political power. First, one needs to integrate the enabling and "superordinating" aspects of theories of power. Second, one must locate and ground discourse on power in essential Christian beliefs. Third, one must critically evaluate the assumptions about power enshrined in the sources and the circumstances shaping one's perspective.[19] Hinze suggests three broad elements of what she describes as a comprehensive approach to the notion of power:

1. A *descriptive model* of power that "informs thoughts about socio-political power";

2. A *normative paradigm* that "expresses judgments about the good and the right in relation to socio-political power"; and

3. "*Programs for action* that determine . . . what formulations of power-to and power-over best reflect the normative paradigm accepted."[20]

What is crucial for our discussion is the normative paradigm that must shape the "manner in which power is understood . . . how it is exercised, for what ends, and for whose benefit."[21] In the section that follows, we will apply Hinze's three-fold task for a comprehensive approach to understanding power: descriptive model, normative paradigm, and programs for action as we seek to ground our concept of right use of power. How are we to understand and use power? We will now look at power from biblical theological perspectives. How is it to be exercised, for what ends and for whose benefit? These questions will be addressed now.

Biblical and Theological Understanding of Power

Both the Old and New Testaments reject the dominating view of power even though they show it to be widely practiced by rulers. The biblical writers' understanding of power affirms the reformative model of power, even though we see the model of power as domination widely used in the Bible. This teaching or affirmation of the biblical notion of power is grounded in the nature and character of God. God's use of power becomes a paradigm for our own use of power.

Old Testament Understanding of Power

The Old Testament Hebrew words translated power is *Hayil, koah* and *'oz*. These Hebrew words conceive power in two ways:

1.   abstract realities such as transgression (Job 8:4), or Sheol (Ps. 49:15); or
2.   "concrete objects or beings" that have ability to perform certain deeds such as
     a.   human persons, who have abilities to perform certain duties that include political authority and military power; and
     b.   God; and other spiritual beings such as angels, and demons.[22]

The verb form of the word מָשַׁל means to rule, govern, have dominion over, and have authority. The noun means dominion. The word carries the ideas of "control" or "dominance" over something (Dan. 11:3–4), right execution of power (Judg. 8:23, Ps. 89:9), and abuse of power (Prov. 28:15). The notion of power as dominating is common in the Bible (Gen. 1:22) even though this was not how God intended for humanity to use power. Our concern in this section will focus on divine and human exercise of power. What is the nature of God's power? How does God exercise power and for whose benefit? How do humans exercise power?

New Testament Understanding of Power

The language of power pervades the whole of the New Testament.[23] The common Greek word for power in the NT is *dunamis*. It derives from *dunamai*, which means "to be able." As in the Old Testament, power means the "ability to carry out an action"; in the case of a supernatural being expressing power, it can mean military or political power, or spiritual forces, like the angelic "army" or "host" of God. God was the Lord of the Powers.[24]

The New Testament uses other words like *Arche* and *archon*. These words relate to "organization of power." In their normal use, they describe the "political, religious, and economic structures and functionaries with which people have to deal."[25] The terms apply to spiritual powers as well, whether good or evil.

The other Greek word rendered power is *exousia*, which means authority. *Exousia* may refer to "human arrangements of power" or to a structural dimension of existence.[26] Authority, according to Wink, gives "ideological justifications, political or religious legitimizations, and delegated permissions" and is occasionally used to designate spiritual powers.[27]

Similar to the Old Testament understanding of power as delegated and having its source in God, the New Testament affirms that God delegates his power and authority to civil authority. Civil authorities are a means God uses to exercise his authority. Rulers must be aware that they have been appointed into the positions they hold by God and they are accountable to him. They must not think of their power in absolute terms, believe that they hold this power as something inherent in themselves, or "confuse divine authorization with a transferred right to do all things at will." Rather, civil authorities must recognize that "authority can be properly exercised only according to the Word of God and within the sovereign authority that God always reserves to Himself."[28]

Political power as Jesus understands it does not reside in human beings. It is beyond human beings. It resides in the realm of the divine. Authority and power truly belong to God. In contrast to this authoritarian and dominating notion of power in his day, Jesus encouraged his disciples to have a different attitude concerning the use of power or authority.

So we see that both Testaments that power may refer to human power, divine power, and spiritual beings exercising power. God is the source of both power and authority, and he uses his power to save lost humanity through his supreme act in Jesus Christ and in the power of the power of the Holy Spirit (Luke 1:49). The New Testament adds a Trinitarian dimension to the source of power. Power is attributed to the triune God—Father, Son, and Holy Spirit. All three work to redeem humanity to God and are concerned about the well-being of God's people.

The Nature and Use of God's Power

Power is attributed to God. How do the biblical writers view God's power? God's power is viewed in six different ways in the Bible. These are all in relation to God's activities. God's power is seen, according to the Malawian theologian, Felix Chingota, as "God's acts, as God's royal rule, as God's empowering wisdom, as God's holy presence, as God's vindication of the poor, and as God's renewing judgment."[29] Throughout the Bible, God uses his power not to oppress, but to save, protect, build, and to seek the well-being of his creation. This is reflected in the six ways that the biblical writers characterized his power. God's power is a creating power, "saving power" (Ps. 67:2), transformative power, and restoring power. God uses his power to execute justice—he does not violate justice (Job 36:22).

God demonstrates his power and authority in his capacity as creator and ruler of the universe. As creator and ruler, he exercises his power for the good and well-being of his creation. As Lord over creation, he is the sole source of all other authorization and power (Luke 12:5). God controls the natural processes of nature for the good and well-being of his creation. He causes his rain to fall on the land so people can get food to eat. Creation itself reflects God's power. He created the vast universe with all its beauty and host of luminaries (Ps. 148:5). His power sustains creation (Ps. 65:5-8) and brings deliverance to his people and creation (Exod. 15:16, Deut. 5:15), and he provides the basic needs of his people. God exercises his power by combining divine power and compassionate love. These two, power and compassionate love, must be understood in an integrated manner and not in a dualistic framework. Love should be seen "as the shape in which divine power appears" and operates.[30]

Divine power is not, says American theologian Elizabeth Johnson, "dominative or controlling power, nor as dialectical power in weakness, nor simply persuasive power, but as the liberating power of connectedness that is effective in compassionate love."[31] God has demonstrated this by liberating humanity from the oppression of spiritual forces, sicknesses, and poverty and all that threatens the well-being of humanity by sending his Son Jesus Christ to bring us his salvation and shalom. God's power is therefore "immanently relational rather than coercive."[32] God does not abuse creation and humanity in using his power. Rather, God uses his power to deliver the oppressed, to strengthen, to appoint human leaders, and to punish the arrogant (Isa. 50:2, Job 37:23, Ps. 33:16).

God in exercising his power and authority does not rape, exploit, and replete the resources of his creation for his own benefits; rather, he nourishes, cares, renews, and uses these resources available in creation to serve and meet the needs and promote the wellbeing of his creation. What underlines this understanding of power has something to do with the essential nature and character of God, as the God of love, justice, and mercy.

Theological Foundations

The notion of power as "transformative" finds its affirmation in the nature and character of God as loving and just. True power, the ability to exercise authority effectively, belongs to God alone (Ps. 62:11). The Old Testament viewed "human power in light of God's sovereignty." Its message is summarized in Zechariah 4:6: "Not by might (*hayil*) nor by power (*koah*), but by my Spirit, says the Lord of hosts."[33]

God's Transforming Power

The right use of power is grounded on God's own ways and laws. He is one who gives power to humanity. God's power is multidimensional. God is both transcendent and immanent to humanity and human activity. God's power reflects his transcendence and immanence in relation to his creation and his activities among humanity.[34] With this understanding, God's power is set over and against all human power. "God as ultimate power is creator, protector, ruler, judge, and the one who determines destinies." Here, God's sovereignty and majesty, evident in his mighty acts, reflects his power over his creation.[35]

God works freely with humanity, and he has delegated his power to humans to enhance their lives and activities. The human person is a dependent creature, and one created in the image and likeness of God. From the point of view of God's power, God's agency as transformative power is illuminated by his "effective capacity to engender and sustain creation, and God's ongoing, immanent presence upholding and enabling human existence and human activity. . . ."[36] Hinze argues, in light of his ontological nature, divine power has a "direct relation to a Christian understanding of human power."[37] Hinze avers, "Humans' creaturely power is framed, negatively, as derivative of and subordinate to divine sovereignty."[38]

In this sense, the exercise of human power is under God's rule. "Positively, humankinds as *imago dei* are seen to reflect divine power-over lower orders of creation, and in capacities for rational self-rule in moral judgments and actions."[39] However, when it comes to human beings, they are not to mistreat and dominate them. Humanity's use of power should reflect God's creative abilities to "engender, sustain, and promote the flourishing of life." This is where many leaders falter in their use of power. Leaders face the temptation to use power in absolute way. Hinze observes that people who hold power "face a constant temptation to exercise prerogatives over others in an irresponsible and self-serving fashion. Powerholders also tend to forget that power and authority are given by God and subject to God's prerogatives."[40]

Jesus and Power

Similarly, Jesus did not use his power and authority to his own advantage, even though he is the source of all authority and power. He did not lord it over his disciples and the people he came to serve. In Christ, we see an integration of divine and human power in the person of Jesus Christ. The way Jesus expressed these capacities in exercising authority is instructive. Jesus does not "lord it over," but comes as "one who serves" (Mark 10:42–45, Luke 22:24–27). Jesus used his power to perform mighty works by healing the sick, casting out demons, and performing many miracles that restored humanity to enjoy the shalom of God (Luke 5:17).

The death and resurrection of Jesus demonstrates God's power over death, sin, and all that militates against human life. Jesus in his ministry demonstrates his power and authority over demons, sickness, and death. In his service and ministry to humanity, Jesus demonstrated the right use of power by enhancing the well-being of people. He did not use his power and authority to disadvantage his disciples and the people to whom he ministered. Jesus' use of power demonstrates a "collaborative, transformative capability," that enhances the well-being of others.[41] As disciples and followers of Jesus, they were to re-enact this pattern in their lives and in the communities in which they serve. What are the implications of this understanding and use of power by the triune God for how humanity exercises power?

Human Power as Derivative and Delegated Power

We learn from studying God's power, first off, that human power is delegated power. Therefore it must be exercised in accordance with God's purpose and rules. Human power is a delegated authority from God. God gives humanity some of his power (Gen., 1:26-28; Ps., 8: 5-8; Ps. 115:16), and God expects those he has given such privilege to reflect his being and character. Therefore, all power exercised by humanity, as derived power, must be used as God intends it. Leaders must understand their power as being delegated and exercise their rule in a manner that reflects God's own rule over creation and humanity. God requires that rulers, kings, presidents, and leaders rule in justice and righteousness and mercy. His instruction to the nation of Israel is instructive.

In Deuteronomy, God sets up a standard for the kings of Israel in relation to how they must exercise their political power and authority over the people and maintain justice for the well-being of the citizens. He expects them to rule as he has instructed them. God sets at least six limitations on how the king must exercise his power. All these limitations have something to do with the king's relationship with the people:

1. The Lord must select the king.
2. He must not be a foreigner.
3. He must not acquire great numbers of horses.
4. He must not take many wives.
5. He must not accumulate large amounts of silver and gold for himself, and
6. He must write on a scroll a copy of the law for himself. (17:15–19)

It is clear from the passage that God rejects the notion of leaders using their power and authority to enrich themselves by accumulating large amounts of money, large military hardware, and many wives. Africans pointedly understand the importance of this restriction on the king. In a continent where corruption is rampant and has become a cancer destroying many countries, political leaders are siphoning billions of dollars out of their countries to fatten their accounts in European and Western banks, leaving their countries in utter poverty. There must be stringent measures and policies put in place against such leaders and their accomplices.

Of importance is the emphasis on the Law of God. The king was to make a copy of the law for himself, to read it daily for three reasons: first, to help him fear the Lord and obey all his commandments; second, so he may humble himself and not become proud and act as if he is above his fellow citizens; and third, so his obedience to God would ensure the positive value of his reign for generations to come.

These criteria set by God for the Israelites contain certain implications for all political leaders. The relevance of these instructions is obvious for African leaders who break all the instructions of God and who rule disregarding the constitutions that brought them to power. They do not follow the law. They disregard it and rule as if they are above the law. They treat the other citizens as if they are second-class citizens. God requires those who rule to follow and live by the constitutions of their countries. Breaking this basic mandate calls for God's judgment on the leaders.

The love for power has made many leaders in African countries allocate almost three-quarters of national budgets to military infrastructure. This is one way to keep these dictators in power for life, while basic needs such as education, health services, communications, hospitals, roads, electricity, water, and job creation are neglected. This abuse of power has reduced many African people to gross injustice and poverty and misery beyond human imagination. These political leaders have totally disregarded God's laws.

Many political leaders in Africa reflect a distortion of the good king portrayed in Deuteronomy 17. Their lifestyles conform to the oppressive king outlined in 1 Samuel 8:11–18. Here, the king will be pervert justice and oppress his people by virtue of his monarchical power. He will take what rightly belongs to the people for himself. The result of this dispossession of the citizens' assets by the king will subject them to a life of servitude, distress, misery, and abject poverty. Nevertheless, God will hold the king accountable for this evil.

What happens when leaders abuse their delegated power and authority? How does God respond to such behavior? We will examine some biblical examples of leaders who abused their power and how God dealt with them.

God's Response to Political Abuse

Old Testament Kings

Some kings in the Old Testament abused their political power by enacting public policies that were not good for the community. For lack of space, we will mention King Xerxes in the Book of Esther, who through the schemes of his confidant Haman, whom he wanted to please, ordered all the Jews in the land to be executed in one day because Haman was not happy that Mordecai, a Jew, had refused to bow down or show him respect (Esther 3:1–15). Of course, God overturned the wicked plans of Haman, and he ended up on the gallows he prepared for Mordecai.

Nebuchadnezzar of Babylon was a supremely powerful ruler in his time. The Book of Daniel attributes the source of Nebuchadnezzar's kingdom, power, strength, and glory to God. He conquered many nations, including Israel, and set up his kingdom at Shinar. Nebuchadnezzar had power, and he used this power as he wished. Twice in his reign, he made public policies that were not in the interest of his people but that served his own purpose and pleasure. When no one in his kingdom could tell him his dream and interpret it, he threatened to cut the magicians, astrologers, sorcerers, and the Chaldeans into pieces and burn their houses. On the other hand, if they could tell him his dream and its interpretation, he was willing to honor the person with gifts and rewards. When they failed to meet his demands, he became furious and ordered that all the wise men of Babylon be put to death. At his decree, the executions began. Daniel stopped the violence when he was able to tell and interpret the dream (Dan. 2:1–49). Because Nebuchadnezzer was a wicked, proud ruler who did not care about anybody but himself, God judged him and made him behave and live like an animal until he was humbled and acknowledged God as the only powerful God, the One to be feared by all humanity (Dan. 4:34–37).

God also punished the kings of Israel who violated his instructions for the king to rule and lead the people in righteousness and justice, but who through their bad public policies oppressed of the majority of people. They were destroyed by foreign powers. While we see so many of the leaders in the Bible abuse their power and authority through bad public policies they implemented, there are some good leaders who used their power in building and bringing prosperity to the nation. For instance, Samuel, the priest and judge of Israel (1 Sam .12:1–5), and David, the second king of Israel, led honorably, repenting of sins and seeking God's righteousness. Because of David's heart, God made a covenant with him to establish the kingship in his house forever. The Lord Jesus Christ, the ideal king, comes from the line of David (2 Sam. 7:1–17).

New Testament Kings

King Herod in the New Testament abuses his power by issuing a policy that resulted in the death of many infants. Who after hearing that a king has been born to the Jews wanted to kill Jesus? When the wise men he had planned to use to get access to the baby to implement his diabolic plan left without informing him, he grew angry and commanded that all male children in Bethlehem and the surrounding villages who were two years old and under be killed.

Pilate, the Roman governor of Palestine, demonstrates the dominant notion of power and authority at the time of Jesus. As Bediako rightly observes: "Jesus held a conception of authority that . . . was essentially 'other'" than that of Pilate. Pilate's understanding of power is one of domination that sacralizes power and political authority. He threatens Jesus, saying that he has power to free him or to crucify him. Jesus rejects these notions of power. Such power, Bediako argues, fails to recognize the "essentially derivative character of all earthly power."[42] Jesus' response to Pilate, that he has no power except that which is given from above, affirms that Pilate's "authority, like all human authority, is delegated. Its source is divine and therefore, it is not arbitrary power, which can be exercised capriciously without moral blame."[43] So we see that when leaders turn away from the God's laws by taking bribes and kickbacks and perverting justice in the courts, they face God's judgment.

What are the implications of our study on power for public policy? How are rulers supposed to use power to make laws that benefit society? What role should Christians play in ensuring that power is used by those in authority for the purpose God intends for it to be used? The last section will address this issue.

Contemporary Implications

The message of the Bible and biblically derived Christian theology and ethics is clear. Today's leaders must use their power to enact laws and policies that address the social, political, religious, and economic concerns that affect the well-being of their citizens. Rulers are put in their positions to defend and protect the vulnerable in society and to provide for their needs. Government policies must address the needs and well-being of its citizens. Leaders are not to make policies that advance their own agendas and prosperity. Rather, they must serve the people with integrity. Power is abused when leaders fail to act on issues that affect the well-being of people within the society. Governments' inaction in making good policies to address societal problems is abuse and misuse of power. Many African leaders abuse power this way. They fail to address the pressing issues facing their respective countries and citizens.

Power Is Delegated for the Benefit of All

Leaders do not have absolute power. They have delegated power. For that reason, they must exercise their power for the purpose it was given. God placed them in positions of power so they can provide for the needs of his people. They are to serve the people, not themselves. God will hold leaders accountable if they abuse their power and mandate. Enacting laws, making policies, and allocating resources justly must happen at all levels of society.

Rulers Are Not Sacred

We must seek to de-sacralize the African conception of power that often makes rulers behave as demigods. Both Old and New Testament writers de-sacralized power. The monarchy in ancient Israel provides instructive examples of the impact of the Hebrew prophetic religion on the notion of authority and the exercise of power in human society. Bediako points out that the Old Testament de-sacralized all human authority and power. Kings were mere humans among fellow humans, and they could be summoned to appear before God. The implication of this was to say that there is a higher kingdom, the Kingdom of God, to which all other kingdoms must submit.[44]

We must continue the de-sacralizing of authority and power in our own contexts as Jesus and other prophets did. In doing this, we recommend, as Bediako puts it,

> Jesus' way. Jesus engaged and involved himself through a new way of overcoming the conception of power at his time, that of domination. He introduced a new and unique concept of power—the power of forgiveness over retaliation, of suffering over violence, of love over hostility, of humble service over domination. . . . Jesus' conception of power is non-dominating power.[45]

By his death on the cross, Jesus, as Bediako observes, de-sacralized all human and worldly power by

> relativizing its inherent tendency, in a fallen universe, to absolutize itself. . . . The Cross desacralizes all the powers, institutions, and structures which rule human existence and history—family, nation, social class, race, law, politics, economy, religion, culture, tradition, custom, ancestors—stripping them all of any pretensions to ultimacy.[46]

Bediako thinks the recognition that power belongs to God can liberate politicians and ennoble politics. Leaders who exercise power and authority must follow the "way of Jesus." The way of Jesus is "the way of non-dominating power." The mind of Jesus concerning power is "not a dominating mind, not a self-pleasing or self-asserting mind, but rather a serving mind, a redemptive mind, a servant mind."[47]

Christian theology sees God as the source of all power. Biblical teaching affirms that true use of power is non-dominating. When leaders acknowledge these truths and see the people they lead as fellow humans and partners in governance, they can serve them with laws and policies that address our common wellbeing.

Human Tendency to Abuse Power and Authority

Of course, there are few times that we see such virtues sustained in government for long. Human fallenness makes it easy for humanity to abuse power. The urge for control and the greed for more are recipe ingredients for one to misuse power. So God wisely places a limitation on the king's power, in terms of what he can and cannot do (Deut. 17:14–20). Christians must play a prophetic role, like that of the Old Testament prophets, by warning and reminding kings and presidents, civil leaders, religious leaders, and all public officers about the responsibility to serve the interest of the people they are governing. It is important to remind leaders of their divine responsibility. The prophets of Israel constantly reminded the kings when they erred and department from God's laws and ways. This is costly work, as we see in the fate of many of the prophets.

Political leaders must use power the way God himself uses it. God exercises power with compassion and love, seeking to advance the prosperity and well-being of his people and creation. Political leaders must develop a concept of power that demonstrates "compassionate love that resists tragic suffering." Leaders must use their power to reduce the sufferings of humanity. God has raised them up as leaders for this purpose. If they exercise compassion towards the marginalized and destitute, they find that this is "empowering power," providing the ability for transforming people and institutions.[48]

Leaders who have such godly attitudes would enact policies that will improve the living conditions of people and give them and their children hope for the future. As the American theologian, Sallie McFague rightly points out, the right use of power is not "the power of control through either domination or benevolence but the power of response and responsibility."[49] Elizabeth Johnson aptly describes the right use of power as expressing vitality: "empowering ... stirs up and fosters life and one that builds up and transforms people, and makes them into better people."[50] In short, all who exercise power must do so in love. Love is the most profound and constructive motivation and foundation of power.

Responding to Abuses of Power as the Church

The Church in Africa has often sat back without speaking to the abuse of power and issues facing their respective countries. This position may be attributed to some of the legacies inherited from the missionaries who brought the gospel to Africa. African Christians were taught to obey governments and leaders and submit to their rule. So, many Christian leaders have not taught the church members to know their civil responsibilities. This is true with most evangelical Christians.[51] Some Christian communities have argued that Christians are not supposed to entangle themselves in the affairs of the world and so Christians have lost their prophetic voice. Contrary to these views, we propose that God has called the church to ensure that justice and righteousness prevail in the land in which we live. So, the church has the mandate to ensure that God's purposes are fulfilled on this earth.

The Church Must Respond

The Church must provide a prophetic critique to the abuse of power and authority by those who exercise it. To do this, it must develop a critical distance necessary to offer a prophetic critique.

Following the example of the Old Testament prophets and Jesus, they should speak against the abuse of power by the political elite of their day. The prophets reminded the kings about their responsibility to the society and challenged the gross abuse of power against the poor, the widows, and the less privileged in society. The Church must always stand against those who abuse power and remind them that their exercise of power must be accountable to God who is the source of all power. The Church should encourage the state to build strong institutions to handle its affairs in the area of developing policies that are efficient, accountable, and address the needs of its citizens.

A major aspect of public policy is law. African governance often focuses on rulers, but good governance, we learn from the Old Testament, makes the ruler subject to the law. The church should insist that right laws and policies are enacted, and that proper care is taken to protect the rule of law by assuring a balance of power between the executive, judiciary and the legislature in government.[52]

It should encourage the government to enact just economic policies and prudent use of resources to eradicate disease and reduce poverty and ignorance in many African societies. Where leaders are oppressive and they have lost their mandate and authority, the Church must press such leaders to hand over leadership to others. In nations where such oppression exists, these stands will be costly. May we find the courage of our convictions.

God's use of power is always transformative. We who are Christian thought leaders must teach a biblical power ethic, and help political scientists and those who exercise political power to reformulate a biblical and theological foundation of right use of sociopolitical power. The church should conduct seminars for this purpose of clarifying the idea of divine power and show how it relates to human agency and its implications for sociopolitical activity and structures including the structures of the church itself. Many African Church leaders are often perceived as demigods themselves, abusing the powers God has given over his flock to exploit them. We must condemn such behavior in the Church as well as in the government.

The African churches have used their "prophetic office" very reluctantly, but they have a role to play in shaping public policy through education and public advocacy. They should encourage groups that work in the area of public policies and provide the moral environment and guidance required for their work. The Church should work with advocacy groups, encouraging them to educate the public as well as public policy makers about the problems facing the people, what legislation is needed to address the problems, and the funding required for providing services or conducting research.

For a long time now, the older mission-founded churches, Catholic and Protestant, have accepted this public responsibility and have engaged in social and political advocacy. Many more pietist and evangelical groups have been critical of this practice, saying in effect that it was a worldly and even spiritually deadening line of activity for the church. But as this study makes clear, God cares deeply about the exercise of power, and God calls the Church to be a transforming agent in this realm, as well as in others more traditionally under its watch and care.

Notes to Chapter Nine

[1] "Power," *Webster's New World Dictionary* (London: Pocket Books, 2003), 505.

[2] The prophets of the Old Testament had one word for this blessed state of affairs: *shalom*.

[3] Many contemporary historians and social scientists comment on the colonial legacy in African governance. See for example, George B. N. Ayittey, *Africa in Chaos* (New York: St. Martin's Griffin, 1998).

[4] Jeffrey Gettleman, "Military Coup Succeeds Easily in Guinea," *New York Times*, December 26, 2008 A14 (L). Francois Grignon, "Guinea: The Junta Must Leave," posted by the International Crisis Group, November 17, 2009, http://www.crisisgroup.org/en/regions/africa/west-africa/guinea/guinea-the-junta-must-leave.aspx

[5] Quoted by Kenneth Ross, "The Transformation of Power in Malawi 1992-94: the Role of the Christian Churches," in *God, People and Power in Malawi: Democratization in Theological Perspective*, edited by Kenneth R. Ross (Blantyre: CLAIM, 1996), 18–19.

[6] Paul Gifford, *African Christianity: Its Public Role* (Indianapolis: Indiana University Press, 1998), gives examples of this pattern of religious complicity in chapters on Ghana, Uganda, Zambia, and Cameroon. See also Gifford, *Christianity and Politics in Doe's Liberia* (Cambridge: Cambridge University Press, 1993).

[7] That is one of the main arguments in K. A. Busia, *Africa in Search of Democracy* (London: Routledge & Kegan Paul, 1967).

[8] Busia later returned and became Ghana's prime Minister after the military overthrow of Nkrumah, but then fell prey to another military coup after only three years.

[9] Kwame Bediako, "De-Sacralization and Democratization: Some Theological Reflections on the Role of Christianity in Nation-Building in Modern Africa," *Transformation* 12 (1995): 8.

[10] See also M. Fortes and Evans-Pritchard, eds., *African Political Systems* (London: KPI, 1987), 16.

[11] Bediako, "De-Sacralization and Democratization," 7.

[12] Accusations and rumors circle a number of leaders, but in the case of Mobutu of Zaire, these practices were well-documented. See, e.g., Michela Wrong, "The Emperor Mobutu," *Transition* 81/82 (2000): 92–112; and Wyatt MacGaffey, "Aesthetics and Politics of Violence in Central Africa," *Journal of African Cultural Studies* 13.1, In Honour of Professor Terence Ranger (2000): 63–75.

[13] Walter Wink, *Naming the Powers: The Language of Power in the New Testament* (Philadelphia: Fortress Press, 1984), 5.

[14] Ibid., 3.

[15] Christine F. Hinze, *Comprehending Power in Christian Social Ethics* (Atlanta: Scholars Press, 1995), 1–5. See also Robert Dahl, *Who Governs? Democracy and Power an American City* (New Haven: Yale University Press, 1963); Steven Lukes, *Power: A Radical View* (London: Macmillan, 1974); Thomas Wartenberg, *The Forms of Power* (Philadelphia: Temple University Press, 1990).

[16] There are many accounts of both creditor nations' arrogance and bad policy and African leaders' corrupt complicity, but for a very capable summary and argument, see George B. N. Ayittey, *Africa Unchained: The Blueprint for Africa's Future* (New York: Palgrave Macmillan, 2005).

[17] Hinze, *Comprehending Power*, 267.

[18] Ibid., 268.

[19] Ibid., 270.

[20] Ibid.

[21] Ibid.

[22] Edward Laarman, "Power, Might," *The International Standard Bible Encyclopedia*, Vol. 3 (Grand Rapids: Eerdmans, 1986), 926.

[23] Walter Wink has demonstrated this; see his *Naming the Powers*, 7–12.

[24] Laarman, "Power, Might," 927.

[25] Wink, *Naming the Powers*, 14

[26] Ibid., 15.

[27] Ibid., 16.

[28] Geoffrey W. Bromiley, "Authority," *The International Standard Bible Encyclopedia*, Vol. 1 (Grand Rapids: Eerdmans, 1986), 370.

[29] F. L. Chingota, "The Use of the Bible in Social Transformation," in *God, People, and Power in Malawi: Democratization in Theological Perspective*, edited by Kenneth R. Ross (Blantyre: CLAIM, 1996), 41.

[30] Elizabeth A. Johnson, *She Who Is: The Mystery of God in Feminist Theological Discourse* (New York: The Crossroad Publishing Company, 1999), 269.

[31] Ibid., 270.

[32] Peter. G. Heltzel, "Power," *Global Dictionary of Theology*, edited by William A. Dyrness and Veli-Matti Karkkainen (Downers Grove: IVP Academy, 2008), 699.

[33] Laarman, "Power, Might," 927.

[34] Hinze, *Comprehending Power*, 270–271.

[35] Ibid., 271.

[36] Ibid.

[37] Ibid., 270.

[38] Ibid., 271.

[39] Ibid., 272.

[40] Ibid., 275.

[41] Ibid., 274.

[42] Bediako, "De-sacralization and Democratization," 8.

[43] Ibid.

[44] Ibid.

[45] Ibid.

[46] Ibid.

[47] Ibid.

[48] Wendy Farley, *Tragic Vision and Divine Compassion* (Louisville: Westminster Press, 1990), 86.

[49] McFague, *Models of God*, 85.

[50] Johnson, *She Who Is*, 269–70.

[51] It must be said, however, that the trend is changing in some of the African countries (Ghana, Kenya, Nigeria, and South Africa, to mention a few) where evangelical Christians have taken a leading role in shaping the public policies of their nations and speaking to the social, political, and economic issues facing their countries. See for example Terence O. Ranger, ed., *Evangelical Christianity and Democracy in Africa* (New York: Oxford University Press, 2008).

[52] Here I found the South Africa constitution as a model for African countries. There is a clear boundary between the judiciary, the executive, and the legislative branches. This helps to check the abuse of power by any one of the branches. Here, the judiciary body must play its vital role to ensure justice prevails and the executive body does not abuse its power by interfering with the work of the courts, as we find in many African countries. This was made clear by the ruling of Deputy Justice Dikgang Mosenke of the Constitutional Court against the state, in favor of a South African citizen who sued the government for neglect after losing his property in Zimbabwe.

CHAPTER TEN

NEGOTIATING
A PLURAL POLITICS

South Africa's Constitutional Court

Paul Brink

The building that contains the Constitutional Court of South Africa is an imposing structure, though not in the ways that Supreme Courts elsewhere are imposing. There are no great marble floors here, no classical pillars that testify to the majesty, authority, and permanence of the law. Such features can certainly be found elsewhere among South Africa's great public buildings, but the Constitutional Court, completed only in 2004, imposes itself in a very different way.

Rather, as the visitor approaches the Court, it is the history and suffering of South Africa that she confronts. The Court is built upon the site of the Old Fort Prison in Johannesburg, where hundreds of thousands of people were incarcerated before it was finally decommissioned in 1983. Nelson Mandela first visited there as a young lawyer, then as prisoner, and finally as president of South Africa, when he revisited the old site. Rather than simply replace the old prison, obliterating any sign of the site's former function, its history was incorporated into the new design. Staircases and walls from the prison were retained, complete with prisoner graffiti, and the original bricks were reused throughout the building. The past is acknowledged also by the physical situation of the Court buildings. Three other prisons of the Old Fort complex remain and stand next to the Court, including the notorious Number Four ("Native") Prison, as well as the Women's Prison, which today houses the Commission for Gender Equity. The result is that as South Africans enter into the great hall of justice that is the Constitutional Court, they encounter their own history, and with it, one hopes, signs of a more just future.

There is a further distinctive to the building also not typical of Supreme Courts elsewhere. From the large exterior sign that announces the Court in all eleven official languages to the cowhide that decorates the court chambers, the building itself responds to and celebrates the diversity of South Africa. In contrast to previous high courts, the justice of *this* Court will be directed toward the good of all South Africans. Plurality is here not something to be overcome; it enters the very heart of the state.[1]

We shared tea with Deputy Chief Justice Dikgang Moseneke in this place, and it was a powerful and moving experience. Justice Moseneke, who has served on the Court since 2002, and as Deputy Chief Justice since 2005, began his career in law at age fifteen, when he was sentenced to a ten-year term for anti-apartheid activity. His entire term was served on Robben Island, the prison island off Cape Town that held Moseneke, Mandela, and many other political prisoners for decades during the apartheid era. Today, Justice Moseneke is an impressive figure, soft-spoken, dignified, generous with his time, and unusually hospitable to our group of visiting academics.

Justice Moseneke is also a gifted speaker. His opening comments with us emphasized how much had changed in South Africa in so short a time. The apartheid regime had sought to shape South Africa with a single vision and resulted in intolerable oppression. Now, however, the new constitution honored the diversity of South Africa, opening up space where all could participate, and where no single theocratic or other vision imposed itself on all. Our questions for him ranged over some delicate topics: the Court's role in protecting the rights of Zimbabwean refugees, the relationship between the Court and the President's office, and the Court's responsibilities to protect South Africa's young democracy. These he handled easily and well, acknowledging the tremendous difficulty of these topics, but emphasizing the Court's task—and its success—to rule decisively and clearly on these questions. Indeed, that very afternoon, he handed down judgment on behalf of the Court on a case relating to the President's responsibility to protect South African farmers in Zimbabwe.

An impressive conversation with an impressive Justice in an impressive building provided much room for hope, and our group marveled at what had been accomplished in so little time, and we spoke together optimistically of what Moseneke and the other members of the Court might be able to accomplish.

It was not until later, however, when I was able to think more about our conversation in that beautiful, unusual space, that I became struck by an interesting juxtaposition, one that perhaps ought to have tempered our enthusiasm—a juxtaposition between the Court building and certain of the comments of Justice Moseneke. To be precise, the most troubling point was one that the Justice did *not* say. Whether he was unable, or merely unwilling, to do so is difficult to judge—and it is, of course, always dangerous to read too much into a conversation over tea. But at one point, noting the Supreme Court nomination hearings that would be beginning shortly in the United States for Sonia Sotomayor, I asked a question occasionally posed to American soon-to-be Justices, a question concerning the source of the authority of law in a democratic society. The question is an old one, and an important one, and it's also a favorite for Christian political theorists who also appreciate the blessings of democracy: can the affirmation that all authority originates in God be reconciled with the principles of a liberal democracy? The question is also one that has recently assumed a higher profile as democracies in Europe, North America, and elsewhere consider new threats to political authority coming from religious faith.[2]

In answer to this question, the Justice had exactly nothing to say. Or, if we had something to say, he was curiously reticent on the subject. He did make clear that the new constitution should not be understood to be based on Christian revelation; it is, in fact, secular. This can be seen, he explained, by its strong affirmation of the diversity of South Africa, both cultural and religious. In contrast to the previous regime, the new constitution opens for all South Africans a space that is genuinely secular in nature.

Now, to a great extent, this emphasis on a new secular space that did not exist before is understandable. Justice Moseneke is quite correct to emphasize the contrast between the apartheid regime and the new era represented by the

1994 constitution. The exclusionary theocratic vision of a South Africa whose public was reserved only for certain groups was one from which he, like the rest of us, recoiled. Such a vision must be rejected in favor of a public space in which all can participate on equal terms.[3] Unfortunately, however, proclaiming the virtues of such a new vision does not avoid the question as to the source of the authority of law within such a plural society—indeed, its importance only increases, particularly in the South African case, where the authority of law was for so long voided in the hearts and minds of so many. But in his answer, the Justice offered us little.

He is not alone in this respect. Indeed, the broad traditions in which the democracies of Canada, the United States, and Europe are rooted struggle also on this question.[4] Part of the reason is rooted in their history. In the European case, the painful experience of the religious wars led many theorists, particularly in the seventeenth century, to the conviction that no longer could religious doctrines be permitted to achieve such a high political profile that society would be split into parties of war. Some foundation for law independent of theology would have to be sought: the only question concerned the nature of that foundation. The figure of Thomas Hobbes looms large here. The significance of Hobbes's attempt to tame religious conflict by accommodating it within the framework of the nation-state is not merely that he set forward a new doctrine, but that he initiated a major philosophical-political response to the challenge of pluralism that still today remains dominant.[5]

What was that early modern strategy? Faced with a situation of radical religious plurality, early liberals sought to establish political order on whatever else might be found that people have in common, and thereby ensure a framework in which widespread assent to some "commonness" might enable those who disagree on so much to live together within the same society. Their impulse seems sound: from the ancient Greeks onward, a widespread consensus on matters of identity had long been understood to provide—and, very likely, actually did provide—a stable foundation, perhaps the only possible foundation, for peaceful society, for a unified cohesive polity, and for the possibility of civic virtue. Given the breakdown in this consensus and its fearful consequences for politics, the search for a new consensus that might provide an alternative foundation was a natural step.

We later moderns can be said to follow a similar "politics of abstraction." We seek to find an abstract basis that is separated from all that divides us, a source of political authority that is independent of any and all religious views, and similarly independent of any other plural identities or loyalties that might threaten our political stability. Indeed, many believe that we have no other option: faced with great disagreement on matters both religious and secular, do we not require a basis for our politics rooted on something else—anything else—that we might be said to have in common? And so in the public space, we are encouraged to retreat from arguments based upon faith or even ideology. Instead we search for a language common to us all—one that is presumably secular, though not stridently so, and almost certainly liberal.[6] Similarly, in our public meetings with each other, we seek to pretend away our other differences—race, gender, ethnicity—appealing instead to some abstract concept of the person, a person we have never met and to whom we cannot relate. Says one modern proponent of this approach, "the deeper the conflict, the higher level of abstraction to which we must ascend to get a clear and uncluttered view of its roots."[7]

The parallel to the situation faced by Justice Moseneke and his fellow justices is striking. Emerging out of the wreckage of South Africa's own version of the religious wars, the Court must now consider how the continuing plurality of South Africa is to be handled. The situation in which the Court and all South Africans find themselves, however, is one where Enlightenment liberalism can help but little. My concern of course is that in Justice Moseneke's hesitation to speak of the source of constitutional authority in the new South Africa, in his desire to make a sharp break with the past, and in his evocation of a secular public space established by the constitution, the Justice makes clear just how tempting is the view that says a healthy public life is one wherein people depend upon the things they have in common, rather than their differences.

The dangers of such an approach are manifold. The chief difficulty is that any basis for political authority robust enough to do the work required of it is bound to be controversial, and cannot fail to privilege certain groups or perspectives over others. Ironically, such privilege is established and perpetuated by the language of tolerance. In the concern to establish the foundations for political order on something other than religion, we search for some even lower common denominator that can somehow unite the population: reason, nature, contract, and individual freedom have all been candidates. Once that foundation has been established, then any difference (cultural, religious, racial, or other) can be tolerated, so long as it does not violate that commonality undergirding the regime. Somehow, the fact is overlooked that to pursue such a strategy of "tolerance" is actually to relegate vital aspects of human identity to the realm of public indifference, while at the same time the various candidates proposed for the common basis become ever more abstract and ever more thin.[8]

Note the contrast between this liberal politics of abstraction and the alternative vision that guided the design of the Court building. The building does not seek to overcome or shrink from the history of South Africa; rather it faces the horrors of the past steadily, and even so, offers hope for a society to move beyond them. Similarly, the reality of South African pluralism in all its complexity is not presented as a threat to society or as a problem that the Constitution must overcome, but rather is invited into the very heart of the building: the court chambers themselves. The building celebrates precisely what liberalism considers to be threats, and it refuses to offer a universal identity that can triumph over the particulars of history and culture.

Is it possible to imagine ways in which the new South African Constitution might be understood that come closer to how the Court building was designed? Given the relative scarcity of models for genuine pluralist democracy, Justice Moseneke and his colleagues have been presented with an unusual opportunity to pry open the door for approaches to politics rooted in traditions of political thought that are less concerned with strong consensus and its achievement, emphasizing instead the importance of plurality in public life, where the recognition of our plurality becomes a vital part of our public consciousness.[9] The challenge is to put aside the assumption that we must look for a politics that establishes a community with a united vision. Such an assumption may have made sense or been a logical move for Hobbes or other early moderns who sought to posit various forms of unity that might substitute for the once integrative, now shattered, religious consensus on matters of state. But the great difficulty involved in finding and developing such a new consensus, and this strategy's general lack of success in persuading different communities that they might take part without becoming secular liberals themselves—the very point of a political theory that attempts to respond justly to pluralism—suggests that this assumption must be abandoned. The attempt to posit a new form of commonality at the foundation of politics will only weaken or threaten the very communities it claims to recognize and include. So what potential does South Africa have for doing something different, for forming a genuinely pluralist democracy?

A place to look for an answer might be with the new constitution itself. The question for Justice Moseneke that prompted these reflections concerned the source of authority underlying the constitution. Why should citizens see it as authoritative? The presumed historical and philosophical reasons behind governmental authority have varied over the years, but one central opposition has been between the so-called "divine right of kings"—we might recall Romans 13—and "natural rights"—we might recall John Locke. Obviously, we are simplifying considerably, but these two alternatives clearly find the authority of the state in very different places. Perhaps Justice Moseneke's reticence may have stemmed from an unwillingness to adjudicate this opposition, at least publicly, but the problem itself is clear enough. In a democratic, pluralist state, it seems inappropriate to assert (a) the nation's dependence on God when there are many who clearly disagree with that claim, even without considering what such dependence might imply. But for the reasons noted above, it seems similarly inappropriate—and perhaps risky—to base the regime on (b) popular will alone, as the people are, in fact, not always right. And of course, to find the source of political authority to lie in (c) some collective idea of "nation" or "ethnic group" is particularly inappropriate, especially in a nation with the history of South Africa.

Such are the problems of a democratic plural society. But consider for a moment the nature of the new constitution. When Justice Moseneke suggests that the constitution of South Africa is "secular" in nature, what does he mean? Is it his suggestion that arguments by advocates of the first position (a) are out of bounds because of their religious character, while the other two (b) and (c) are permissible? Surely not, for the risks and the dangers inherent in both majoritarianism and ethnic nationalism are well known. The liberal approach might be to suggest that all three must in fact be rejected in favor of an even deeper basis, rooted perhaps in individual freedom, upon which we can develop a principle of toleration to adjudicate between the three rivals.[10] But here's another consideration: does the constitution itself need to adjudicate the matter? Is it critical that in the political agreement that we call the constitution we find included some sort of strong moral claim concerning the source of the authority of the document? My question posed to the Justice might suggest that such a declaration is vital. But is it necessary that in the debate one of the proponents be found *right*, that one actually *"wins"*? Or might it be possible that *all of them are right*?

Obviously, philosophically, theologically, this cannot be the case. These three competing claims are mutually exclusive, or largely so. Politically, how-ever, and constitutionally, we need make no such declaration. Besides giving us another reason to explain Justice Moseneke's silence on this point, this strategy offers us the considerable advantage of avoiding a ruling against citizens or groups of citizens on the *grounds* for their views or arguments—an action that could not help but increase resentment and threaten stability. We also avoid asking citizens to downplay their particular identities in favor of some theorized universal, thereby relegating these identities—and the people who hold them dear—to the realm of public indifference. Instead, allowing citizens their varied grounds for affirming the government's authority is no small thing; indeed, it evokes the same inclusive theme that graces the structure and fur-nishing of the Court building.

More difficult may be the requirement that we change our understand-ing of what a constitution is. By loosening the standards for what is included within the constitutional consensus, we are loosening control, removing the constitution from the "gatekeeping" function that perhaps we assumed it had or otherwise sought for it. We may find, in fact, that the reasons people hold to the authority of the new constitution and the government it prescribes may vary as greatly as they do themselves—and in a country as pluralistic as South Africa, that variance may be great indeed. Liberalism, which has long held the established position in Western democracies—it's why they're called *lib-eral* democracies—and might have expected to assume such a role also within the new South Africa, may object to such a risky strategy. People will join the constitutional consensus for their own reasons—and there is nothing to ensure that their reasons will be liberal reasons. We might actually encounter the Romans 13 Christian, the Lockean bearer of natural rights, the ethnic nationalist, all as members of the consensus. On the other hand, if most people in society are liberals, it is likely to be the consensus. But there can be no guarantees.

Liberals may take comfort, however, in the fact that all are similarly "disestablished." If there is no substantive, shared common basis for the constitution rooted in liberalism, neither is there such a basis rooted in Christianity, nor in nationalism, nor collectivism. Nor, for that matter, in secularism. However, if all of these can recognize that genuine respect for pluralism demands that liberalism, Christianity, nationalism, collectivism, and secularism all be denied pride of place, then something like this notion of constitutionalism begins to make more sense. Considering these examples also makes clear that not only is the constitutional consensus unlikely to reflect a single conception, but further than that, what is at issue here is the shape of a politics that does not even pretend to operate within the confines (as well as the security) of a society-wide moral consensus.

Is the risk entailed in this understanding of the constitution too great? Perhaps, but only if we believe that what most fundamentally holds a political order together is an ideological or other "strong" agreement among citizens concerning the nature of that order. Liberals perhaps have a special propensity toward this belief, though they are certainly not alone in this habit. If the belief is true, then, given the extent of South African pluralism, the situation is truly alarming, and the risk is that much greater. On the other hand, the truth of this belief is not obvious, and it is certainly not necessary. There may be many more things that sustain a constitution or, more broadly, a political order, most of which have little to do with a strong moral consensus on ideological or identity questions.

Rather, we might imagine a conception of the political that depends simply upon the willingness of the participants to respect the rules of a constitutional democracy as they are developed, rather than upon a larger integrative moral vision for politics that all must share. Of course, citizens enter into the political fray accompanied by their visions—indeed, politics can be about the contest of visions of politics, as much as about anything else. But the point is that the basic constitutional guarantee of equal opportunity of democratic participation for citizens is more important than a prior agreement among them concerning the character or nature of that participation. Indeed, what else is a polity, we might ask, as distinct from other forms of human community, than a structure that embraces all who reside in a territory, regardless of their race, religion, gender, ethnicity, and all the other distinctions that divide? And if the state embraces all, without regard to particularities, then the emphasis should be placed upon enabling all to participate, without regard to these particularities, and especially without an insistence that participation be in terms of a particular common basis. The call therefore is for a constitution that is a human agreement—and, particularly in the South African case, this means not an agreement between free, rational (and identical) individuals, but rather one between persons who have a race, a gender, a faith, a history. It is a constitution that respects that these persons have their own reasons for supporting the democratic experiment that is South Africa.[11]

Can genuine understanding be possible in such an environment? Can participation in such a constitutional conversation possibly hope to come to an agreement on anything? Our ability to answer such questions positively depends on our willingness—and the Court's willingness, frankly—to let go of the terms of the debate and to give up our concern to proceed on that common basis. Once we have done so, agreement and understanding remain very much within the realm of possibility. This is because it is very possible, even likely, for people to agree on a particular point or conclusion or policy without coming to an agreement on the underlying reasons for that point or conclusion or policy. Citizens can then be encouraged to enter into political dialogue with all their particularities intact, although they cannot demand that others support their views for those same reasons. Happily, there is no reason why this plurality cannot be seen as a strength, rather than a weakness, recognizing that the plurality of bases need not be seen as a problem to overcome, but rather as signs of widespread support for the political enterprise.[12]

What makes the South African situation so vital is that although we have been contrasting the exciting South African constitutional possibilities with the old liberal strategies of Europe and North America, in reality those older democracies are becoming more South African with every passing identity crisis. The plural realities that make the liberal strategy unappealing in the South African context are present elsewhere—they simply stand out less clearly, and the liberal establishment is more entrenched. As the United States continues to re-imagine itself with respect to racial and ethnic diversity, as "old Europe" comes to grips with the reality of Islam, and as Canada comes to terms with its treatment of First Nations peoples, these countries' traditional liberal strategies of positing new forms of unity to paper over identity divides will increasingly be found wanting. It is to South Africa that they may come—not only for football, but also to seek out new possibilities for a pluralist politics. Reflecting the statement already made by its new Constitutional Court building, South Africa can show others how to imagine a constitutional democracy that accepts, and even rejoices in, a world of plural communities.

Notes to Chapter Ten

[1] Indeed, the building ably reflects the spirit and thrust of the new South African Constitution, which begins:

> We, the people of South Africa,
> Recognise the injustices of our past;
> Honour those who suffered for justice and freedom in our land;
> Respect those who have worked to build and develop our country; and
> Believe that South Africa belongs to all who live in it, united in our diversity.

[2] With respect to France, the United Kingdom, and Canada, for example, see Danièle Hervieu-Léger, "France's Obsession with the 'Sectarian Threat,'" in *New Religious Movements in the Twenty-First Century: Legal, Political, and Social Challenges in Global Perspective*, edited by Phillip Charles Lucas and Thomas Robbins (New York: Routledge, 2004), 49–59; Rowan Williams, "Civil and Religious Law in England: A Religious Perspective," February 7, 2008, http://www.archbishopofcanterbury.org/articles.php/1137/archbishops-lecture-civil-and-religious-law-in-england-a-religious-perspective; John Winterdyk and Kiara Okita, "Mixing Sharia Law with Canadian Legal Traditions," *LawNow* (December 2005/January 2006); online version found at http://www.lawnow.org/Downloads/documentloader.ashx?id=3239

[3] Efforts to articulate this new vision of South Africa's public space are ongoing, from a variety of perspectives. A consideration of five distinct evangelical South African contributions is offered by Anthony Balcomb in "From Apartheid to the New Dispensation: Evangelicals and the Democratization of South Africa," in *Evangelical Christianity and Democracy in Africa*, edited by Terence O. Ranger (Oxford: Oxford University Press, 2008), 191–223.

[4] Consider, for example, questions concerning the limits of democratic action: may the people, in principle, collectively will *anything*? Or are there limits on democracy that arise from an authority other than the people? A particularly clear example of this concerns issues where a democratic majority attempts to act against the rights of a minority—upon what basis can these laws be overturned? Natural rights, tradition, natural law, divine law, scientific authority—all these and others have been proposed as alternative sources, but in a democratic age, all remain controversial. Consider, for example, debates concerning the arguable right to same-sex marriage articulated against democratic majorities, or the appeal to tradition made by Native American tribes seeking court action to halt land development.

[5] Kenneth D. McRae, "The Plural Society and the Western Political Tradition," *Canadian Journal of Political Science* 12.4 (1979): 682.

[6] This language has been described by John Rawls and others as "public reason" and would require, for example, that arguments for prayer in public schools be based not on a "private" reason related to claims about God and education, but rather on an "appropriately public" reason: that prayer in public schools leads to less violence

during recess, for instance. This might be seen as an extension to the realm of political arguments what the Supreme Court's "Lemon test" (in *Lemon v. Kurtzman*) requires for legislation concerning religion: that "the government's action must have a secular legislative purpose"(403 U.S. 602 (1971)).

[7] John Rawls, *Political Liberalism* (New York: Columbia University Press, 1993), 46.

[8] With respect to one proposed foundation, for example, consider the complaint of communitarianism against liberalism's focus on the individual and the individual's rights. Once the principles of justice are established on this basis, complains Michael Sandel, a leading communitarian critic, concerns such as family, friendship, faith, and community are considered too shallow to be constitutive of identity except as patterns of individual choice and are not permitted within the public square. The result is very close to George Grant's depiction of liberal society:

> As for pluralism, differences . . . are able to exist only in private activities:
> how we eat, how we mate, how we practice ceremonies. Some like pizza,
> some steaks; some like girls, some like boys; some like the synagogue,
> some like the mass. But we all do it in churches, motels, restaurants
> indistinguishable from the Atlantic to the Pacific.

George Grant, *Technology and Empire* (Toronto: Anansi Press, 1969), 26, quoted in *Liberalism and the Limits of Justice* by Michael Sandel (Cambridge, U.K.: Cambridge University Press, 1982), 182. See also Paul A. Brink, "Selves in Relation: Theories of Community and the *Imago Dei* Doctrine," in *The Re-Enchantment of Political Science*, edited by Thomas W. Heilke and Ashley Woodiwiss (Lanham: Lexington Books, 2001), 85–120.

[9] Where might we find these traditions? The study of constitutionalism in divided societies is growing also in the global South. But within the Western tradition of political theory, Kenneth D. McRae suggests exploring political traditions in those countries where the Reformation was at best partial or incomplete: parts of the Holy Roman Empire, Switzerland, the Netherlands, and other countries farther away from the mainstream of the Western liberal tradition. Asks McRae:

> [I]s there any evidence of *other* streams, of lesser channels, eddies,
> backwaters, or even swamps, where different and possibly more interesting
> life forms may be discovered? Have we, under the 400-year old spell of
> national sovereignty, unwisely neglected other sectors of Western thought
> that are more relevant to societal pluralism? . . . Should we devise an
> alternative curriculum in political thought that would stress Althusius over
> Bodin, Montesquieu over Rousseau, von Gierke over Hegel, Acton over
> Herbert Spencer, Abraham Kuyper over T. H. Green, Karl Renner and
> Otto Bauer over Marx and Engels? In short, have we been studying the
> wrong thinkers, and even the wrong countries?

McRae, "The Plural Society and the Western Political Tradition," 685–86.

[10] Indeed, this is very close to the strategy of American political philosopher, John Rawls, who suggests that the time has come to apply the principle of toleration "to philosophy itself" (*Political Liberalism*, 10).

[11] Of course, this also means that even with regard to the "rules of engagement" described here, we should expect political discussion and debate. Even the products of an agreement to establish basic rules for political debate cannot be placed beyond debate.

[12] Ironically, even in a strongly liberal nation such as the United States, it is unclear whether most or even any political decisions actually are made according the narrow liberal standard. Even in the U.S. Congress, representatives vote for a great variety of reasons, to the dismay of observers, while citizens themselves are even more decidedly lacking in civic virtue, if such virtue is defined according to the liberal creed. Of course, from the perspective of the other unitary visions we might care to name—nationalism, the Christian right, socialism—this is equally a problem. In contrast, the pluralist vision outlined here attempts to turn such a reality into a virtue, as well as warn of the dangers that lie in attempts to cleanse politics of religious and other unshared political visions. Such delegitimizing arguments are most unlikely to inculcate habits of civic friendship and tolerance, virtues that remain in short supply in the U.S. and South Africa alike.

CHAPTER ELEVEN

THE POLITICAL VOICE OF CHURCHES IN A DEMOCRATIC SOUTH AFRICA*

Tracy Kuperus

In June 2009, I participated in a two-week seminar that introduced participants to South African Christians who were working for positive change in their society and politics. We visited the Central Methodist Mission in Johannesburg and heard Bishop Paul Verryn discuss the struggle to serve Zimbabwean refugees. We met Guguletu township residents who provided loving and supportive homes to children orphaned or otherwise negatively affected by HIV-AIDs. And we heard judicial and political leaders—Justice Dikgang Moseneke of the Constitutional Court and the COPE Party's presidential candidate, Mvume Dandala—describe their efforts to serve the common good.

Sprinkled among the high-profile contacts were some separate "side visits" to places like the Parliamentary Office of the South African Council of Churches (SACC). Here we listened to Keith Vermeulen, the Director of the Office, explain the SACC's involvement in monitoring legislation and engaging in advocacy around issues of interest to SACC member churches. As we heard Mr. Vermeulen explain the range of issues (e.g., macroeconomic policy, the Basic Income Grant, land redistribution, and Zimbabwe's human rights record), it became clear to us that his office was responding to a vast policy landscape with exceedingly limited resources. One member of the group asked the question, "With so many critical issues facing South Africa, where is the church?" Several among us asked that question numerous times along the two-week journey, often with a nostalgic tone of lament—"If South African churches were active and influential during the apartheid era, why is their voice and witness so diminished and seemingly inconsequential in a democratic South Africa?" We were heartened by the work of some intrepid people and committed congregations, but we saw little evidence of "the Church" acting in its more collective and nationwide forms. I was currently spending the year in South Africa to follow up on some previous research in which I examined the role of churches in South Africa,[1] and this question hit right at the heart of my research.

This chapter seeks to answer the questions above by exploring the post-apartheid political voice and public engagement of four churches and church-based organizations within South Africa. These are

- the *Nederduitse Gereformeerde Kerk* (NGK- a.k.a. the Dutch Reformed Church or DRC),
- the South African Council of Churches (SACC),
- Rhema Bible Church, and
- the Zion Christian Church (ZCC).[2]

To find out why the churches' national public influence seems diminished, a number of sub-questions probe further:

1. What is the political voice and public engagement of the NGK, SACC, Rhema, and the ZCC in a democratic South Africa, particularly related to issues of macro level public policy advocacy?[3]

2. Does each group's political role in a democratic South Africa differ significantly from the apartheid era, and if so, why?

3. Is the political voice and public engagement of South African
    churches indeed diminished and marginalized, or merely more
    diverse and pluralistic within a democratic context?

This study responds in part to a growing body of research that explores
relationships between Christianity and democracy in the Global South. Some
of the broader questions addressed in this study relate to that field of inquiry:
How do the trends within and among South African churches affirm or differ
from the growth of Christianity elsewhere in the Global South? Do church
and parachurch organizations in South Africa help or hinder the consolidation
of democracy in the country?[4]

The answers to these questions led to intriguing conclusions. Churches are
still active in the political arena in South Africa; however, their political involvement is far more diverse and less binary than it was during the apartheid years.
Moreover, South Africa resembles many other countries in the Global South
regarding the growth and influence of evangelical, Pentecostal, and independent Christianity.[5] Finally, the political influence of all forms of South African
church-based organizations regarding the consolidation of democracy must be
assessed on a contextual basis, leading to an outcome of church and religious
organizations that do *not* always serve the political interests of society as a
whole. To unpack this argument, we turn first to an overview of some trends
regarding Christianity and democracy in the Global South.

Christianity and Democracy in the Global South

Numerous studies over the past decade point to the phenomenal growth of
Christianity in Asia, Latin America, and Africa over the past century. Philip
Jenkins argues that because the great majority of Christians live in the Global
South, "our traditional concept of the Christian world as a predominantly white
and Euro-American world of western Christianity, in fact—is no longer the
norm."[6] But the growth in Christianity, he argues, involves more than ethnic
and geographical shifts; it involves changes in class and belief systems as well.
Christians in the Global South tend to be poorer and more conservative than
their Western counterparts. The most dramatic growth among Christian

churches in the Global South is among Pentecostal and evangelical Christians, where conservative beliefs and moral teachings dominate.[7]

Although one may be familiar with the statistics regarding Christianity's growth in Africa, they are still worth recounting. Timothy Shah reports that "Christians numbered 10 million in 1900 and 30 million in 1945, but then jumped to 144 million by 1970 and further to 411 million by 2005."[8] And by far, the most impressive growth is among Pentecostals and evangelicals. Joel Carpenter states, "In Africa, where Christians now make up half of the continent's total population, Pentecostals and evangelicals account for more than a third of the Christians."[9]

One of the more recent debates among scholars interested in the growth of Christianity in the Global South concerns the relationship between Christianity and democracy. Evangelical Christians, for example, have become increasingly involved in the public arena in the Global South, but does their political and public involvement contribute to the consolidation of democracy?[10] On the one side, scholars like Paul Gifford argue that within Africa historically, "it is the mainline churches that have challenged Africa's dictators; the newer evangelical and pentecostal churches . . . have provided the support."[11] In a more recent work, Gifford points to mainline Protestant churches and the Roman Catholic church being more in tune with issues of structural justice in the African public arena, whereas evangelical churches tend to focus on personal and public integrity and the newer Pentecostal churches emphasize a "faith gospel" that detracts from structural injustice. For Gifford, African countries are in desperate need of sociopolitical restructuring. Although evangelical and Pentecostal churches may offer evidence of cultural dynamism, Gifford argues that the individualistic and sometimes triumphalistic nature of their religion will likely *not* bring about the social change needed for political reform or democracy's consolidation in Africa.[12]

Other scholars, notably Jeffrey Haynes and Terence Ranger, disagree with the analysis as portrayed by Gifford. Haynes argues that most leaders within the mainline churches, in an effort to "maintain their hegemonic domination over society,"[13] work with political elites to preserve the status quo. Mainline religious leaders support fundamental political reform only if it forwards their religious and material interests. New religious movements, whether Muslim or Christian, offer a far different political orientation. They realize that "the best way to achieve individual and collective benefits [is] by practicing methods of self-help."[14] Haynes argues that the many indigenous and independent churches in Africa may not seek a role at the institutional level, but their politicization is at the personal level, which allows for a measure of social, and perhaps more authentic, cohesion.[15]

Ranger's earlier work has tended to affirm many of Haynes' assessments. Ranger argues that the public's perception of the moral credibility of the church and the international, resource-rich, and centralized nature of mainline Protestant and Roman Catholic churches helped them fill the political vacuum of the 1980s and challenge authoritarianism in the early 1990s. However, the decentralized churches of the newer evangelical, independent, and charismatic churches may offer more in the way of consolidating democracy compared with the mainline churches. Independent and evangelical churches are inherently participatory and democratic in nature, and because they are in tune with local realities and contribute to social restructuring, they may be able to build the social capital necessary for consolidating democracy.[16]

Only specific case studies can help answer the question of whether Christianity contributes to democratic consolidation in the Global South. Can South Africa shed light on this debate? How do churches and religious organizations, as important elements of civil society, respond to the ongoing process of South Africa's democratization?[17] What is their political voice and witness, and do their actions and statements help or hinder democracy's consolidation?

To answer the questions above accurately, there would need to be a thorough examination of the political voice and witness of the four featured case studies (NGK, SACC, Rhema, and ZCC) at the macro, intermediate, and micro levels of analysis. That is because the public role of religion includes action at all these levels, including, among other things, public policy statements by religious hierarchies, congregations sponsoring HIV-AIDs forums in their neighborhoods, religious leaders addressing socioeconomic issues in weekly editorials, and rituals associated with public events like funerals. In this chapter, however, I will be concentrating on the political role of the NGK, SACC, Rhema Bible Church, and the ZCC as expressed at the macro level of public policy advocacy. Two reasons explain this choice. One, a focus on the macro level of public policy advocacy among churches in the post-apartheid era offers a good comparison with the apartheid era, and two, public policy statements produced by religious actors are often regarded as the most visible representation of public religion or political engagement within a society. In Robert Wuthnow's words, policy statements, carefully crafted, seek to influence "the public arena directly. The news media are expected to give these papers wide coverage, and religious leaders hope in the process to influence not only their own adherents but also the public officials who set the direction of national policy."[18]

Of course, public policy advocacy does not represent all or even the majority of political responses by Christian churches in their sociocultural context, and a concentration on public policy advocacy is inevitably biased in favor of bureaucratic or institutional responses to the modern political environment. This chapter acknowledges the need to explore the intermediate and micro levels of public religion, as well as how the micro and intermediate levels interact with and shape the macro level. Together these offer a far more holistic vision of the relationship of religion and politics in South Africa. Despite these limitations, it is important to examine the public policy advocacy of prominent Christian organizations in South Africa. They remain a critical element of the churches' political voice and public engagement.

The Political Voice of South African Churches

According to the 2001 Population Census data, 79.8 percent of South Africa's population claims to be Christian.[19] A breakdown of the main Christian groupings (i.e., mainline denominations, African independent churches, and Pentecostal/charismatic churches) shows a gradual decline in mainline denominations, and an increase in the numbers of African independent and Pentecostal/charismatic members—trends that mirror the growth of Christianity in the global South.

During the apartheid years, the political role of Christian churches was defined by whether they affirmed, condemned, or tried to offer a neutral position vis-à-vis the apartheid state.[20] South Africa churches today interact with a democratic state that respects religious pluralism rather than Christian nationalism. This political shift has corresponded with some dramatic changes in the profile of Christianity in South Africa, noted in James Cochrane's work. These changes include new "leadership patterns, the new dominance of forms of Christianity not bound to the original mission churches, the rise of neo-Pentecostal influence, the confusion of identity and purpose in the ecumenically-aligned churches, and a shifting local social imaginary."[21]

Many of these changes will be explained in more detail below, but the most significant shift in the profile of Christianity in South Africa revolves around the reversal of status regarding the SACC and the evangelical churches. More specifically, the SACC, whose role in politics was dominant during the apartheid years, has become considerably weaker in a democratic South Africa, while the evangelical/charismatic movement, often positing a "neutral" political position during the apartheid years, has emerged much stronger in terms of political influence. To explore these developments further, we turn to the four main case studies of this chapter.

The NGK: Inconsequential, but not Absent[22]

The Afrikaner Reformed churches hold the dubious distinction of having supported apartheid in the previous political dispensation.[23] Of the three main Afrikaner-Reformed denominations, the NGK was the largest and most influential, with 1.7 million members—representing 65 percent of the Afrikaner population in 1985. Dubbed "the National Party in prayer" during the apartheid years, the NGK was linked to the legitimization of and support for apartheid during Nationalist rule. [24]

Although the NGK advanced a neo-Calvinist, ideological justification for race policy as early as the 1930s, numerous documents during the years of apartheid illustrate the NGK's ongoing theological and biblical support for apartheid. For example, the General Synod's 1974 report entitled *Human Relations and the South African Scene in the Light of Scripture* stated, "A political system based on the autogenous or separate development of various population groups can be justified from the Bible."[25] In addition to providing the moral underpinning of apartheid, the NGK was able to influence public policy "completely out of proportion with the number of members" in areas of education, public morality, and welfare when leaders of the NGK had "silent meetings" with government officials or served on government statutory bodies where discussions on policies beneficial to Afrikaners occurred.[26] In sum, the NGK during the years of apartheid played a key role in justifying and legitimating, and it emphasized the preservation of Afrikaner interests more than structural democratic reform in the political arena.[27]

The NGK's political voice and witness has experienced significant changes in the new South Africa. If the NGK during the years of apartheid spoke with confidence on public policy issues or in support of the government during the years of apartheid, its voice today is muted. The reality is that the NGK no longer has the political platform to speak out on issues in the form of a tight relationship to a ruling party. Its loss of credibility in the public eye has added to its reluctance to speak out. Within the NGK leadership there has been a conscientious effort to allow ecumenical organizations like the SACC to take positions on the NGK's behalf. In the words of Coenie Burger, former moderator of the NGK,

> I knew we lost credibility due to our support for apartheid, so we had to change tactics. . . . There were some political issues that arose and I often took the issue to the SACC, so they could "speak" for us. There were some individual NGK statements during my tenure, but generally, we tried to make statements with the SACC and URCSA, so we would have more credibility.[28]

Besides a more muted political voice, the NGK's political witness today is divided and shifting. After apartheid's demise, the NGK, like other Afrikaner institutions, was forced to reassess its nature and identity. Theologian Piet Naude argues that this reassessment led to "a dramatic 'pluralization' . . . in a very short time period."[29] No longer could the NGK be considered one church. There was now diversity in theological thought (e.g. Reformed, evangelical, liberal, post-modernist) as well as "congregational differentiation: examples are mega-city-churches, so-called community churches, traditional suburban and rural churches, and experiments in small alternative house or family churches."[30] The NGK's diversity regarding theological perspectives and worship styles has contributed to a multiplicity of political witness inside the denomination, although two forms are dominant, namely, the NGK as "preserver of the flock"[31] and the NGK as a "promoter of societal transformation."

For most of the 1990s, the NGK public policy witness, whether expressed through synodical statements, bilateral meeting with political leaders, or *Kerkbode* editorials, was as a 'preserver of the flock.' Its position on sociopolitical issues reflected the concerns of NGK members and was fairly predictable— alarm regarding "the high incidence of violence and crime, the abolishment of the death penalty, the discrimination against members that is conducted in the name of affirmative action," and the loss of Afrikaans as an official language.[32] Less attention was given to issues that were important to the government at the time, for example, poverty, the Truth and Reconciliation Commission (TRC), or the equitable distribution of resources in education.

The NGK's reluctance to embrace transformative political change in the 1990s was demonstrated most clearly in its position toward the TRC. Although initially supportive of the TRC, the NGK struggled to submit a statement on the role it played during the apartheid years, and hesitated, but eventually sent, a representative to the TRC hearing on faith communities.[33] In a critical analysis of *Kerkbode* articles on the TRC in the 1990s, Christine Anthonissen points to the overall pattern of skepticism expressed toward the TRC: would the TRC be one-sided? Why should the nation pour its energy into an experiment like the TRC that focused so heavily on the apartheid sins when "new morality" concerns (e.g. violence, crime, abortion, pornography) desperately needed attention? Although intended to bring national healing, wouldn't the TRC be too traumatic for the country? In Anthonissen's perspective, the *Kerkbode* articles skirted principled engagement with the nation-building exercise because the NGK "was concerned about stating its own views and defending its own positions."[34] Thus the church missed an important chance to participate in the reconciliation experiment.

A change in leadership in the 2000s led the NGK to embrace a more inclusive public policy witness. At the 2002 General Synod, the NGK recommitted itself to the African continent and South Africa's political transformation. It also acknowledged the need to engage with issues like poverty and HIV/AIDs as well as the more traditional concerns of white South Africans like crime and violence.[35] Another example of the NGK's shift away from defensive engagement on public policy was the NGK's submission to parliament regarding amendments to the Marriage Act and the law enabling civil unions

for homosexual couples. Rather than expounding on the biblical defense of heterosexual marriage, as many would have expected the NGK to do, the submission acknowledged the variety of positions within society and among Christian
communities regarding homosexuality and urged the government to respect
religious freedom, including churches that supported a heterosexual structure
of marriage, in the process of devising a new bill.[36]

Besides tackling public policy issues in a more inclusive way, the NGK
recommitted itself to ecumenical relations in the early 2000s. It sought and
was restored into the SACC's fold in 2004, and it pursued unification talks
within the Reformed family of churches. Differences between the NGK and
URCSA leaders regarding the NGK's unconditional acceptence of the Belhar
Confession (a statement denouncing racism in all its forms, including apartheid) were seemingly resolved in 2006, making the prospects for its acceptance
at NGK local churches higher than ever before.

More recently, however, it appears as though the NGK's public witness
may be shifting back to a position as "defender of its flock." First, unification
talks with the Reformed family of churches have stalled after a newly constituted NGK moderature (an NGK governing body comprised of its leadership) expressed less desire for organic unity with URCSA.[37] Second, there
has been a backlash by NGK members, revealed primarily in *Die Kerkbode*,
to the NGK's submission on the Marriage Act. Finally, there have been concerted efforts to expose "liberal theological forces" at the School of Theology
at the University of Pretoria (the so-called "Evangelical Initiative").[38] As
Johann Symington, previous editor of the *Kerkbode*, states, "The NGK is in
the headlines at a fairly steady rate, but for all the wrong reasons, and for all
the wrong issues!"[39]

In sum, the NGK's political voice is far more muted in a democratic South
Africa compared to the apartheid years. Although the NGK has broken its
relationship of co-optation with the state, becoming a more autonomous civil
society actor in a democratic South Africa, its political role since 1994 has
been fairly inconsequential due, in large part, to its divided nature and its
long–standing commitment to being a "preserver of the flock". When the
NGK's political witness embodies the role of "preserver of the flock," it is
regarded by many who assess religion and democratization to be on the

sidelines of political and social transformation. We will return to that assessment toward the end of this chapter.

The SACC: Still Prophetic, but Marginalized

The South African Council of Churches (SACC), representing roughly half of all Christians in South Africa through its twenty-seven member churches and organizations, is an ecumenical organization "committed to expressing . . . the united witness of the church in South Africa, especially in matters of national debate and order."[40]

Unlike the white Afrikaans churches, the SACC took a leading role in the struggle against apartheid, serving as one of the main conduits of anti-apartheid activity in the 1980s.[41] This prophetic engagement was built upon earlier forms of resistance. In 1968, the SACC, along with NGK dissident theologian Beyers Naudé's Christian Institute, issued the controversial "Message to the People of South Africa" that declared that apartheid was an unjust political policy and contrary to the biblical message of reconciliation.[42] By the mid-1970s, theologians Desmond Tutu, Alan Boesak, and Manas Buthelezi were ascending in the SACC's leadership and offering a critical voice through the development of Black Theology, with its particular emphasis on the poor and the hope for liberation.[43] Throughout the 1980s, as political oppression increased, the SACC stepped up its opposition. It provided support for conscientious objectors to military service, commended international economic sanctions, and resolved that churches should withdraw from cooperation with the state in all those areas and organizations where the law of the state contradicted the law of God's justice.[44] The SACC's actions, rooted in what became known as contextual prophetic theology, were directed toward transforming unjust power structures and developing and mobilizing the resources of the oppressed, mainly black, communities.

If the SACC's political role was fairly influential and deeply appreciated within the broader liberation struggle and within the ANC during the apartheid years, its political role today is much "diminished and sometimes marginalized." Indeed, says religion scholar James Cochrane, "Ecumenical churches and agencies . . . have suffered a serious loss of influence and voice in the public square."[45] The SACC's decline was glaringly evident when it was bypassed during the formation of National Interfaith Leaders Council (NILC)—an interreligious group intended to partner with the government for improving public service—in 2009.[46] In an August press release, the SACC stated that it was "neither informed of, nor invited to the recent formation of the NILC."[47] The exclusion of the SACC from the initial meetings of NILC is remarkable, considering the SACC's historic commitment to eradicating poverty and empowering the marginalized. How and why has the SACC, an organization that played such an important political role during the struggle years, arrived at this diminished political status?

Some of the reasons lie in developments external to the SACC. The ecumenical movement worldwide has weakened considerably—not only in terms of reach and public impact, but also because of a "crisis of vision, mission, and mandate . . . in a post cold war era."[48] Ecumenically oriented churchesin Europe and North America and a variety of other philanthropic agencies provided major support (financial and otherwise) to the SACC during the apartheid years, but since the birth of democracy in South Africa, interest and support has dropped considerably.

Moreover, in a religiously pluralist and democratic state, the SACC has had to share the public space with Pentecostal, charismatic, and evangelical churches that are often technologically savvy, connected with the grassroots, and increasingly willing to engage the government on political issues. The latter churches are more newsworthy in a democratic South Africa. John De Gruchy, a South African theologian and ecumenical leader, says,

> During the 1970s and 1980s, we [the SACC] couldn't keep the media away. The media was interested in our message because we were anti-apartheid. But things are different in a new South Africa. Take churches talking about HIV/AIDs. If the SACC talks about the issue, the SACC is not heard, but if evangelical churches talk about it, the media picks up on it. Why? Evangelical involvement in politics is new and interesting. The SACC's political voice isn't new or interesting.[49]

Along with changes in global and local Christianity, there are developments internal to the SACC that have contributed to its diminished voice. After 1994, quite a few prominent leaders left the SACC and other organizations in the anti-apartheid movement for academic or governmental positions. With considerable overlap existing between the SACC and the ANC-led government on policy issues, an identity crisis grew within the SACC. How would the SACC weather this political change? Should it be a social partner to the government, a critical watchdog, or both?

For some in the SACC, there was a desire to pull back some of the public advocacy focus and "let the church be the church again." Those taking the latter position, particularly prominent in the early years of democratization, argued that the SACC faced a liberated and democratic South Africa with politicians in office who embraced the same causes as the SACC. This meant the SACC no longer needed to confront government; instead, it could embrace a supportive political role.[50] These voices, however, did not represent the SACC's evolving official position, a position which has been shifting from "critical solidarity" to "critical engagement" over the years.[51] The important but subtle differences between these positions made it clear that the SACC intended to support the government in nation-building exercises if social justice and the common good were upheld, but because the SACC's solidarity ultimately rested with the poor, the SACC reserved the right to criticize the government if the poor were being marginalized or human rights were being trampled. And while the SACC has indeed supported the government in efforts of nation-building since 1994 (the SACC was one of the TRC's strongest proponents),[52] its advocacy stance on issues like economic justice—for example, its significant leadership in the People's Budget Campaign, which presents a people-centered, redistributive economic vision, compared with South Africa's fiscally conservative, elitist-driven economic framework,[53] or its consistent opposition to arms deals based on the fact that military spending diverts money from much-needed developmental projects[54]—indicates the survival of the SACC's contextual and prophetic voice regarding public policy.

Indeed, the SACC's insistence on maintaining its "watchdog status" vis-à-vis the government may be another reason the SACC is currently being sidelined in the political environment. The ANC-led government has made it perfectly clear over the years that it prefers South African churches adopt a supportive, partnership role with the government in nation-building efforts in lieu of a "watchdog" role.[55] Even the newly minted Zuma administration, through the voice of Vusi Mona, formerly the media spokesperson at Rhema Church but now one of Zuma's communications directors, has called on churches to be "unequivocally committed to collaboration with the government" in the new service delivery project fostered by NILC.[56] It appears that the government is less willing to work with the SACC because it has resisted collaboration and maintained a more critical witness, especially when compared, as we shall see, to other religious actors in South Africa.

Of course, an alternative explanation that might explain the current sidelining of the SACC in the political arena rests in shifting political alignments within the ANC, with Jacob Zuma now as party leader. Evidently the ANC cannot completely trust the SACC to be a loyal political partner. Some have suggested that the SACC got too close to the ANC faction led by Thabo Mbeki over the years—evidenced by the SACC's lack of criticism regarding Mbeki's disastrous position on HIV/AIDS or the ANC's movement toward hierarchical authority and suppression of dissent under Mbeki.[57] SACC leaders have acknowledged mistakes in this regard. Tinyiko Maluleke, current President of the SACC, says,

> We lost our credibility when some of the SACC folks or mainline church thinkers ended up working for the government (e.g. Frank Chikane, Molefe Tsele) and then we were too polite to criticize their errors. . . . In some ways, we look like we're in bed with the government.[58]

More recently, a number of high-profile leaders that had been associated with the SACC, notably Mvume Dandala, the former Methodist presiding bishop, and ecumenical leader Allan Boesak, ran for office under the banner of Congress of the People (COPE), political party formed in 2008 made up primarily of Mbeki allies. These moves only cemented the perception in the minds of some ANC members that the SACC was more supportive of Mbeki than Zuma.[59]

Although the SACC has certainly missed some opportunities regarding prophetic engagement since South Africa's democratic transition, its record over fifteen years is fairly consistent. It tries, albeit imperfectly, to be faithful to the vision of a more just, participatory democracy in a new South Africa. Its public influence, although significantly diminished from the previous political era, is still vitally important in South Africa. As John De Gruchy says,

> Maybe the role of the mainline, ecumenical churches/SACC is the critical role. They won't be popular or be invited into the circle of power. Their range of issues (e.g. poverty, homosexuality) is important. Church growth won't happen, but maybe these issues will eventually end up in the churches that *do* have political clout.[60]

In sum, the SACC's political voice continues to be shaped by a critical stance on many public policy issues related to its advocate on behalf of the marginalized,[61] The SACC also seeks to maintain its autonomous status vis-à-vis the government, but its political influence as a religious actor that the ANC listens to and respects is diminished, even marginalized, in a democratic South Africa compared with the apartheid years.[62] Ironically, a church that promoted 'apolitical' engagement during the apartheid years has strengthened its political position in a democratic South Africa. It is to this case study that we now turn.

Rhema: Influential but Potentially Co-opted

Rhema Ministries, led by Ray McCauley, was started in 1979. It was a reflection of the white-oriented Christianity of the Charismatic Renewal Movement that arose in South Africa during the late 1960s and the mid 1970s.[63] Starting with thirteen people in 1979, Rhema Bible Church has grown to forty-five thousand members and ranks as one of the most prominent "prosperity gospel" churches in South Africa.[64] Perhaps the most remarkable aspect of Rhema's history is its intentional and high-profile political involvement since the early 1990s, a surprising development considering its position during the apartheid years.

In general, white evangelical churches, like the Baptist Church, the Assemblies of God, and Rhema Bible Church, "were at best apolitical and at worst upholders of the status quo in the old regime."[65] Churches like Rhema emphasized personal salvation and imminent return eschatology that translated into a minimal desire for immediate sociopolitical engagement. Literal interpretations of Romans 13 also meant evangelical churches tended to preach order and respect to the government of the day rather than rebellion. If Christians were to engage in resistance, it should be against communism, the "social gospel," and atheism.[66] The political voice and witness of Rhema, then, during the apartheid years rarely questioned, and often supported, the policies of the apartheid regime.[67]

At the Rustenburg Conference in 1990, Ray McCauley made a dramatic turnaround when he confessed the errors of Rhema's apolitical and pietistic stance during the apartheid years and resolved "to play an active and positive role . . . in the new South Africa."[68] As a prominent church leader, McCauley contributed to South Africa's democratic transition by serving as a political broker between the ANC negotiating team and individuals (e.g. Brigadier Gqoza and Chief Buthelezi) who were reluctant to join the peace process.[69] After South Africa's democratic transition, McCauley maintained his commitment to numerous public initiatives, for example, "the Stop Crime Campaign, . . . the Moral Summit of 1998, . . . and the Cape Peace Initiative, which attempted to bring gang leaders together to stop gang violence."[70] And, like many of the member churches of the SACC or the NGK's diaconal ministries, McCauley provided leadership in ensuring that Rhema Ministries offered a variety of social development programs. Its "Hands of Compassion" ministry, for example, offers substance abuse rehabilitation programs, literacy training, and employment opportunities for the purposes of empowering the poor and marginalized in South African society.[71]

Events in 2009 only confirm McCauley's and Rhema's influential public engagement. McCauley, in particular, has been involved with a number of newsworthy responses and actions; for example, he invited ANC President Jacob Zuma to Rhema Bible Church a few weeks before the 2009 national elections. The influential pastor said he welcomed the National Prosecuting Authorities' decision to drop charges against ANC President Jacob Zuma in April 2009, and that he was "breathing a sigh of relief" at a Judicial Service Commission review that dropped misconduct charges against a Zuma ally, Western Cape Judge Hlophe.[72] Moreover it is McCauley who in July 2009 launched the National Interfaith Leaders Council (NILC), a mass-based interreligious group intended to partner with the government in improving service delivery.

This brief overview of the political involvement of Rhema Ministries in public policy advocacy indicates that the political voice and witness of Rhema has changed considerably over the decades. From an apolitical and pietistic stance that accepted the status quo during the apartheid years, Rhema's leaders today promote political involvement, working to "align their evangelical following with South Africa's progressive direction under the ANC."[73] This latter-day stance could be the result of a genuine change of political perspectives or of more opportunistic and pragmatic considerations.[74] Whatever the case, the bigger question is whether Rhema's approach to politics will contribute to the consolidation of democracy.

Anthony Balcomb has written a convincing portrait of Rhema, showing that however much Rhema "encourages its membership to become positively engaged in the transformation of society,"[75] its ability to actually nurture democracy is limited. The reason comes down to race. For as much as Rhema boasts of a "multi-racial" ministry, it is still "largely white and middle-class in composition" and unlike some of the older Protestant denominations, it has "little impact on the black community."[76] In essence, Rhema's white, middle-class composition means it is unable to "enhance the sociopolitical cooperation and harmony—essential to the effectiveness of democracy—across South Africa's ongoing racial divide."[77]

But could McCauley's new role as leader of NILC change things? Since McCauley's new political platform is much bigger than Rhema's, perhaps McCauley, representing the strength of the *multi-racial* charismatic-Pentecostal phenomenon in South Africa—notably its ability to mobilize the grassroots and build social capital—can embark on projects that can nurture South Africa's democracy in the realm of social development. Ray McCauley himself says, "Our expertise is to mobilize thousands of churches across the country to get involved with partnerships at grassroots level, with councils, mayors, and so forth to help them deliver."[78] John De Gruchy affirms the potentially positive role of NILC: "If McCauley can do service delivery, that's all to the good, for the country and church as a whole!"[79]

However, there are already worrying signs that the new partnership between the ANC and Rhema (through NILC) may not be good for South Africa's democracy.[80] It is widely agreed that the NGK lost its credibility due to its collusion with the NP government during the apartheid years. As civil society actors, churches and church leaders can play a positive role in democratization *only if* they maintain a voice autonomous from the government. Can McCauley maintain the church's autonomy? At this point, it's not clear. From inviting Jacob Zuma to Rhema prior to the election, and actually refusing to allow other political leaders the opportunity to address his congregation, to stating that the National Prosecuting Authority's ruling in Jacob Zuma's favor regarding a notorious corruption case involving an arms weapons deal was "a victory for the rule of law" when it was a far more ambiguous outcome,[81] to producing a media statement on behalf of NILC in support of the JSC ruling on Judge Hlope from a site *in the headquarters of the ANC*.[82] McCauley appears to be cozying up to the ANC. Where is McCauley's voice, for example, when ANC officer Julius Malema utters words that insult women? Or where is McCauley's voice when ANC politicians purchase luxurious, expensive vehicles using government funds? To date, McCauley's silence on these and other matters that make it appear as though his political voice is partisan and selective.[83] Rather than being an honest broker among pluralistic religious voices, one that seeks the common good in a new South Africa, McCauley (and the Pentecostal-charismatic churches under his influence) appears to be co-opted to do the government's bidding—a detrimental outcome for the consolidation of South Africa's democracy.

The ZCC: Nationally Aloof, Locally Reconstructive?

A focus on the African Independent Churches (AICs), which can be described as African-founded churches with both African traditional and Pentecostal-type traits,[84] is essential if we are to grasp the "emerging global face of Christianity."[85] In South Africa, AICs loom large in terms of size, constituting 40.8 percent of Christians and 47.6 of black South Africans.[86] The largest of the AICs is the Zion Christian Church (ZCC) with close to 5 million members, by far the largest single denomination in South Africa.[87]

Similar to the evangelical-charismatic churches described above, AICs were thought to be have adopted an "apolitical" or reactionary stance with regard to the government during the apartheid years.[88] While many AIC leaders discouraged political participation, some AICs seemed to accommodate the

Nationalist government. The ZCC, for example, was charged by those on the left as being explicit collaborators with the apartheid regime due to the visit by President Botha in 1985 to a large ZCC gathering in which Botha addressed the crowd about the need to be obedient to government.[89] Others have argued that a more comprehensive picture of the ZCC, if one removes the anomalies of Botha's visit, illustrates the protest character of independent churches. A less binary framework suggests that the ZCC "functioned as a haven in the heartless world of white political power, urban stress and economic exploitation,"[90] offering avenues of cultural protest in the form of transformative rituals that allowed for the healing of oppressed lives. The ZCC, then, from this author's perspective, presented an ambiguous political voice during the apartheid years—it offered personal and communal resistance to a white-dominated society, but its non-confrontational political witness at the macro level also meant that it did not pose a threat to the apartheid regime.

The ZCC's political voice and witness in the post-apartheid era has not changed considerably. It still remains nationally aloof—direct public engagement with or in macro political events is mostly absent—but many scholars have argued that the strength of the ZCC (and other AICs) is its influence on society "from below."[91] Some believe, for example, that the ZCC contributes to the cultivation of social capital (i.e., the normative values citizens share) that helps strengthen democracy. AICs like the ZCC create trust and cooperation among their members within their tight-knit, disciplined church organization as they care for each other in often hostile and uncertain environments.[92] The values embedded in these interactions form the moral foundation that indirectly strengthens South African society. Another way churches like the ZCC contribute to the consolidation of democracy in South Africa is by acting as agents of community development. The ZCC, and other AICs, have a remarkably strong local presence that offers great potential for socioeconomic enhancement.[93] Finally, churches like the ZCC encourage members to make significant lifestyle changes, like abstaining from alcohol and drugs or honoring hard work, that contribute to the social and economic mobility of individuals in South Africa's economy.

Unfortunately, evidence also confirms the negative "below ground" influences the ZCC may have in the sociopolitical realm. For example, as surely as the ZCC contributes to the building of trust and cooperation among its communities, it also contributes to the forwarding of exclusivity, authoritarianism, and patriarchy that hurt efforts at consolidating democracy.[94] In addition, for some Christians in South Africa, the fact that the ZCC does not take a bold public position on national issues central to its membership, like poverty, HIV/AIDS, or violence, diminishes its credibility and the significance of its local witness.[95] Time will tell if the ZCC will become an important, albeit indirect, partner in the support of South Africa's multi-religious, multi-cultural society, an observation to be commented upon further in the last section of this paper.

Christianity and Democracy: An Ambiguous Relationship

So what do these studies reveal regarding religion and politics in South Africa and the relationship between Christianity and democracy? They show, first off, some dramatic changes in the profile of Christian churches and parachurch organizations in South Africa since the end of apartheid.

Under the apartheid regime, the NGK operated as a state church, the SACC operated as a struggle church, while the majority of African independent and evangelical churches either supported or did not overtly challenge the status quo. Under a democratic regime, the NGK's political role is inconsequential but not absent, the ZCC is nationally aloof but locally formative, and the SACC and the evangelical churches—albeit maintaining many similarities with the apartheid era, namely, the SACC's political voice, is still contextually prophetic, and Rhema's political engagement appears coopted—have experienced dramatic shifts in terms of macro-level political status. More specifically, the SACC, whose role in politics was influential and prominent during the apartheid years, has become increasingly marginalized in a democratic South Africa; while the evangelical/charismatic movement, whose role in politics was marginal compared with the SACC or the NGK during the apartheid years, has emerged with stronger political influence in a democratic South Africa.

One of the outcomes, the muted and inconsequential political role of the NGK, is to be expected, given the demise of apartheid and the loss of its political platform. A second outcome, the growing appreciation of African

Independent Churches like the ZCC, whose political voice and witness hasn't changed considerably, opens up new avenues for public and private sociopolitical engagements in a democratic South Africa. The most dramatic turnaround in church-state relations since the apartheid era involves the diminished, even marginalized, status of the SACC and the more influential political status of evangelical churches like Rhema.

So we return to the question that provided the foundation for this chapter, namely, "With so many critical issues facing South Africa, where is the church?" We have discovered that the churches are still active in the political arena; however, their political involvement is far more diverse and less binary than it was during the apartheid years.

But what do these changes signify regarding South Africa's democratization? It is generally understood that actors in civil society, like religious associations, help contribute to democracy's consolidation when they maintain an autonomous relationship with the state and, among other things, foster civility, hold governments accountable, and promote the welfare of the populace at large.[96] How effective, then, are South Africa's church and interdenominational organizations, as examples of civil society, in building or consolidating democracy? Based on the evidence provided in this chapter, the impact of South African church-based organizations regarding the consolidation of democracy is decidedly mixed.

The NGK, for example, mired in debates involving its identity, more often than not promotes issues that serve its constituency, the Afrikaners, more so than the South African populace as a whole. Thus, if one examines the NGK's narrow sociopolitical interests or its continued resistance to church unification in the Reformed family across racial lines, the NGK continually misses opportunities to build a strong platform for its Afrikaner constituents as committed and constructive partners in the process of South Africa's reconstruction and democratization.[97]

What about the ZCC? Although this chapter cautions against the tendency to romanticize the "below ground" contributions of AICs, this author also acknowledges the important role that the ZCC embraces whenever it assists marginalized communities in meeting their basic needs. This outcome, whenever it happens, by AICs or other religious communities, needs to be recognized as contributing toward the moral and social foundation of South Africa's democracy.

But how should the ZCC's lack of leadership within the formal, public level on important matters like the AIDS epidemic or poverty be interpreted?[98] On the one hand, one can acknowledge that public engagement in a democracy makes room for a variety of responses from religious associations. Not all churches, for example, need to be politically involved at the macro level, thus allowing for the ZCC's relative silence on such matters.[99] Although this argument certainly situates the ZCC's local witness, given what we know about the crucial role that civil society and religious organizations can play in the building of democracy, the publically aloof role of the ZCC diminishes its amazing potential as a civil society actor. Because of its considerable presence and credibility within marginalized communities, the ZCC potentially be doing much more than it is in terms of shaping public policy debates, playing the role as a social partner, a critical watchdog, or even some combination vis-à-vis the ANC-led government, rather than remaining relatively absent on the national scene.[100]

Rhema's Ministries's increasingly influential political voice and witness also reveals a mixed picture. On the one hand, Rhema has been involved with projects (e.g., Hands of Compassion) that encourage its members to promote the welfare of the populace as a whole. On the other hand, Rhema's recent socio-political engagement (through NILC) offers evidence of its co-optation by the ANC-led government, one of the more destructive state-civil society outcomes regarding democracy's consolidation. Moreover, if Rhema is in fact using the NILC to strengthen the position of the more religiously intolerant element of the evangelical-charismatic tradition in the public realm, the values of religious pluralism could be seriously undermined in the new South Africa.[101]

The SACC must also be critiqued for missing opportunities to hold the ANC-led government accountable when it had extraordinary access to the Mbeki regime. On the other hand, the SACC probably offers the most laudable witness regarding a religiously-based civil society actor playing a positive role regarding democracy's consolidation. It has tried over the last fifteen years, through public pronouncements on arms deals, meetings with government officials on issues like Zimbabwe, or projects like the People's Budget

Campaign, to hold the ANC-led government accountable to a vision of public justice that promotes the welfare of the populace at large, but particularly those who are marginalized. The SACC also cultivates a political culture of tolerance, respect and civility among a diverse populace. As noted above, the SACC certainly falls short of this goal, and in size, resources, and influence vis-à-vis the ANC, it is a much diminished organization today. This means its potential to impact public policy debates is, unfortunately, negligible, but its active support for and encouragement of participatory democracy remains largely intact.

In conclusion, this examination of religious organizations in South Africa undercuts the sweeping generalizations about Christianity and democracy made by scholars like Paul Gifford and Jeffrey Haynes. To argue, for example, that the inherently participatory worship style and structure of evangelical-charismatic and independent churches cultivates the social capital that supports democracy, or that the hegemonic structure of mainline churches causes them to uphold the status quo, is far too simplistic. Rather, it is far more accurate to acknowledge the contextual, varied, and ambiguous relationship between Christianity and democracy.[102]

But, beyond that conclusion, one could propose a more nuanced version of Paul Gifford's thesis. That is, while mainline Protestant churches and interdenominational organizations like the SACC continue to offer a relatively mature sociopolitical voice and witness in the public arena compared with their peers, developments within churches like Rhema indicate that evangelical churches also have the potential to help strengthen South Africa's democracy when they embrace a political witness that moves beyond moral issues and narrow group interests to one of the broader welfare of the nation. However, the potential co-opting of prominent evangelicals in South Africa by the ANC-led government means this opportunity has not yet been realized.

Since the relationship between Christianity and democracy in South Africa is uncertain and varied, South African churches and interdenominational organizations, particularly the increasingly influential evangelical churches, have plenty of room for improvement in fostering good governance. What we can see from this brief examination of their current witness, is that they must continue to work hard at

- maintaining a critical, independent voice vis-à-vis the government,
- developing sound principles of political engagement,
- building ecumenical bridges in public affairs discourse, and
- affirming the public role of theology.

These tasks are easier said than done. But there is a hopeful element within South Africa's religious approaches to public affairs. The nation has a tradition of prophetic witness. When particular church organizations fall short of maintaining a voice that is autonomous from the government and serve their own interests instead of the public good, there have always been theologians, activists, and religious organizations that powerfully contest the current realities, offering what Ann Loades calls a "politics of grace," or "a political dispensation in which we accept the 'pain of understanding religious difference,' drawing on 'all the resources of our imagination and sympathy we can muster,' to impel us to meet and embrace each other in our differences for the sake of that which binds us as a society."[103] As long as South African churches foment a "politics of grace," they will continue to contribute to the consolidation of democracy. The journey will be long and arduous, but as this chapter has indicated, we have seen glimpses of this hope within each of the case studies.

Notes to Chapter Eleven

*An earlier version of this paper appears in *The Journal of Church and State* 53.2 (2011): 278-306.

[1] Tracy Kuperus, *State, Civil Society, and Apartheid in South Africa: An Examination of Dutch Reformed Church-State Relations* (New York: St. Martin's Press, 1999).

[2] The focus of this chapter is on formal Christian institutions. Christianity in South Africa is pervasive and quite diverse, so it is difficult to capture a truly representative group, but here we have the start of one, at least among Protestants. It features, respectively, the largest of the Afrikaner Reformed denominations, the premier ecumenical Protestant grouping dominated by the older English-speaking Protestant denominations, a large and influential charismatic-evangelical network, and the largest of the African Instituted Churches (AICs).

[3] The political voice and public engagement of a church could also be referred to as its political role. Although my assessment of different church's political roles is fairly descriptive, I have tried to measure a church's political voice by whether it is muted or active, status quo or prophetic. Public engagement at the macro level is assessed by a church's relationship with the state (co-opted or autonomous) and the issues it promotes, among other things. What this paper does not address directly, only indirectly, are the factors contributing to a church's political response, some of which include theological commitments, class and racial make-up of laity, historical interactions with the state, church polity and socio-political context. Indeed, I will tend to concentrate in this paper on how churches are responding to (and shaping) the political environment, but, of course, the inverse also happens and needs further investigation.

[4] Democratic consolidation is a critical concern for emerging democracies. It is the lengthy process of strengthening democracy, and it involves sustaining democratic elections and other democratic measures (e.g., an independent judiciary) over time without reversal. For more on democratic consolidation, see Michael Bratton and Nicolas van de Walle, *Democratic Experiments in Africa: Regime Transition in Comparative Perspective* (Cambridge: Cambridge University Press, 1998). To begin a review of South Africa's decidedly mixed picture of democratic consolidation, see Rod Alence, "South Africa after Apartheid: The First Decade," *Journal of Democracy* 15.3 (2004): 78–92.

[5] For purposes of this essay, I acknowledge the definition of evangelical provided by Anthony Balcomb that highlights Biblical authority, personal conversion, the centrality of evangelism, personal piety and a reliance on doctrines like imminent return eschatology. See Anthony Balcomb, "Evangelicals and Democracy in South Africa," *Journal of Theology for Southern Africa* 109 (2001): 4–5. This definition of evangelical includes charismatic churches (like Rhema Bible Church) and both classical Pentecostal and neo-Pentecostal churches. The latter two traditions emphasize the evangelical elements noted above as well as the miraculous power

and working of the Holy Spirit. A more encompassing definition of evangelical is provided in the work of David Bebbington.

[6] Philip Jenkins, "Believing in the Global South," *First Things*, December 2006, 1.

[7] Some of the conservative moral beliefs embraced by Pentecostal and charismatic churches concern matters of homosexuality, divorce, and abortion.

[8] Timothy Shah, "Preface," in *Evangelical Christianity and Democracy in Africa*, edited by Terence Ranger (New York: Oxford University Press, 2008), x.

[9] Joel Carpenter, "Now What? Revivalist Christianity and Global South Politics," *Books and Culture*, March/April 2009, 26.

[10] What follows is a discussion among African scholars. For an overview of others who have contributed to this debate, particularly the prominence of Latin American scholars, see Paul Freston, *Evangelicals and Politics in Asia, Africa and Latin America* (New York: Cambridge University Press, 2001), 110–13; 298–311.

[11] Paul Gifford, "Introduction: Democratisation and the Churches," in *The Christian Churches and the Democratisation of Africa*, edited by Paul Gifford (Leiden: E. J. Brill, 1995), 5. Matthew Schoffeleers' scholarship on the AICs makes a similar point to Gifford's on the collaborationist nature of South African AICs during the apartheid years. See for example, J. M. Schoffeleers, "Ritual Healing and Political Acquiescence: The Case of the Zionist Churches in Southern Africa," *Africa* 61.1 (1991): 1–25. For a more positive assessment of the AICs, see the Comaroffs' work, notably Jean Comaroff, *Body of Power, Spirit of Resistance: The Culture and History of a South African People* (Chicago: University of Chicago Press, 1985); and Jean Comaroff and John L. Comaroff, *Of Revelation and Revolution* 2 vols., especially vol. 2, *The Dialectics of Modernity on a South African Frontier* (Chicago: University of Chicago Press, 1991).

[12] Paul Gifford, *African Christianity: Its Public Role* (Indianapolis: Indiana University Press, 1998), 306–48.

[13] Jeff Haynes, *Religion and Politics in Africa* (London: Zed Books, 1996), 7.

[14] Ibid., 133.

[15] Ibid., 181.

[16] Terence Ranger, "Conference Summary and Conclusion" in *The Christian Churches and the Democratisation of Africa*, 14–35; and Ranger, "Introduction: Evangelical Christianity and Democracy in Africa," in *Evangelical Christianity and Democracy in Africa*, 3–35.

[17] Civil society refers to the associations and societal spheres engaged in activities like economic production, civic education, and social networking in an effort to preserve social identity, reach collective goals, demand governmental responsiveness, or hold it accountable. Civil society can include but is not limited to trade unions, churches, women's groups, and cultural organizations.

[18] Robert Wuthnow, *Producing the Sacred: An Essay on Public Religion* (Urbana: University of Illinois Press, 1994), 79.

[19] Jurgen Hendriks and Johannes Erasmus, "Religion in South Africa: The 2001 Population Census Data," *Journal of Theology for Southern Africa* 121 (2002): 91.

[20] For a detailed examination of church-state relations in South Africa, begin with John De Gruchy and Steve De Gruchy, *The Church Struggle in South Africa* (London: SCM Press, 2005).

[21] James Cochrane, "Reframing the Political Economy of the Sacred: Readings of Post-Apartheid Christianity," in *Falling Walls: The year 1989/1990 as a Turning Point in the History of World Christianity (Einstürzende Mauern. Das Jahr 1989/90 als Epochenjahr in der Geschichte des Weltchristentums)*, edited by Klaus Koschorke (Wiesbaden: Harrassowitz Verlag, 2009), 95.

[22] Ibid., 103.

[23] These churches included the NGK, the *Nederduitsch Hervormde Kerk* (NHK), and the *Gereformeerde Kerk* (GK). The "NGK family" was divided into churches for whites, coloureds, blacks, and Asians. The political voice of the so-called "daughter churches" diverged considerably from the NGK, with the NGSK, or NGK for "coloureds," in particular offering a prophetic voice against the theology of apartheid and the government in the 1980s. See Allan Boesak, *Black and Reformed* (Johannesburg: Skotaville Publishers, 1984) and J. Christoff Pauw, *Anti-Apartheid Theology in the Dutch Reformed Family of Churches* (Amdsterdam: Free University Academic Dissertation, 2007).

[24] Kuperus, *State, Civil Society and Apartheid in South Africa*, 166. Today the NGK's membership is 1.5 million members, representing 39 percent of white Christians. See Hendriks and Erasmus, "Religion in South Africa: The 2001 Population Census Data," 93.

[25] *Human Relations* (DRC Publishers, Cape Town, 1976), 71.

[26] Etienne De Villiers, "The Influence of the Dutch Reformed Church (DRC) on Public Policy during the late 80s and 90s," *Scriptura* 76 (2001): 52–3. De Villiers also points out that significant voices of political reform arose within the NGK in the 1980s.

[27] For more insights into the NGK during the years of apartheid see Kuperus (cited above) or Johann Kinghorn, "The Theology of Separate Equality: A Critical Outline of the DRC's Position on Apartheid" in *Christianity Amidst Apartheid*, edited by Martin Prozesky (St. Martin's Press, New York, 1990), 57-80.

[28] Interview with Coenie Burger, Stellenbosch, South Africa, September 10, 2009. The URCSA, or the Uniting Reformed Churches in South Africa, is a merger of the former colored and African "mission churches" of the NGK.

[29] Piet Naude, "Constructing a Coherent Theological Discourse," *Scriptura* 83 (2003): 195.

[30] Ibid. It would be a fascinating and worthwhile exercise to examine the public and political witness of these various types of congregations at the local level.

[31] See Julie Aaboe, "The Other and the Construction of Cultural Identity: the Case of the DRC in Transition," (PhD dissertation, University of Cape Town, 2007), 201.

[32] De Villiers, "The Influence of the Dutch Reformed Church (DRC)," 59.

[33] Piet Meiring, "The Dutch Reformed Church and the Truth and Reconciliation Commission," *Scriptura* 83 (2003): 250–57.

[34] Christine Anthonissen, "A Critical Analysis of Reporting on the TRC Discourses in *Die Kerkbode*," *Scriptura* 83 (2003): 273.

[35] Coenie Burger, "The Dutch Reformed Church Looks Ahead," *Challenge* 78 (September/October 2004): 9.

[36] "NGK Presentation to the Portfolio Committee of the Department of Home Affairs Regarding the Amendment to the Marriage Act: Response Regarding the Civil Unions Bill," October 3, 2006. Document received by author from Ben du Toit, Stellenbosch, South Africa, August 5, 2009.

[37] Moreover, the NGK moderature presented a survey to URCSA showing that the Belhar Confession was not viewed favorably by the majority of NGK congregations. See "Report of the Executive Committee on Church Unity to the Fifth General Synod in Session, September 29 to October 5, 2008, in Hammanskraal," location unknown. These actions lead some in URCSA to wonder how authentic the NGK's earlier commitments to reunification were.

[38] See, e.g., "'Marriage Act Proposal Causing a Stir," *Die Kerkbode*, October 27, 2006, or "Dialogue on Resurrection Continues," *Die Kerkbode*, November 17, 2009.

[39] Interview with Johann Symington, Welgemoed, Cape Town, August 26, 2009.

[40] "About the SACC," South African Council of Churches, accessed November 11, 2009, http://www.sacc.org.za/about.html.

[41] Peter Walshe, *Prophetic Christianity and the Liberation Movement in South Africa* (Pietermaritzburg: Cluster Publications, 1995). While the SACC's leadership was engaged in the struggle against apartheid, the laity of mainline churches, often captive to a culture of white privilege, was not necessarily supportive of its actions. See for example, Charles Villa-Vicencio, *Trapped in Apartheid: A Socio-Theological History of the English-Speaking Churches* (Maryknoll: Orbis Books, 1988).

[42] John De Gruchy, *The Church Struggle in South Africa*, second edition (Grand Rapids: Eerdmans, 1986), 120.

[43] See David Chidester, *Religions of South Africa* (London: Routledge, 1992); or Bonganjalo Goba, *An Agenda for Black Theology: Hermeneutics for Social Change* (Johannesburg: Skotaville Publishers, 1988).

[44] Walshe, *Prophetic Christianity*, 111–14. See also Tristan Anne Borer, *Challenging the State: Churches as Political Actors in South Africa, 1980–94* (Notre Dame: University of Notre Dame Press, 1998).

[45] James Cochrane, "Research Challenges on Religion in South Africa," *Religion, Politics, and Identity in a Changing South Africa*, edited by David Chidester, et. al. (New York: Waxmann Munster, 2004), 229.

[46] "National Interfaith Leaders Council," July 28, 2009, unpublished document received by author from Roy Harris, Brackenfell, South Africa, August 20, 2009.

[47] "S. African Council Uneasy of Exclusion from Zuma's Interfaith Group," *Ecumenical News International*, August 20, 2009.

[48] Tinyiko Maluleke, "Ecumenism Seeking Justice in and for Our Times," address delivered to the Conference of the Christian Council of Zambia in Lusaka, Zambia, August 16, 2009, 4.

[49] Interview with John De Gruchy, Stellenbosch, South Africa, August 13, 2009.

[50] Simanga Kumalo and Daglous Dziva, "Paying the Prince for Democracy: The Contribution of the Church in the Development of Good Governance in South Africa," in *From Our Side*, edited by Steve De Gruchy, et. al. (Amsterdam: Rozenberg Publishers, 2008), 175, 181. See also Allan Boesak, *The Tenderness of Conscience* (Stellenbosch: Sun Press, 2005), 133–70.

[51] See Dirk Smit, *Essays in Public Theology* (Stellenbosch: Sun Press, 2007), 65–67; or James Cochrane, "Reframing the Political Economy," 5–7. See also Barbara Bompani, "Mandela Mania: Mainline Churches in Post-Apartheid South Africa," *Third World Quarterly* 27.6 (2006): 1137–49.

[52] Tracy Kuperus, "Building Democracy: An Examination of Religious Associations in South Africa and Zimbabwe," *Journal of Modern African Studies* 37.4 (1990): 658.

[53] Doug Tilton, "The People's Budget Calls for a New Anti-Poverty Program," *Challenge* 68 (April 2002): 4–5. Numerous articles in *Challenge* from 2000–2007 illustrate the SACC's consistent efforts at promoting economic justice, from articles on the People's Budget to its support for a Basic Income Grant to calling for a variable rate VAT. The SACC's Public Liaison, Doug Tilton, and the Ecumenical Service for Socioeconomic Transformation (ESSET) were instrumental in these campaigns.

[54] Nico Koopman, "Defence in Democracy: A Church Perspective on the Post-Apartheid Defence Review Process," *Nederduitse Gereformeerde Teologie Tydskrif* 45.3/4 (2004): 609–19.

[55] See Boesak, *The Tenderness of Conscience*, 159–70; or Kumalo and Dziva, "Paying the Price," 177. See also Bernard Sprong, "A New Role for the Churches," *Challenge* 78 (Sept/Oct 2004): 20–21. In the latter article, Thabo Mbeki's address to the SACC's 2004 Triannual Conference is recounted where he directly urges the SACC to shun the "watchdog" role and take up a "partnership" role.

[56] Vusi Mona, "The Third Wave," *City Press*, August 15, 2009. Vusi Mona writes the editorial in his personal capacity, but his links with both Zuma and McCauley suggest otherwise. Accessed August 27, 2011 at http://152.111.1.87/argief/berigte/citypress/2009/08/17/CP/18/Mona-Aug13-Faith.html.

[57] For more on democratic centralism, see Anthony Butler, "How Democratic is the African National Congress?" *Journal of Southern African Studies* 31.4 (2004): 719–36.

[58] Interview with Tinyiko Maluleke, Stellenbosch, South Africa, August 31, 2009.

[59] Mmanaledi Mataboga, "Why the ANC Dumped the Council of Churches," *Mail & Guardian*, September 18–23, 2009, http://www.mg.co.za/article/2009-09-18-why-anc-dumped-council-of-churches. Indeed, one government spokesperson, commenting on why the SACC had been sidelined in the development of NILC, said, "relations between the ANC and the SACC had deteriorated because of suspicion that the SACC was becoming 'a springboard' for the opposition—COPE, in particular."

[60] Interview with John De Gruchy, August 13, 2009.

[61] Jo Mdhlele, "A New World," *Challenge* 87 (2007): 21.

[62] Admittedly, member churches within the SACC will be dedicated to the grassroots public actions (e.g. HIV-AIDs programs, literacy training, economic enterprise) that the SACC isn't directly engaged with. And these locally-based involvements can and do influence the SACC's public policy advocacy (e.g. the Central Methodist Mission's work with Zimbabwean refugees has probably contributed to the SACC's statements on xenophobia), but critics of the SACC will argue the SACC as an institution is too far removed from these churches and too limited in its form of political engagement.

[63] Glen Thompson, "Transported Away: The Spirituality and Piety of Charismatic Christianity in South Africa (1976-1994)," *Journal of Theology for Southern Africa* 118 (2004): 131. Pentecostal/charismatic Christianity has grown considerably in South Africa. The 2001 population census depicts 7.3 percent of the Christian population belonging to Pentecostal/charismatic churches, although the percentage is probably higher given serious compilation errors. See Hendricks and Erasmus, "Religion in South Africa," 91. According to *Spirit and Power: A Ten-Country Survey of Pentecostals* (Philadelphia: Pew Charitable Trusts, 2006, online), 10 percent of South Africans are Pentecostal and 24 percent are charismatic. It is important to note, however, that black and white Pentecostal/charismatic worship and sociopolitical outlooks vary considerably. My focus on a white charismatic church like Rhema is rooted in its visible macro-oriented political involvement since the early 1990s.

[64] Niren Tolsi, "Inside Rhema: For Church and Country," *Mail & Guardian*, November 13–19, 2009.

[65] Anthony Balcomb, "Evangelicals and Democracy in South Africa–Helpers or Hinderers, Another Look, Another Method," *Journal of Theology for Southern Africa* 109 (2001): 10.

[66] See Anthony Balcomb, "Left, Right, and Centre: Evangelicals and the Struggle for Liberation in South Africa," *Journal of Theology for Southern Africa* 118 (2004): 147–8.

[67] Thompson, "Transported Away," 137.

[68] Ray McCauley, "IFCC Submission," TRC Faith Community Hearings, November 18, 1999 (personal document).

[69] Anthony Balcomb, "From Apartheid to the New Dispensation: Evangelicals and the Democratization of South Africa," in *Evangelical Christianity*, edited by Ranger, 201. See also Thompson, "Transported Away," 140–142.

[70] Balcomb, "From Apartheid," 201. McCauley's current political voice is far more "liberal" than many of his counterparts. For this reason, his political stance is not supported by all evangelicals. The African Christian Democratic Party, for example, represents a more fundamentalist evangelical position with its focus on public morality (e.g, abortion, homosexuality, death penalty) and battling the secular state. See Balcomb's work for a more detailed description of the ACDP as well as the rich variety of evangelical public expression. For example, he shows that there are also "radical evangelicals" who have their concerns with McCauley and Rhema, mainly related to its promotion of the "prosperity gospel."

[71] E. M. K. Mathole, "The Charismatic Evangelical Response to Poverty in South Africa" (PhD dissertation, University of Pretoria, 2005), 274–81.

[72] Ray McCauley, "Is God Too Dainty and Delicate for Politics?" *Mail & Guardian*, March 19, 2009; "McCauley Congratulates Zuma," *Cape Times online*, April 6, 2009; and "McCauley Concerned by Hlophe Saga," *Cape Times online*, September 6, 2009.

[73] Balcomb, "From Apartheid to the New Dispensation," 203.

[74] Evidence for the latter includes McCauley's late "conversion" in 1990, when he had nothing to lose and much to gain, by aligning himself with South Africa's political changes, as well as his outreach to high profile ANC members throughout the years, including Frank Chikane, Carl Niehaus, Mathole Motshekga, Vusi Mona, and Jacob Zuma.

[75] Balcomb, "From Apartheid," 203.

[76] Ibid., 204.

[77] Ibid., 204.

[78] Quoted in Chris Brown, "So Many Questions," *Sunday Times*, August 2, 2009.

[79] Interview with John De Gruchy, August 13, 2009.

[80] It is important to remember that NILC may not be effective or influential. It could be as politically inconsequential as the National Religious Leaders' Forum in South Africa or the U.S. White House Office of Faith-Based and Community Initiatives.

[81] "McCauley Congratulates Zuma," *Cape Times online*, April 6, 2009.

[82] Jacques Rousseau, "Prayer to Cherish Diversity," *Mail & Guardian*, September 18–23, 2009.

[83] J. J. Tabane, "What is Pastor Ray up to?" *Mail & Guardian Online Network*, September 20, 2009.

[84] Hennie Pretorius, "Ukhonza Phi na? Comments on Church Typology," in *Traditional Religion and Christian Faith*, edited by G. Lademann-Priemer (Hamburg: Verlag an der Lottbek, 1993), 135–47. Considerable debate regarding AICs revolves around definitions, typologies, and reasons for their origin. To begin a review of these debates see Dawid Venter, "Concepts and Theories in the Study of African Independent Churches," in *Engaging Modernity*, edited by Dawid Venter (Westport: Praeger, 2004), 13–43. The development of AICs sometimes has been seen as part of the story of evangelicalism, but in this chapter, I treat AICs as separate from the mainly Western-oriented evangelical Christianity of South Africa.

[85] Tinyiko Maluleke, "Pushing the Boundaries in AIC Studies," in *Zion and Pentecost: The Spirituality and Experience of Pentecostal and Zionist/Apostolic Churches in South Africa* by Allan Anderson (Pretoria: UNISA Press, 2000), ix.

[86] Hendriks and Erasmus, "Religion in South Africa," 91.

[87] Ibid., 98.

[88] Walshe, *Prophetic Christianity*, 110.

[89] Freston, *Evangelicals and Politics*, 172–73.

[90] Walshe, 110. The work of Jean Comaroff and R. Petersen stress the implicit protest character of the AICs broadly or the ZCC specifically.

[91] See Robert Garner, "Religion as a Source of Social Change in the New South Africa," *Journal of Religion in Africa*, 30.3 (2000): 310–43.

[92] See Garner in *Engaging Modernity*, edited by Venter, 84.

[93] Hennie Pretorius' book *Drumbeats* (Pretoria: UNISA Press, 2004) offers a wonderful window into the beliefs and practices of the Zionists in the Cape Flats, as well as their efforts in community welfare. A similar book is needed on the ZCC!

[94] Khotso Kekana's article, "The ZCC: 82 Years of Mystery and Secrecy," in *Challenge* magazine (June/July 1992) explains some of the patriarchal and authoritarian values of the ZCC. The ZCC, in essence, operates like other religious organizations that forward both negative and positive social capital values. My argument is not to denigrate the ZCC specifically, but to caution against romanticizing it.

[95] For commentary on the public silence of the AICs, see Adam Ashcroft, *Witchcraft, Violence and Democracy in South Africa* (Chicago: University of Chicago Press, 2005), 192.

[96] For more on civil society's relationship to political, social and economic development, both positive and negative, see Emmanuel Gyimah-Boadi, "Civil Society and Democratic Development," in *Democratic Reform in Africa: The Quality of Progress*, edited by Emmanuel Gyimah-Boadi (Boulder: Lynne Rienner Publishers, 2004), 99–119.

[97] Jonathan Jansen, Vice Chancellor of the University of the Free State, made a similar pronouncement regarding the NGK in the latter part of 2009.

[98] Freston, *Evangelicals and Politics*, 298.

[99] Along these lines, some might argue that churches like the NGK should be allowed to pursue the interests of a narrower constituency within the broader mantle of South Africa's democracy for the sake of retaining minority rights.

[100] Interview with Alan Boesak, Stellenbosch, South Africa, November 16, 2009.

[101] Ibid.

[102] For examples of this more nuanced approach, see Freston, *Evangelicals and Politics*, 281–321; and Ranger, *Evangelical Christianity and Democracy in Africa*, 3–35.

[103] Quoted in James Cochrane, "Religious Pluralism in Post-Colonial Public Life," *Journal of Church and State* 42.3 (2000): 454.

CHAPTER TWELVE

BEYOND SPEAKING

A Challenge to Public Theology

Stephen W. Martin

Introduction

One of the more striking conversations we had during our sojourn in South Africa in June 2009 was with Mvume Dandala, the former Presiding Bishop of the Methodist Church of Southern Africa, now a member of Parliament, who had been a candidate for the nation's presidency. Mr. Dandala was under no illusions about entering this role and realm. He knew full well how the political system, even at its best, can compete for believers' hearts and minds. And South Africa's political system is in trouble. Once a harbinger of democratic renewal, the sheen of the new South Africa has faded as members of the ruling party, once grassroots activists who mocked National Party politicians surrounded by "protection," now speed through town in bullet-proof Mercedes autos, the infamous "blue light convoys." By early 2010, the Congress of South African Trade Unions was calling for "lifestyle audits" for government ministers, news media were investigating so-called "tenderpre-neurs"—officials who have enriched themselves through business-government connections—and grassroots protests were flaring over lack of basic services. Furthermore, as Dandala told us, government seemed to have turned a deaf ear to faith communities. It's time, he said, for Christians to go "beyond speaking," to action. For him, this meant "entering public life," setting aside his clerical collar and joining the political fray as leader of the Congress of the People (COPE).

This chapter offers a critical look at the church's public witness to the world. It will offer a kind of "public theology" deeply recognizable to Dandala who, after all, served for several years at Central Methodist Mission in Johannesburg,[1] but different from the academic discourse usually associated with the term.[2] The starting point will be a very brief sketch of a theological understanding of "public" that allows us to see the distinctive ways the church contests, creates, and sustains space, and forms a people that bears public witness to the Kingdom of God. A Christian does not "enter public life" by becoming a professional politician, for the church is already "public" insofar as it bears witness to the Kingdom of which its members, regardless of their race, class, or nationality, are citizens. To see the church or its members as "private" (and therefore as needing to do something else to "go public") is to misunderstand its nature and mission. This claim fundamentally changes our understanding of what Christians are doing—and ought to be doing—when they engage other publics, including taking up the vocation of political office.

A "public," wrote St. Augustine, is "an assemblage of reasonable beings bound together by a common agreement as to the objects of their love."[3] Public theology, then, would be a theological articulation of the shape of this "common agreement." It would look at the directedness, or *aim* of the love shared by such an assemblage.[4] For Augustine, such a shared aim is indexed to a *civitas*, or city.[5] And since there are only two possible kinds of objects of love, the Source of all creation, or some thing within creation, there are only two cities to which humans may belong.[6] The one city, the *civitas terrena*, or city of this world, aims its love at things within this world; the other, the *civitas Dei*, or city of God, aims its love outside this world, toward the Eternal. Since setting its love on things within the world means a competition for possession of limited goods, the life (and politics) of the *civitas terrena* is characterized by *libido dominandi*—the desire to dominate, to master, to control.[7] Citizenship in the City of God does not mean a lack of concern with the world, or the things of the world, only that the world and the things therein cannot be of *ultimate* concern.[8]

Christians confess themselves to be members of the City of God, called in Scripture "Jerusalem," or "Zion."[9] In the Christian eschatological imagination, that City is not immanent in the world. It is not "a competitor for space" in the world, nor does it belong to the world (John 18:36). It does not boast a political party, nor does it set up a throne from which to rule. And yet, it is neither a mere ideal nor a vague hope. The City of God has a real presence in the gatherings of those who belong to it. In these gatherings and the practices that mark them off, the City of God is visible. The visibility of this city consists in its reconfiguration of space and its contestation of the public. We see these actions most clearly in Christian liturgies—sacred dramas or rituals that reshape their participants by correcting the "aim" of their loves, and remind them of their true belonging.[10] Liturgies reorient life in the here and now—"during the world"—and shape citizens for the world to come.[11] Indeed, this shaping is toward the human destiny figured in Jesus Christ himself.

But on their pilgrimage through the present world, Christians also find themselves involved with a diversity of communities within it. As workers, students, professionals, shoppers, and sports fans, they inhabit multiple spheres of belonging. Christians pay taxes, carry passports, and claim the benefits of national membership. But they differ from those who belong to the city of this world precisely in their practiced awareness that the present configurations of world and public belong only to the present age. So their citizenship is negotiated, and their loyalty is conditional. And yet they continue to seek the welfare of the city wherein they find themselves (Jer. 29:29), all the while aware that it is neither final, nor their final destination.

What does it mean to negotiate citizenship during and within the world? In what ways is this provisional, contingent, and ultimately temporary world confirmed and upheld by the people called to be citizens of the eternal City of God? How is their public "agreement as to the common objects of their love" aimed *through* these restless and penultimate loyalties, to God? These are questions for a public theology that understands "public" in the theological sense I've outlined. Such a theology would resist the mere re-shaping of the Christian message in order to address the institutions and issues that make up the social and political affairs in this age. But it would engage those realms, finding ways to point to the proper use, and the misuse, of God's created world, those things given us all for our common good.

What follows are snapshots of such a public theology in action, taken of a particular set of churches in South Africa: the African Initiated (or Independent) Churches (hereafter called "AICs"). I want to focus in particular on those churches that claim a sacred center in "Zion, city of our God."[12] The AICs, we shall see, interrupt the world as presently constituted, resituating the things of the world through a renegotiation of time and space, in liturgy. They reorient the things of the world toward the City of God, where there is healing and restoration. The people gathered around these things are transformed into the political subjects of that city, longing for its full arrival. But the AICs do this from a place of radical dispossession, and in ways that speak profoundly to mainline evangelical and ecumenical churches, which have, in South Africa and North America, settled into the city of this world. Often misunderstood as "sectarian" during the apartheid years, research is showing that the AICs' liturgical practices enact symbolic resistance to racial oppression and that AICs are revitalizing grassroots activism in South Africa. This chapter suggests that "reading" the AICs with an Augustinian view of public affairs can open up new possibilities for public theology—in South Africa and beyond.[13]

The Puzzle of the AICs

The AICs are a huge presence in South Africa, and their spectacular Easter celebrations have become tourist attractions. One tour agency breathlessly reports:

> The worship of the Lord over Easter is zealously attended, and members use whatever mode of transport they can find to get there—some come by donkey cart, others by bicycle, bus, car, taxi, train and on foot. Spoornet apparently runs a number of 20-coach high speed passenger trains the 380 kilometres between Johannesburg and Polokwane, whilst the church hires thousands of 100-passenger buses for its members.[14]

According the 2001 census, just under 40 percent of South Africa's Christians belong to African "Independent" ("Initiated" or "Indigenous") Churches.[15] While there are different ways of classifying these churches, scholars agree that the most important differentiation is to be made between Ethiopian churches on the one hand, and Zionist and Apostolic churches on the other.[16] The former represented a first wave of African self-assertion in the late nineteenth century, and make up churches that started essentially as African-led versions of mission denominations; the latter arose as Africans creatively and subversively appropriated the early twentieth century revivalist preaching associated with John Alexander Dowie's Christian Catholic Apostolic Church in Zion, a town he founded in Illinois. Dowie's church, as Jean Comaroff has shown, was itself engaged in protest against the corrosive effects of modernization,[17] and the Zion Cities that sprang up as a result were attempts to embody an alternative, "holy" space. At times calling themselves the *iiKonzo zoMoya* ("churches of the Spirit"), as opposed to *iicawe zomthetho* ("churches of the law" or "churches recognized by government"),[18] independent churches were considered politically dangerous by South African officials during the first half of the twentieth century. Their greatest threat was the simple fact that they represented Africans outside the control of established state and religious structures, presenting a challenge to the identity of Christianity as the "soul" of a white-dominated society.[19]

A radical, millenarian spirit initially infused a number of AICs.[20] However, by the end of the 1920s, these radical movements had died out in favor of others who sought redemption in what David Chidester calls "a separate, alternative sacred order that accommodated itself to white political domination in South Africa, yet provided powerful spiritual resources of healing, purity, and protection from a hostile world."[21] Paradigmatic of this is the Zion Christian Church, with its sacred site at "Moria" near Polokwane (formerly Pietersburg) in the north. This sacred space, currently a pilgrimage site for members who each Easter make the trek there, "stood apart from the political center of Pretoria and the economic center of Johannesburg in the ZCC's spiritual geography of South Africa."[22] While churches following in the Zion Cities tradition find a power center, the particular places where members of these churches meet locally can vary from conventional buildings to township shacks to miners' hostels to trees in the veld.[23] These too are symbolic choices. Says Chidester, "African initiated churches [practice] their religion in the 'leftover spaces' in the [secular] city,' establishing their own 'cosmopolitan centres' in open lots, under motorways, or on a beach, where 'a line in the ground is often the only edge between sacred space and the city.'"[24]

What transpires inside these spaces also shows a marked contrast with other churches. In the dusty township of Gugulethu near Cape Town, for example, a candle-lit healing service at St. John's Apostolic Faith Mission begins with the unfolding of a large, white cloth with blue borders, similar to the blue and white uniforms of the members. The cloth is held high by three members on each side, forming a canopy, while the prophet blesses ordinary water, to which ash and salt have been added, by stretching forth his staff. The congregation lines up and approaches the water, passing under the canopy. Each cleanses their hands with the water, then drinks some of it. The water has healing and cleansing properties, while the flickering of the candles evoke the empowering presence of the Holy Spirit. Members who live in an area bereft of basic health care and sanitation hail the healing abilities of the water.[25] Bottles of the blessed water are taken from the service, and specialists in the theology and ritual of the church extend its healing powers into the township, forming networks of care, prayer, and support.[26] Indeed, healing—physical, emotional, spiritual, and social—is unquestionably the dominant note in the practices of AICs.

Outside their meetings, members of AICs maintain distinctive attire and lifestyle. The members of the iBandla lamaNazaretha may be found wearing Western clothes or simple skins.[27] But their prohibition (per Num. 6:2ff.) against cutting their hair is a visible sign of their difference and has marked them for persecution.[28] Members of the ZCC are distinguishable by the star-shaped badges pinned to their clothes. Men are neatly attired and clean-shaven. In other AICs, however, men may grow distinctive beards, while women wear headgear or wristbands.[29] While their attire differs depending on the church, AICs share a strict code of behavior that marks them all equally distinct in places where drunkenness, sexual impropriety, and other abuses are all too common.

This "independency" in appearance and conduct is largely responsible for the disparaging treatment some members of AICs receive. But whether well-treated or ill-treated, there's little question about the class location of most AIC members: they are among the poorest of the poor. And yet they are also committed givers, as evident in their practices of offering. Unlike the mission churches, where the taking of an offering is shrouded in privacy, members of the Full Witness Apostolic Church in Zion present their offerings one by one, dancing and displaying their coin to the assembled.[30] In other AICs, the donor will announce how much he or she is putting in, and the purpose for which it is intended.[31] Other items are also presented for sanctified use, including "shoes, blankets, and foodstuffs."[32]

Once sanctified, the money that members of the ZCC church have earned as painters, sweepers, and diggers[33] builds alternative institutions. When the apartheid government was closing mission schools and creating "Bantu Education," the ZCC created its own schools, a bursary fund to allow children to attend University, and adult literacy programs.[34] These initiatives were open to the entire community, whether Zionist or not. During the apartheid years, the ZCC developed a mill for local subsistence farmers to process their grain, a bus company operating in and around Pietersburg, a medical clinic, and even a post office.[35] All these initiatives were concrete ways of building community and responding to the impoverishment of Africans.

For much of the 1980s, the AICs represented a puzzle to mainline theologians.[36] Liberation theologians looked to them for an authentic expression of Black working-class theology, but the AICs' liturgical practices mystified— and their refusal to participate in the struggle against apartheid in the same way frustrated—many theologians and activists. During its testimony to the Truth and Reconciliation Commission, the ZCC admitted that it "did not lead people into a mode of resistance against apartheid. But as a church the ZCC taught its people to love themselves more than ever, to stand upright and face the future, to defy the laws of apartheid."[37] In other words, asserting human dignity was its response to injustice, and its people, so formed, translated this dignity into defiance. The church itself, however, refused to take sides publicly, or to so instruct its members.

The ZCC's seeming deference to the apartheid regime turned mystification and frustration into downright suspicion. The most notorious event was the invitation to P. W. Botha to address the annual Easter gathering in 1985, an invitation he accepted. For this to happen during a national State of Emergency, while other religious bodies sharply opposed the regime, seemed to be a coup for the apartheid government. Broadcast live on SABC TV, it certainly sparked strong reaction from the United Democratic Front (UDF) and other anti-apartheid movements.[38]

That same year, leading theologians published *Challenge to the Church: The Kairos Document*.[39] Here a different kind of church was imagined: prophetic and activist-based. This was not a church that goes on long pilgrimages to obscure sites, much less invites the chief oppressor to join them. It confronts the state, on the state's own turf. *The Kairos Document* challenged churches that stayed clear of the struggle, hoping thereby to occupy some safe, middle ground. It called them to declare their independence from their traditional role of state legitimation,[40] and to renounce their citizenship in the old South Africa. Furthermore, the *Document* called on churches to challenge the state by declaring their solidarity with the liberation movements. When it came to the AICs, however, their "independence"—granting a few exceptions—made them positively complicit in apartheid. The events at Moriah had only confirmed this. The *Document* expressed condemnation not only of what it saw as accommodationist theologies, but of liturgical practices that were powerless in that they failed to explicate the crisis of the moment and to spell out the prophetic action necessitated by it.[41]

Recently, scholars have begun to challenge the idea of what resistance looks like, suggesting that the practices of AICs once thought representative of their "quietism" could also be read as quietly subverting dominant structures, and providing a new, distinctively African, basis for struggling against injustice. Robin Petersen's sympathetic reading of the AICs tries in this regard to recover a thicker understanding of resistance. Following a distinction made by David Tracy, Petersen contrasts the "prophetic" discourse of the *Kairos Document* to the "mystical" orientation of "the churches of the Spirit."[42] While mysticism might connote unhealthy otherworldliness that leads churches into collaborations with the powers that be, the distinctively *African* mysticism of the AICs is communal and embodied, a mystical excess that spills over, and breaks through, colonial containments.[43] It bursts the boundaries between private and public, domestic space and civic space. But it also refuses confinement to the liberation struggle.[44] While valuing the contribution of prophetic theologies, Petersen, who was himself an activist during the 1980s, complicates the terrain of struggle. He also argues that the quest for human dignity transcends the division between the "old" and the "new" South Africa. Both periods find the church existing *during the world.*

The mysticism of the AICs, in Petersen's view, is also *apocalyptic*—living from, and looking toward, God's interruption of a rebellious world regime. Radical theologians criticized apocalyptic theology for producing passivity and escape.[45] Yet with the AICs, this is not the case. Their apocalyptic politics is enacted in liturgies that map the church and world as sites of dispossession. Apocalyptic outlook, liturgical enactment, and an identity of dispossession—these three concepts suggest a framework for a fresh negotiation of Christian citizenship, one that disputes the public-private dichotomy and revives prophetic action.

The AICs and Contested Citizenship

Apocalyptic Eschatology

Contemporary theology has seen a resurgence of interest in an apocalyptic outlook, that is, pointing to God's once and future invasion of history in Jesus Christ. Walter Lowe, for example, cites Barth's study of the Epistle to the Romans to argue that postmodern theology is "apocalyptic without reserve." By this he means an understanding of the crisis of the day—in Barth's case, "the self-dismantling of modernity by mustard gas and Gatling gun" during World War I—points to the crisis of God's invasion. That invasion puts modernity in its place, as a limited and passing outlook.[46] Barth's great enemy was the ethical eschatology of modern liberalism, seeing modernity as the culmination of the ages. Liberalism sought to transform the world into the kingdom of God through ethical and political action.[47] It defined religion as operating within the limits of reason, as that source of "values" that steers humanity toward its secular utopia.

Thus conceived, "religion" is in the service of "the modern world" and its body politic, serving to animate it, to give it its *soul.* But religion has, on this reading, no "body politic" of its own. The body of Christ is displaced or spiritualized, reduced to the category of "religion."[48] Such religion must be kept separate from "politics," understood as the bureaucratic management of the world by an elite, acting on behalf of that abstraction called "the people.""The secular city"—modernity's utopian project—confines religion to private space, away from public affairs. People may appeal to other citizenships; but all other citizenships are made relative to that one sphere of belonging: the nation-state. In a world where the logic of capitalism drives progress, the image of the "citizen" is rapidly giving way to the "consumer" of state services.[49]

That's why "apocalyptic" is modernity's nightmare. As a radical interruption of "the world" and its settled understanding of the social and political order, apocalyptic eschatology re-centers history not on the slow-but-inevitable march of progress, but on a rupture—God's interruption of the course of the world in the singular event of Jesus Christ. In apocalyptic perspective, Jesus does not stand before Pilate with a plan to help Rome more justly manage the world; he stands before Pilate as Pilate's—and Rome's—judge.[50] All projects that seek to bring the world under control are judged as rivals to the Kingdom of God. And as Jesus before Pilate, so the Church before the world. Or at least that's how a Christian apocalyptic imagination sees it.[51] Because it celebrates God's intervention in history, the Church knows it doesn't need to seize control of history. Its mission is, consequently, not to try to establish its own truth, but "to testify to the truth" that has *already* been manifested. Hence the Church is precisely *for* those in society who don't count within the bureaucratic calculus of history, who otherwise are a "drain" on society's resources: the unemployable, the physically and developmentally challenged, "the unproductive aged."[52] This theology is far from apolitical. Rather, it sees, lives, moves, and is sustained in the world by another regime: the City of God.

The centrality of this other polis for AICs is evident in their choice of names, including "the African Baptist Church in Zion," the "African Faith Mission Apostolic Church in Zion," "Cornerstone Catholic Zion Church," "First African Apostolic Church in Zion of South Africa," and so on.[53] Zion is both transcendent spatially and temporally—pointing to origins outside the closed system of "the world," but also available in the present. Zion manifests itself spatially in the cracks and fissures of the secular city. "We have no place of our own," says one member.[54] This "placelessness" in the terrain of the modern *civitas* is mirrored where AICs gather. Unlike established churches that one can find by consulting a map, "[Even] an ordinary home is transformed into a sacred space, the sacred centre of Zion."[55] This amounts to a double subversion. First, the classical separation of *oikos* (household) and *polis* (city-state) is undone, for the household is now also a place wherein a city gathers itself. Zion, the City of God, is God's "homestead" within the dusty sprawl of a South African township.[56] It was this same kind of subversion in early Christianity that worried the political theorist Hannah Arendt, who saw that Christianity undermined the public order as conceived in Hellenic world.[57] All the baptized are made members of the household of God *and* made its citizens, regardless of their earthly status, thus giving slaves, women, and foreigners equal standing with male property-owners in the early church. This idea is indeed reflected in the original understanding of the word *ekklesia*, which English Bibles translate as "church." The *ekklesia* was the assembly of citizens called together to make important decisions about life in the *polis*.[58] The AICs remind us of this seminal point. Wherever the church gathers, its members are simultaneously "at home" and citizens of God's new polis. The church thereby points to the *destruktion* (dismantling) of one polis by another.[59]

Secondly, the conjuncture of *oikos* and *polis* subverts the easy modern distinction between religion and politics, and forms an alternative center around which to orient life. All penultimate loyalties are reoriented around that ultimate *loyalty*, that *identity*, *manifested* within the church and given to its members in baptism. As I indicated above, Christians inhabit multiple centers of belonging, each competing for loyalty. James Kiernan's research in kwaMashu found that Zionist identity was "a marker subsuming, dominating and taking precedence over all others, acting 'as a mold which reshapes and shapes the other layers of identity.'"[60] In both KwaMashu and the Cape Flats: "[Zionist] religious identity is primary and also total. '. . . there is no situation to which he or she will not react primarily as a Zionist. The Zionist is at all times first and foremost a *Zionist* and only secondarily a Zulu or a migrant or a worker.'"[61] Moreover, all of life is seen in the light of Zion's reality. Taking issue with the tradition of interpreting AICs as eschewing politics (a tradition that on Bonpani's view includes Kiernan), Barbara Bompani claims that "African independent churches do not just produce *spiritual answers* but also different *centers of interpretation* of forces that shape church members' lives. These forces are also *political*."[62] As Bompani discovered in her research in Jabulani, ". . . politics was not just public political discourse, but also a daily constant of work not publicly recognised."[63] This radical remapping of the political is perhaps best captured in her research by Archbishop Ngada, President of the African Spiritual Churches Association: "I think to be political, to some people, is to put on a tie around the collar, sitting in an office and bringing all the media around. We are the voice of the voiceless, *we are politically minded but we haven't a political organisation.*"[64] In my reading, this "political-mindedness" is related to the AICs' self-understanding as a body politic by virtue of their membership in Zion.

Zion is, in the words of historian Bengt Sundkler, "a place of longing,"[65] which implies an apocalyptic sort of dislocation in space and time. But we've seen that there's also a prominent *present* orientation: the New Jerusalem in the here and now.[66] Believers experience the presence of the new city of God in the communal performance of worship that early Christians called liturgy. It is in *liturgy* that the time and space of Zion are brought to bear on life here and now.

Liturgy and the Reforming of Desire

Contemporary theologians are more and more convinced of the centrality of liturgy in shaping and sustaining a Christian imagination, and some see it forming the basis for a new politics.[67] It's in liturgy that the body of Christ participates in the future City of God. They represent Zion on pilgrimage, reorienting their desires away from things as rendered within the world as it is and toward things as imagined in the light of their future. Perhaps Evangelist Mpanza of the AmaNazaretha tradition put it best when he told the Truth Commission, "I have seen many warlords not throwing away their sticks but changing their sticks into staffs, and using these staffs for healing instead of beating. The shields used for fighting are then used for dancing for the Lord. The war cry is then changed into praise of the Almighty."[68]

While the world in the experience of AIC members is a place of disorienting brokenness, defilement, and danger, Zion is an outpost of reorienting, filled with healing, cleansing, and purification.[69] Liturgy effects this transformation in three ways. First, liturgy marks a boundary and constructs a site within which healing can occur.[70] Pretorius observed that the significance of *baptism* in the churches he studied goes beyond a rite of initiation. It is a practice of "the literal washing away of sin and that if one is not baptised, one is not rid of one's sin and therefore not saved."[71] Baptism *transforms* the person—sometimes in remarkably physical ways. *Communion* is usually done at night, only involves "members in good standing," and is preceded in most cases by washing of feet.[72] Again, the theme of cleansing is prominent, as is the careful maintenance of boundaries. But members participate in the liturgical marking off of space in other ways. The body forms part of this marking off through distinctive manners of dress. Worn during worship, the uniform is a sign of belonging to that space of healing. A member is under discipline is permitted to wear the uniform and must "remain passive" during services.[73] A special service will restore members to their privileges (including special washing and prayers). All this contributes to the consolidation and expansion of the City of God.[74]

A second function of liturgy concerns the re-situation of desire, its "aiming" toward the City of God.[75] AICs share the prohibition of alcohol, tobacco, and pork with certain other Christian groups. But Jean Comaroff argues, at least with reference to the Tswana churches she studied, that these proscriptions do not indicate a mere moralism. In a South African context, such things are rendered "outside" as symbols of white, colonial control.[76] And the ritual "baptism" of other commodities "[which] are brought to the church [and] placed on the table for the duration of the service and then are ritually processed" removes them from the control of the world by liberating their very meanings."[77] These offerings are, we might say, cleansed, *sanctified* in ritual as they are thereby translated from one meaning-system to another. They are made the property of the community, to be redistributed apart from the control of the market. Thus the temporal world of capitalism is subverted.[78] AIC strategies for resisting capitalism's domination during apartheid are of course still applicable today. The communal identity "marked by the wearing of uniforms, the forms of ritual dance, the communal singing, and the very practical mutual aid of the members" is a profound resistance to the social isolation people feel as workers in large and functionally abstract commercial enterprises.[79] These may be to a large extent unselfconscious strategies, but indeed, they plot "paths in the cracks of this order, creatively poaching and hence remaking these forms in their own image."[80] In sum, says Petersen, "the source of [the AICs' resistance] is the convoking of another time, ritual time, in which the work-week is radically interrupted, the subject-object split is mediated by the re-enchantment of things and the creation of a *communitas*, and the domination of commodities is brought under ritual control."[81]

It is within the time and space mapped by this liturgy that new light is shed on the things of this world and the use to which they *ought* to be put. This is the third function of liturgy: to provide a basis for social criticism. Indeed, the liturgical practices of AICs *are* social criticism. And so Bompani writes that "attending the liturgy on Sunday at Jabulani was not an escape into a different world, a world of ahistorical and spiritual truths." It meant, rather, "going through the debate on the nation building process, discussion on corruption, on unemployment, on the government" according to a narrative of scarcity.[82] This passage issued forth in a kind of grassroots activism that effected a different politics, breaking with "the traditional (Western) way of considering political action as a well-organized and public intervention, ignoring the value and the political nature of actions, rituals and symbol of resistance in the everyday life of these religious communities."[83]

An Ecclesiology of Dispossession

But the serious conversations of this Christian public are done from the edges, rather than society's centre. The AICs, engaging in "tactic," not "strategy," locate themselves in the fissures of settled places. "We, the Zionists," says one leader, "are not distinguished people."[84] Indeed, the AICs are pilgrim people, "travellers," moving locally and translocally.[85]

This *ecclesiology of dispossession* held by "undistinguished people" constitutes my third motif. An ecclesiology of dispossession claims that the church only exists insofar as it configures a space where power is given differently: to those who have renounced a claim to control the world *as it is*, and are enacting, rather, the world as God has said *it will be*. For God was incarnate as a dispossessed member of a tiny people under imperial domination. So the church of God, as bodily manifestation of Jesus, makes God present in its refusal to distinguish itself in terms of the this-worldly city.

This does not, however, mean that the church is thereby rendered "invisible." Such a creature is theologically problematic, reflecting the modern disjuncture between externality and internality, body and soul, public and private. But it's also *empirically* untrue when looking at AICs. For while it may not always be possible to identify their buildings, the gathering of the AICs is certainly evident to all nearby. Their colors, sounds, and rhythms create "a politics of praise" (to use a phrase of Kerr's), out of doors, that publicly demonstrates the presence of Zion, the *polis* of God.

Perhaps this points to something churches in the global North need to think about, namely, the possibility that church buildings as settled places locatable on a map—and indeed the church's ownership of substantial property—might actually disguise the church's public witness to the gospel. And perhaps also the struggle to be faithful against the legacy of establishment—embodied in the unsettlement that I feel even in writing these words—is a sign that the church should be a place of disturbance, of discomfort, in its refusal to participate in the desire for domination characterizing the city of this world. The transformation of desire within worship ought to create profound dissonance when it is encountered; it ought to issue in debate about the just distribution of goods. The AICs Bompani studied were sensitized to the corruption of desire—and the desire for corruption—especially in the settled and secure places of the new South Africa. Popular disquiet about corruption is creating an "insurgent" style of democracy,[86] where ordinary people, who have experienced in everyday things extraordinary grace, are empowered to demand they be treated with the dignity promised by and tasted in Zion.

The profiling of the AICs around these three elements—apocalyptic eschatology, desire-reforming liturgy, and dispossessionist ecclesiology—presents them as a contrast to the established church of "place" assumed in the public theologies I spoke of earlier. Unlike theologians who struggle over what the place of the church in society might be, the AICs don't inquire as to their "place" in society, *for they have no such place*. They simply *are the church* wherever they happen (to be). Put perhaps more theologically: they are the church *wherever God happens*. And God happens in places of pain and displacement, bringing healing and hope. This is not the Church as a settled institution, locatable on a map. Rather, as Rowan Williams puts it, church is

> the event of Jesus' presence with its characteristic effect of gathering people around him and making them see one another differently as they see Him. The church is the immediate effect of Jesus being there.

And hence St Paul can write about the new creation which happens when people are drawn into fellowship, into relationship with the risen Jesus and encourages us therefore to think that the church itself is the beginning of the new creation.[87]

Thus, Williams insists, the Church is able to offer "a 'citizenship' distinct from any kind of belonging in a merely human political community."[88] And yet it seeks the human good while it is on pilgrimage during the present age. Indeed, the seeking of the human good represents a radical counter to the sovereignty of goods that call forth today's post-humanist "citizen-consumers."

Public Theology and Contemporary Post-Liberal Democracy

If my theological judgment is correct, the African-initiated churches present a challenge to today's "oldline" churches, both in South Africa and in North America. Their construction of time and space in liturgy is reminiscent of that in early Christianity, as is their challenging of settled constructions, including the "public." Far from being "quietist," they confront the daily assaults on their dignity that make up life in the new South Africa with the dignity nurtured within their community. They also form part of an "insurgent" democracy, which is arising in South African civil society. I want to describe this briefly, and the contribution that churches so constituted can make to it.

Democracy has grown old in those parts of the world where it once flourished. With declining participation in elections, more and more cynicism about "career politicians," and a growing sense that political parties differ little from the marketing machines of large corporations, liberal democracy faces a crisis of legitimacy.[89] Liberal democratic emphasis on majority rule makes it to feed on the statistically gathered opinions and votes of individual citizens. But given the growing awareness of how such choices are shaped, liberalism's critics argue that these statistics do not constitute the will of the people. However, *liberal* democracy doesn't exhaust the possibilities for *democracy* as a vision of people participating in their governance. There are other kinds of democracy. Within the past decade or so, a series of theorists have explored possibilities for renewing the direct engagement of citizens in matters of governance, coining the phrase, "radical democracy."[90] This is democracy not as a set of institutions (elections, political parties, constitutions) but as an ever-evolving goal, as—one might say—*eschatological*.[91] Publics are not established and settled, but contested and unsettled, continuously created and recreated as more voices speaking their particular languages are heard. And the more genuinely different voices are heard and contested, the thicker the public becomes.[92] Moreover, these voices speak not the abstract, managerial language of career politicians, but languages particular and local, articulating communally-grounded visions of human good. Democracy in this view is "a generative activity in which people seek to reinvent it in challenges and contestations concerning the question of what it might become."[93] As an eschatological goal (and yet at the same time as a reality in which democratic movements participate), radical democracy constructs its public in a way analogous to the church. Just as the meaning of the church is understood insofar as it participates in the Kingdom of God, so in the process of "doing" democracy, people participate in the goal of democracy.

In the late-1990s, a series of new social movements began to arise in South Africa, identified not as much with large-scale structural change as with matters of "service delivery." Provoked by the government's embrace of neo-liberal policies, its slowness in fulfilling its promise of "a better life for all," and its inability to act decisively in addressing HIV/Aids,[94] these radical democratic movements constructed new kinds of citizenship, not from "above" by constitutions, human rights lawyers, and government decrees, but from below.[95] Here, "citizenship is not bestowed by the state or by a set of legal norms, but is enacted in a set of diverse practices and spaces, and involves multiple identities and struggles around concrete issues."[96]

But theologian Stanley Hauerwas puts a crucial question to political theorist Romand Coles: where do radical democrats come from? They "do not drop from the sky but rather become who they are through training in practices that form the habits of their hearts and tongues."[97] In saying this, however, Hauerwas implies that radical democratic movements do indeed have something to say to the church. As "parables of the kingdom,"[98] such movements can remind the church of its true calling, of that to which its existence bears witness. So do the AICs, I have argued, with reference to the "oldline" churches.

But might the Church in turn have a unique witness with reference to new social movements? In a recent address to the Christian-Muslim forum in Cambridge, Rowan Williams identified civil society as "the recognized shorthand description for all those varieties of human association that rest on willing co-operation for the sake of social goods that belong to the whole group, not just to any individual or faction, and which are not created or wholly controlled by state authority." But the presence of the Church in civil society—and in this regard especially those churches "in Zion"—is unique in that, being truly dispossessed, it rests on something beyond the political, "to which any and every human society is finally answerable."[99] Even more than this, the church's formation will point beyond all local and particular concerns, to that human concern which is named as "the common good"—the flourishing of human beings, and the creation through the use of its goods ordered to the enjoyment of its highest Good. The AICs exemplify this kind of vision. They tacitly resist bureaucratic attempts to manage them as much as they refused to be co-opted into the agendas of the 1980. Nevertheless, they engage in disciplined reflection and action that makes present our broken experience on pilgrimage through this world, wherein we have no abiding city, and the world to come, made available in Zion.

The AICs point to the deep connection between eschatology and worship, between the desire for the reign of justice and the daily experience of injustice, and between practices of space- and time-making and actions in the world. This is, of course, something all churches should know. But the way modernity has co-opted the Church so as to "fit" into a certain way of imagining the world has rendered such things as quaint, idiosyncratic, and ultimately powerless private rituals. If the AICs have a message, it is to show that the very practices that mark Christians as a peculiar people are *themselves* a public theology that challenges the enclosure of the world, confronting its abuse of the things God has made for human flourishing, and calling it to a more human way of being in anticipation of the renewal of all things in Jesus Christ.

Conclusion

We started this journey with Mvume Dandala, presidential candidate and member of Parliament, who believes with some reluctance, given his prior call to church ministry, that he has been called to work in politics. What does our line of thought here have to say to him, and to many other Christians who participate intensively in politics and government? Perhaps this is the first thing to note, *reluctance*. St Augustine thought that Christians should neither seek public office, nor refuse to serve there if the duty was placed on their shoulders.[100] Leaving to others the question of the particular policies a Christian should pursue, the question following from our study above is, *how* should a Christian serve in such a place as Parliament? The interpretations at which we've arrived do provide some clues.

First, the Christian public servant must recognize that his or her confession that Jesus is Lord means that something decisive for the world happened in Jesus Christ and his crucifixion by the powers of this world. The cosmos is ruled by something that the "normal" politics of the world beheld, rejected, and crucified. After the vindication of Jesus Christ in his resurrection and ascension, all human politics becomes relativized as a politics of the interim, taking place "during the world," and subject to God's judgment at the end. And that judgment will concern how "the least of these"—who image Christ himself—are treated (Matt. 25:31–46).

Second, the Christian public servant must be formed by fellowship, teaching, and especially liturgies that radically reorient his or her desire away from the lust for domination and toward the caring regard for others that makes a true politics. These liturgies constitute a counter-formation to much that is experienced in Parliament.[101]

Third, this reorientation means the Christian public servant takes on this role as a kenotic, self-emptying calling. He or she will not be a competitor for glory, but will "take the form of a slave" (Phil. 2:7). As paradoxical as it sounds, the politics of a faithful Christian public servant will, I think, be a politics of dispossession.

All this is difficult, to say the least! But there were encouraging signs in the meeting of our group with Mr. Dandala. He recognized the enormity of the challenge of bearing witness to Christ in Parliament, and while he had "laid aside" the mantle of Bishop, he knew he could not proceed without the church. And so he told us of his relationship of prayerful accountability to a group of spiritual advisors—not to advise him on policy matters, but to ensure that he stayed true to his calling as a Christian disciple. Perhaps there is hope that he might be able to put his ethical principles into practice. Perhaps there might be in his witness some good news for the South African people, who are fast growing cynical at the enrichment of their political figures. Perhaps he might also become a parable of the Kingdom to the Church, reminding it of *its* calling to continually spend itself for the sake of the world.

Notes to Chapter Twelve

[1] April Oliver, "Mission is Small Symbol of Unity in South Africa," *National Catholic Reporter*, April 15, 1994, 9.

[2] The American theologian, Max Stackhouse, described public theology as a theology of mediation. The ideas and values embedded in Christianity need to be translated into terms that all reasonable people can understand. See for example, Max Stackhouse, "Civil Religion, Political Theology and Public Theology: What's the Difference?" *Public Theology* 5.3 (2004): 275–93. My complaint about this model is threefold: first, it assumes that a "matter of fact," "here and now" view of the world common to public affairs is the "reality" into which the Christian vision must fit. Second, it leaves out Christians' existence as a "public" community and Christian identity as a citizenship that stands in tension with other citizenships and loyalties. Third, it makes public discourse a conversation between elites, furthering the alienation of the poor—who comprise the great majority in the Church—from those who govern them.

[3] St. Augustine, *City of God*, trans. Henry Bettenson (London: Penguin Books, 1984), xix: 24.

[4] James K.A. Smith, *Desiring the Kingdom: Worship, Worldview, and Cultural Formation* (Grand Rapids: Baker Academic, 2009), 47–52. What follows in this introduction is indebted to Smith's understanding of liturgies and loves.

[5] Augustine, *City of God*, xiv: 28.

[6] Augustine, *City of God*, 595–600, xv: 1–4. For a helpful discussion of these ideas, see Charles T. Mathewes, *A Theology of Public Life* (Cambridge: Cambridge University Press, 2007), 88–94.

[7] Augustine, *City of God*, 5 [i: Preface]; xv: 4–5.

[8] Ibid., xix: 17.

[9] See for example Psalm 48:2; 53:6; 87:5; 149:2; Galatians 4:24-25; Hebrews 12:22; Revelations 21:2-3. These texts (and others) indicate that "Zion" or "Jerusalem" or "the Jerusalem that is above" is the City wherein God dwells, and to which God's people truly belong.

[10] Smith, *Desiring the Kingdom*, 46–52.

[11] Mathewes, *A Theology of Public Life*, 17–18.

[12] Lest the contrast between AICs and other black churches be overdrawn, see Tinyiko Sam Maluleke, "Research Methods on AICs and Other Grass-Roots Communities," *Journal of Black Theology in South Africa* 10.1 (1996): 18–28.

[13] This "reading" is an act of interpretation wherein the practices of African churches are related to larger theological and political issues. I make no pretense of speaking for AICs, nor do I presume that AIC members would articulate their experience in precisely the terms I use. For a similar apologetic, see Robin M. Petersen, "The AICs and the TRC: Resistance Redefined," in *Facing the Truth: South*

African Faith Communities and the Truth and Reconciliation Commission, edited by James Cochrane, John De Gruchy, and Stephen Martin (Cape Town: David Philip, 1999), 114–125.

[14] "Zion City at Moria, Polokwane," SA-Venues, accessed August 27, 2011, http://www.sa-venues.com/attractions/limpopo/zion-city.htm.

[15] South Africa Statistics, South Africa Government, figures downloaded on August 16, 2009, http://www.statssa.gov.za. For more detailed statistical analysis, see Jürgen Hendriks and Johan Erasmus, "Religion in South Africa: The 2001 Census Data," *Journal of Theology for Southern Africa* 121 (2005): 88–111. See also M. L. Daneel, "AICs: Historical Roots and Ecclesial Interconnections," in Daneel, *All Things Hold Together: Holistic Theologies at the African Grassroots,* African Initiatives in Christian Mission (Pretoria: Unisa Press, 2007), 3–20. The figures quoted above exclude Pentecostals.

[16] Hennie Pretorius and Lizo Jafta, "'A Branch Springs Out': African Initiated Churches," in *Christianity in South Africa: A Political, Social & Cultural History,* edited by Richard Elphick and Rodney Davenport (Cape Town: David Philip, 1997), 211–26. A further distinction could be made between Zionist and Apostolic churches, though in this work I will understand these together when I use the term "AIC."

[17] Jean Comaroff, *Body of Power, Spirit of Resistance: The Culture and History of a South African People* (Chicago: University of Chicago Press, 1985), 180ff.

[18] Pretorius and Jafta, "'A Branch Springs Out,'" 211.

[19] For an account of how the state sought to rein in the AICs through bureaucratic management, see Johan W. Claasen, "Independents Made Dependents: African Independent Churches and Government Recognition," *Journal of Theology for Southern Africa,* 91 (1995): 15–34.

[20] Especially among Enoch Mgijima's Israelites, who waited at their sacred site of Ntabelanga—a settlement with houses, a place of worship, schools, and court—for an apocalyptic war which would bring an end to white rule. In 1921, 800 white policemen attacked the 3,000 members of the Israelites, killing 183. David Chidester, *Religions of South Africa* (London: Routledge, 1992), 126–27.

[21] Ibid., 131. As will become evident, I take issue with the term "accommodate."

[22] Chidester, *Religions of South Africa,* 135.

[23] Truth and Reconciliation Commission, "Testimony of the iBandla lamaNazaretha," in *Official Transcript of the Faith Community Hearings of the TRC, November 17–19, 1997* (Cape Town, 1997). Transcripts of all three days of the hearings posted by the Department of Justice and Constitutional Development, Republic of South Africa, accessed August 27, 2011, http://www.justice.gov.za/trc/special/faith/faith_a.htm.

[24] David Chidester, "Mapping the Sacred in the Mother City: Religion and Urban Space in Cape Town," *Journal for the Study of Religion* 13.1–2 (2000): 25.

[25] Linda E. Thomas, *Under the Canopy: Ritual Process and Spiritual Resilience in South Africa* (Columbia: University of South Carolina Press, 1999), 87–90.

[26] Ibid., 103–105.

[27] Truth and Reconciliation Commission, "Testimony of the iBandla lamaNazaretha."

[28] Ibid.

[29] Hennie Pretorius, *Drumbeats: Sounds of Zion on the Cape Flats* (Pretoria: UNISA Press, 2004), 69.

[30] Comaroff, *Body of Power, Spirit of Resistance*, 212.

[31] Robin M. Petersen, "Time, Resistance, and Reconstruction: Rethinking Kairos Theology" (dissertation, University of Chicago, 1995), 230.

[32] Petersen, "Time, Resistance, and Reconstruction," 267.

[33] Truth and Reconciliation Commission, "Testimony of the Zion Christian Church," in *Transcript of TRC Faith Community Hearings.*

[34] Ibid.

[35] Ibid.

[36] See the helpful resume of the views of South African black and liberation theologians on the AICs in Petersen, "Time, Resistance, and Reconstruction," 110–170.

[37] Truth and Reconciliation Commission, "Testimony of the Zion Christian Church."

[38] Botha addressed the pilgrims, but Bishop Barnabas Legkanyane spoke *after* Botha , spoke *twice as long* as Botha, and was *applauded more vehemently* than Botha. In his study of the event, Petersen concludes that Botha was there, but on Legkanyane's terms. Petersen, "Time, Resistance, and Reconstruction," 1–5.

[39] The Kairos Theologians, *Challenge to the Church: The Kairos Document* (Grand Rapids: Eerdmans, 1985).

[40] Charles Villa-Vicencio, *Trapped in Apartheid: A Socio-Theological History of the English-Speaking Churches* (Maryknoll: Orbis Press, 1988).

[41] *Challenge to the Church*, 49.

[42] David Tracy, *Dialogue with the Other* (Grand Rapids: Eerdmans, 1991), distinguishes the "prophetic" and the "mystical."

[43] Petersen, "Time, Resistance, and Reconstruction," 275.

[44] This reading parallels a criticism of Latin American liberation theology: that it accedes to modernity by equating liberation with seizing control of the state. Daniel M. Bell, Jr., *Liberation Theology After the End of History: The Refusal to Cease Suffering* (London: Routledge, 2001); and William T. Cavanaugh, *Torture and Eucharist: Theology, Politics, and the Body of Christ* (Oxford: Blackwell Publishers, 1998).

[45] See Petersen's critique of two such radical critics, Bonganjalo Goba and Albert Nolan, in "Time, Resistance, and Reconstruction," 119–20, 149.

[46] Walter Lowe, "Prospects for a Postmodern Christian Theology: Apocalyptic Without Reserve," *Modern Theology* 15.1 (1999): 23.

[47] Robin M. Petersen, "Theological Reflection on Public Policy: Soweto to the Millennium: Changing Paradigms of South African Prophetic Theology," *Journal of Theology for Southern Africa* 95 (1996): 77.

[48] William T. Cavanaugh, *Theopolitical Imagination: Discovering the Liturgy as a Political Act in an Age of Global Consumerism* (Edinburgh: T & T Clark, 2002), 35–42.

[49] Graham Ward, "Christian Political Practice and the Global City," *Journal of Theology for Southern Africa* 123 (2005): 29–41.

[50] See the stunning exposition of this scene in Rowan Williams, *Christ on Trial: How the Gospel Unsettles Our Judgment* (Grand Rapids: Eerdmans, 2000), 74ff.

[51] Nathan A. Kerr, *Christ, History, and Apocalyptic: The Politics of Christian Mission* (London: SCM, 2009).

[52] Nathan Kerr, "The Politics of Praise," 8–9. This essay was posted at the website of the Graduate Theological Society, Vanderbilt University Divinity School, on May 10, 2006, http://gradtheo.yak.net/12/Nate_Kerr_-_The_Politics_of_Praise.pdf.

[53] Pretorius, *Drumbeats*, 341–352, lists 369 AIC churches on the Cape Flats, of which 247 are Zionist. The names are picked from this list. See also *Drumbeats*, 49–52, for further analysis of the significance of church names.

[54] Ibid., 61. The distinction between space and place comes from Michel de Certeau's *The Practice of Everyday Life* (Berkeley: University of California Press, 1984). Petersen employs this distinction to describe the "positional marginality" of AIC meetings. "The AICs and the TRC," 121.

[55] Chidester, "Mapping the Sacred," 25.

[56] Pretorius, *Drumbeats*, 293. See Ephesians 2:19–22: "So then you are no longer strangers and aliens, but you are citizens (*sympolitai*) with the saints and also members of the household (*oikeioi*) of God, built upon the foundation of the apostles and prophets, with Christ Jesus himself as the cornerstone. In him the whole structure is joined together and grows into a holy temple in the Lord; in whom you also are built together spiritually into a dwelling-place (*katoiketerion*) for God."

[57] Rowan D. Williams, "Politics and the Soul: A Reading of the City of God," *Milltown Studies* 19/20 (1987): 55–56.

[58] Bernd Wannenwetsch, *Political Worship: Ethics for Christian Citizens*, translated by Margaret Kohl (Oxford: Oxford University Press, 2004), 138ff.

[59] I deliberately use the term here to suggest the deconstruction of the secular city by the City of God. It's perhaps analogous to Jacques Derrida's contrast between undeconstructable justice and the orders by which we live. John D. Caputo and Jacques Derrida, *Deconstruction in a Nutshell: A Conversation with Jacques Derrida* (New York: Fordham University Press, 1997), 125–55. See also William T. Cavanaugh, "The City: Beyond Secular Parodies," in *Radical Orthodoxy: A New*

Theology, edited by John Milbank, Catherine Pickstock, and Graham Ward (New York: Routledge, 1999), 182–200.

[60] Pretorius, *Drumbeats*, 129, citing James P. Kiernan, *The Production and Management of Therapeutic Power in Zionist Churches within a Zulu City* (Lewiston: Edwin Mellen, 1990), 211–15.

[61] Pretorius, *Drumbeats*, 130, quoting Kiernan, *Therapeutic Power in Zionist Churches*, 215.

[62] Barbara Bompani, "African Independent Churches in Post-Apartheid South Africa: New Political Interpretations," unpublished paper (2007), 32. My thanks to Prof. Bompani for sending this paper, which is now published as Barbara Bompani, "African Independent Churches in Post-Apartheid South Africa: New Political Interpretations," *Journal of Southern African Studies* 34.3 (September 2008): 665–77. As the published version has left out some pertinent observations and conversations, with Prof. Bompani's permission I am using the original where such material is relevant.

[63] Bompani, "AICs in Post-Apartheid South Africa," 666.

[64] Ibid., 668.

[65] Bengt Sundkler, *Zulu Zion and Some Swazi Zionists* (London: Oxford University Press, 1976), 197.

[66] Pretorius, *Drumbeats*, 125.

[67] See, for instance, Cavanaugh, *Theopolitical Imagination*. The most innovative work in this regard is Stanley Hauerwas and Samuel Wells, eds., *The Blackwell Companion to Christian Ethics* (Malden: Blackwell, 2004), in which liturgy forms the basis for a Christian ethics. Smith's *Desiring the Kingdom* sees liturgical formation as integral to all human formation. Christian liturgy, then, is a counter-formation to the liturgies of the city of this world.

[68] Truth and Reconciliation Commission, "Testimony of the iBandla lamaNazaretha."

[69] Disorientation-reorientation: Walter Brueggemann, *The Message of the Psalms: A Theological Commentary*, Augsburg Old Testament Studies (Minneapolis: Augsburg, 1984).

[70] Bell, *Liberation Theology After the End of History*, 70–74, shows this practice at work within the churches of the poor in Latin America.

[71] Pretorius, *Drumbeats*, 64.

[72] Ibid., 63.

[73] Ibid., 75.

[74] Ibid., 73.

[75] Smith, *Desiring the Kingdom*, 46–52.

[76] Comaroff, *Body of Power, Spirit of Resistance*, 218.

[77] Petersen, "Time, Resistance, and Reconstruction," 267; Comaroff, *Body of Power, Spirit of Resistance*, 235–236.

[78] It would be facile to claim that the practices of AICs are, insofar as they contest commodification, "socialist." Clearly there are strong entrepeneurial currents in the ethics of AICs, and the ZCC in particular encourages African enterprises as part of its call for its members to "stand tall" as self-reliant people in strong communities. See G. C. Oosthuizen, *African Independent Churches and Small Businesses: Spiritual Support for Secular Empowerment* (Pretoria: HSRC Publishers, 1997), 47–48.

[79] Petersen, "Time, Resistance, and Reconstruction," 266.

[80] Michel de Certeau, quoted "Time, Resistance, and Reconstruction" by Petersen, 267.

[81] Petersen, "Time, Resistance, and Reconstruction," 268.

[82] Bompani, "AICs in Post-Apartheid South Africa," 674–75.

[83] Bompani unpublished manuscript, 31.

[84] Pretorius, *Drumbeats*, 61.

[85] Ibid.

[86] The phrase belongs to Romand Coles. Stanley Hauerwas and Romand Coles, *Christianity, Democracy, and the Radical Ordinary: Conversations Between a Radical Democrat and a Christian (Theopolitical Visions)* (Eugene: Wipf and Stock, 2007), 278.

[87] Rowan D. Williams, "Plenary Address," to On the Church, Mission-Shaped Church Conference, June 23, 2004. Posted by Anglican Church Planting Initiative, accessed August 27, 2011, http://www.acpi.org.uk/articles/archbishops%20address.htm.

[88] Rowan D. Williams, "Forum Debate: Is Europe at Its End?" address, Sant'Egidio International Meeting of Prayer for Peace (Palais de Congress, Lyons, 2005), http://www.archbishopofcanterbury.org/958.

[89] See Douglas Rushcoff's excellent (and chilling) PBS documentary, "The Persuaders" (2005; http://www.pbs.org/wgbh/pages/frontline/shows/persuaders/), about the role of advertising techniques in American politics.

[90] See for examples, Chantal Mouffe, *The Democratic Paradox* (New York: Verso, 2000); William Connolly, *Pluralism* (Durham: Duke University Press, 2005); and Romand Coles, *Beyond Gated Politics: Reflections for the Possibility of Democracy* (Minneapolis: University of Minnesota Press, 2005).

[91] Although Mouffe, Connolly, and Coles are all secular, albeit with a love-hate relationship to St. Augustine. I've learned much on this from two Augustinian Christian respondents to radical democracy: Mathewes, *A Theology of Public Life*, and Kristen Deede Johnson, *Theology, Political Theory, and Pluralism: Beyond Tolerance and Difference*, Cambridge Studies in Christian Doctrine (Cambridge: Cambridge University Press, 2007). I suspect they would also have a critical ally in another Augustinian: Rowan Williams—whose entire theological project aims to unsettle.

[92] For a consideration of what this might look like in South Africa, see Ivor Chipkin's provocative book, *Do South Africans Exist?: Nationalism, Democracy, and the Identity of the People* (Johannesburg: Wits University Press, 2007).

[93] Coles, *Beyond Gated Politics*, xi, quoted in *Christianity, Democracy, and the Radical Ordinary: Conversations Between a Radical Democrat and a Christian* by Stanley Hauerwas and Romand Coles (Eugene: Wipf & Stock Publishers, 2007), 18.

[94] The fascinating story of new social movements in South Africa is told in Richard Ballard, Adam Habib, and Imraan Valodia, eds., *Voices of Protest: Social Movements in Post-Apartheid South Africa* (Scottsville: University of KwaZulu-Natal Press, 2006).

[95] Bettina von Lieres and Steven Robins, "Democracy and Citizenship," in *New South African Keywords*, edited by Nick Shepherd and Steven Robins (Athens: Ohio University Press, 2008), 50.

[96] Von Lieres and Robins, "Democracy and Citizenship," 50. See also Steven Robins, "Grounding 'Globalisation from Below': Global Citizens in Local Spaces," in *What Holds Us Together: Social Cohesion in South Africa*, edited by David Chidester, Wilmot James, and Phillip Dexter (Pretoria: Human Sciences Research Council, 2004), 242–73.

[97] Hauerwas and Coles, *Christianity, Democracy, and the Radical Ordinary*, 111. Coles realizes this, and so speaks in fascinating ways in their conversation about liturgies of "the radical ordinary" that form and sustain democracy.

[98] As famously discussed in *Church Dogmatics* IV. For a good treatment along the lines I have in mind, see Nicholas Adams and Charles Elliott, "Ethnography is Dogmatics: Making Description Central to Systematic Theology," *Scottish Journal of Theology* 53 (2000): 339–64.

[99] Rowan D. Williams, "Faith Communities in a Civil Society—Christian Perspectives," *Christian-Muslim Relations* 19.3 (July 2008): 352.

[100] See Williams, "Politics and the Soul."

[101] So what Smith does in *Desiring the Kingdom* for the liturgies (pedagogies of desire) of the Mall and the University, I'm suggesting needs to be done for the Parliament and the Congress as well.

WHAT IS SOUTH AFRICA TO ME?

Confessions of an Amateur Tour Guide

Tinyiko Maluleke

What is Africa to Me?

"What is Africa to me?" So goes the opening line of the celebrated poem by African American lyric poet of the twentieth century Countee Cullen. Cullen's was a question of lament. It was a lament of a speaker three centuries removed—only three centuries(!)—from the land that nevertheless marked and defined everything the speaker was (or was supposed to be). Though uttered by Cullen, this was a question many African Americans knew well. In anguished tones they posed this question to themselves and to one another. The question spoke to the reality of African Americanness—it spoke of, from, and to the "souls of black folk."[2] It is not a comfortable question. No. This was a question to run from—a question from which to escape. This is the question that, at the turn of the twentieth century, occupied the likes of W. E. B. Du Bois, Edward Blyden, Langston Hughes, and others. But it was a dogged question. It would neither surrender nor give up. Throughout the three centuries and beyond, this question pursued African Americans like a bloodhound.

It is not a question African Americans ask; it is a question that asks African Americans. It poses African Americans, not vice versa. This question sprang from the trauma of being removed from Africa and yet marked by Africa. The question comes from Africa itself—the place of darkness, where allegedly "the lowest of human species" roamed. By looks, origins, genes, and spirit, African Americans were African. If they were individually not born in Africa, Africa was born in and borne by them; daily. Daily they had to endure Africa, deciding whether it was a known or an unknown, inside or outside, benign or malign, a curse or a blessing, a life or a death.

What Is South Africa to Me?

In June 2009, I was privileged to be one of the hosts of a group of visiting scholars from a variety of disciplines in the humanities and social sciences, scholars who hailed from around Africa and from around North America as well. As I traveled and engaged with these scholars, I was haunted by the question Countee Cullen posed in the 1920s. In the process of trying to help a group of curious minds make sense of South Africa, the country of my birth, I found myself wondering, in a fresh and strange kind of way, what South Africa is to me.

Unintended Consequences

I was born in South Africa. Yet at that point, in the 1960s, the country called South Africa, as we have come to know it, was not yet born. I was born into the Republic of South Africa—newly and angrily seceded from the British Commonwealth. Even so, I was not a citizen of that country. Like my parents and theirs, I was a foreigner, a sojourner, and a subject, born at Baragwanath Hospital in the South Western Township (better known as SOWETO)—a black reserve, outside Johannesburg. SOWETO was a temporary dwelling, a large-scale dormitory, a ghetto graduated from the single (single because they were not allowed to bring their wives along) men's mine hostels. Like its predecessors, the single men's hostels, SOWETO had no purpose other than to serve as a labor reservoir to Johannesburg's growing white mining and related industries. Its metamorphosis into a home, a place of pride, and a place of struggle was an unintended consequence. Nothing in SOWETO was intended—certainly nothing was intended to last. Not the schools. Not the houses. Not the hospitals. Not the people. The poet Sipho Sepamla captures the tragedy and horror of SOWETO:

I have watched you grow
like fermented dough
and now that you overflow the bowl
I'm witness to the panic you have wrought
You were born an afterthought
on the by-paths of high-ways
and lived like a foster child[3]

Sometimes I think that I and millions like me were rather like footnotes to that massive unintended consequence of history. In 1976, as a naïve and boisterous teenager, I joined thousands of fellow students in what has come to be known as the SOWETO uprisings. This was a furious, unpredicted student revolt against the apartheid system, inspired in part by the Black Consciousness movement but also by the example of the leaders then languishing in jail. This at a time when the struggle against apartheid seemed to be in recess—with all the major black political parties banned and their leaders incarcerated.[4] As a result of the uprisings, the struggle against apartheid received a tremendous boost, as hundreds and thousands of young people fled into exile in order to join the armed struggle against apartheid.

One of the slogans of the SOWETO uprising was: "Liberation before Education," or "Liberation First and Education Later." The education in question was Bantu education, an inferior, poorly funded form of education meant to prepare the black children to become useful cheap labor—drawers of water and hewers of wood. Over weekends, I walked the streets of the whites-only suburbs of Roodeport, a small town northwest of SOWETO, in search of weekend gardening jobs.[5] Alternatively, I held the job of being an "interpreter of maladies"[6] at the Johannesburg dental surgery where my father worked as a laborer and assistant to the orthodontist.

Only thus could I manage to pay for some of the costs for my own schooling. The slogan "Liberation First, Education Later" was as radical as it was foolhardy. The adults of SOWETO were not persuaded by the slogans and methods of the impatient and furious young.[7] "Black Power" was the other slogan of the 1976 SOWETO uprising, and this slogan was accompanied by the sign of a clenched fist. Power? What power? The adults must have wondered what on earth had gotten into our heads. At that time, the might and power of the apartheid state was palpable. Monstrously huge armored police and army vehicles camped in SOWETO. Daily these vehicles full of soldiers and police with long guns in their hands strutted the streets of SOWETO, raiding schools and homes at will. Detainees were being killed by the dozens. Between the obstinate bravado of the students and the cruel methods of the apartheid police, the school system in SOWETO collapsed.

Enough, said my father as he sent me off to the South African Bantustan, the homeland of Gazankulu. There I was to find a more stable school environment and a further taste of what it means to be a second-class citizen in one's own country of birth. Gazankulu was to be found in the space that borders Mozambique to the east and Zimbabwe to the north. There I joined the thousands of surplus, rural, and forgotten people who eked out a living at the mercy of the rains, on the margins of white South Africa.

Betrayed at Birth

When I say I was born in SOWETO, I also mean by it that I was not born in South Africa—not in the South Africa that was unveiled to my inquisitive visiting scholars. But neither SOWETO nor South Africa is innocent. For me, both are at once objects of my undying love and fountains of my traumatic fears. As I burst onto the scenes in SOWETO, Mandela was in hiding, soon to be tracked down and jailed for life. Only half of my short life has been spent in the new South Africa—the South Africa that I tried to introduce to my North American visitors. At many moments, the old South Africa interfered with and disrupted my narrative. Indeed the very tours undertaken by my learned visitors—in Johannesburg and in Cape Town—took them in and out of the old and the new South Africa, sometimes several times in one day. The question of what South Africa is to me is therefore a potent and relevant one. It is a question that arises to a person born into a country that abandons one at birth. Every black child born into apartheid South Africa knows the anguish. It is the anguish of the abandoned child, further complicated by repeated, pathological, and systemic parental abuse.

Journey into Theology

Posing as a tour-guide to my scholarly visitors raised the question of the meaning of South Africa sharply in me. South African nationality is a taste I am slowly acquiring, a dance I am learning fast.[8] It is a country whose actual existence is not always indisputable.[9] Sometimes I think that if the country exists, then I do not exist, and if I exist, then the country does not exist. My very existence is at once a testimony to and an indictment of the very idea of South Africa. And yet there are times when my chest could burst with joy at being a South African. This was precisely the feeling I had the day Nelson Mandela walked out of prison a free man. On that day, I joined members of my congregation at a house in Tembisa Township, to watch in utter amazement the TV broadcasting of Mandela's release. The same feeling of euphoria visited me when, for the first time in my life, I cast my vote as a full citizen in 1994. But I am going ahead of myself.

In the early 1980s, I caught the train from Johannesburg to Pietermaritzburg in Kwazulu Natal.[10] This was my journey into theology—a trip that is still continuing. This journey further deepened the question of what South Africa is to me. As a student of theology in Pietermaritzburg, I had my first taste of education outside of the Bantu education frame. For the first time, my teachers and lecturers asked me, "What do you think?" What a liberating question! With that question, I was enabled to see the possibility of a different South Africa. In this South Africa, it is recognized and it matters not only that I thought, but also what I thought. These were my first tentative steps into citizenship in a country that had denied me from the time of my birth.

After years of worshipping a God who separated blacks from whites, I lived for three years in the Federal Theological Seminary (FEDSEM), Imbali, Pietermaritzburg, a community of students and lecturers of different colors, sexes, and Christian confessions. Inside that isolated island within a country-wide apartheid sea, I began to visualize a new South Africa in which race, gender, and confession was no handicap but part of a rich diversity to be embraced. And yet the island of my theological formation was no utopia. Bitter contestations of a racial, gender, and confessional nature were fought. Inside the four walls of the fort called FEDSEM, there were petty squabbles, rivalry, bigotry, and yes, even racism. If one minimized or underestimated these, all one needed to do was to go out of the gate of FEDSEM and the cold winds of the real South Africa would blow away any romantic illusions about full citizenship in apartheid South Africa. Outside the walls, there were far too many nice places for whites only! In any case, three years later, one had to leave the artificial comforts of the castle of FEDSEM.

Seeing Anew

Back to June 2009 and my visitors. Which South Africans then, given my and their limitations, my and their experiences, were we going to visit and foreground? How could we ensure that we would not end up with a caricature of a country with so protracted, so informative, so painful, so human, and so inspiring a history of struggle for freedom and coexistence? How could we ensure that this would not lead to yet another episode of academic tourism? How could we ensure that we would not end up either with a romantic picture of the country or a stereotypically negative one?

From the intense conversations we shared at the foot of the Voortrekker Monument, the engaging talk of Deputy Chief Justice Moseneke at Constitutional Court, and the tears we shed together at Central Methodist Church Johannesburg, to the courage we witnessed at Kayelitsha, and the visit to SOWETO, it was very clear to me that these colleagues took my country, its promises, and its challenges seriously. Reading through the fascinating essays in this book, it is very clear to me that the colleagues who journeyed with me through the country were no sheer academic voyeurs on tour. They caught a glimpse of my country in its ugliness. They had a taste of the tragedy out of which the country is trying to emerge. For a moment, they basked in the sun of our young and vibrant, if at times fragile, democracy. When they looked deeper and scratched below the surface, they began to see themselves in South Africa. At times, it dawned on them that they had come all the way to South Africa to confront issues they had left back home. South Africa, they found, was not that unique. They discovered that South Africa was very similar to their own countries and that South Africans are much like their own compatriots.

From a Post-Apartheid Country to a Post-Reconciliation Country

In conversation and in journey with my academic visitors across the country, the question of what South Africa means to me took on a new dimension and a new urgency. My country is many things. It has been a prison, a desert, and a graveyard. For millions who remain unable to cash their 1994 freedom check in South Africa, the country remains a prison, a desert, and a graveyard. I am thinking of the millions who are unemployed and increasingly on welfare. I am thinking of women and children who are at the receiving end of violence and abuse. To those who continue to be excluded from the slow-growing economy, South Africa remains a precarious country to live in. As we traversed the land and as we engaged deeply in discussions about the written and human texts we were reading, I was struck by the extent to which the signature of apartheid was still everywhere—not only at the Voortrekker monument. Fifteen years into democracy, townships remained townships (with their schools, churches, and police stations) and white suburbs remained white suburbs—with the proviso that the few blacks who could afford to could now live there. But the apartheid architecture was still stark and in our faces.

I was also struck by the greatness of the danger of political, developmental, and moral stagnation—if not regression. It seemed as if South Africa was reaching a stage (already) where the temptation to settle (for "what we have" [achieved]) was becoming irresistible. There was something in the tone of the elites who spoke to my visitors that seemed to suggest this. Many of the presentations were tall on the achievements and rather curt and short on the challenges. Admittedly, there were sharp presentations about the legacies of apartheid and the failures of government. But there were few comprehensive, honest, and coherent assessments of where we were as a people and as a country. Even where reality was looking us in the face, such as when we met with the wretched inhabitants of the church building that had become a giant bedroom for several hundred African foreign nationals—the Central Methodist Church—words and incisive analyses seemed to escape our interlocutors and ourselves alike. It felt to me as if everyone, ourselves included, was struggling to move beyond the rhetoric and the framework of the transitional arrangements and strategies intended to be midwives for a genuinely new and democratic South Africa.

And yet since 1994, South Africa has become home, to foreign nationals, to blacks, to whites, to men, to women, to the religious, to agnostics, to gays, and to lesbians—in short, home for humanity. The question is whether this "home" is being consolidated and reconfigured even as it is made more permanent.[11] In this, the churches have an important role to play. But we saw already in May 2008, when Afrophobic violence broke out, that the hospitality of South Africa is fragile and not guaranteed.[12] Churches have to work harder to undermine the geography of apartheid—even if all they can do at times is merely to point the scandal out. In other words, churches have a stake in making South Africa "home." The task of championing the cause of the poor and the marginalized still beckons.[13] Included among the marginalized is the earth itself. The time has come for the church in South Africa and everywhere to stand in solidarity with the earth and with all of creation. Having assisted in the creation of a post-apartheid South Africa, we are now called upon to create what Njabulo Ndebele calls a "post reconciliation" South Africa. By this, Ndebele does not mean a South Africa that has no more use for reconciliation. Rather, it is a search for a South Africa that does not stagnate and solidify in the sea of transition symbols, transition rhetoric, and transition arrangements. These symbols served their purpose and laid an important foundation for the new country. However, these arrangements are in danger of being regarded as a permanent state of affairs. Yet clearly they are not sufficient to ensure that South Africa is home to all. If they were, the gap between rich and poor would not be growing; if they were, we as a country would have broken the back of the HIV/AIDS pandemic.[14] If these arrangements were sufficient, South Africans would not have hounded and murdered African foreign nationals in May 2008 only to give people from all over the world a rousing welcome two years later, during the FIFA World Cup. If the transitional arrangements were sufficient, South Africa would not have a steady economic growth that nevertheless fails to create jobs. Indeed if these arrangements were sufficient, the scourge of corruption in both the private and public sectors would not be growing. Nor would the problem of race still dog us.[15]

It is not that South Africa is only and utterly a bad place. It is rather that it is a country *en route* to a greater place. It would be a grievous mistake to settle here and now. Nelson Mandela was speaking for all of us and for the whole country when he wrote,

> I have walked that long road to freedom. I have tried not to falter; I have made missteps along the way. But I have discovered the secret that after climbing a great hill, one finds that there are many many more hills to climb. I have taken a moment here to rest, to steal a view of the glorious vista that surrounds me, to look back on the distance I have come. But I can rest only for a moment, for with freedom comes responsibilities, and I dare not linger for my long walk is not yet ended.[16]

This volume contains a selection of excellent essays that bear testimony not only to a country "on the move" but also to the resonance of issues between South Africa and many other countries in the world.

Conclusion

To conclude, I return to my self-characterization as an amateur tour guide. Since I started with a poem, I wish to end with one. Adrienne Rich is an American feminist poet and essayist who rose to prominence during the second half of the twentieth century. In her poem, "Here is a map of our country," she does what I have been trying to do in this essay and in my role as host to my scholarly colleagues in 2009.

> Here is a map of our country:
> here is the Sea of Indifference, glazed with salt
> This is the haunted river flowing from brow to groin
> we dare not taste its water
> This is the desert where missiles are planted like corns
> This is the breadbasket of foreclosed farms
> This is the birthplace of the rockabilly boy
> This is the cemetery of the poor
> who died for democracy

This is a battlefield
from a nineteenth-century war, the shrine is famous
This is the sea-town of myth and story when the fishing fleets
went bankrupt here is where the jobs were on the pier
processing frozen fishsticks hourly wages and no shares
These are other battlefields Centralia Detroit here are the forests
primeval the copper the silver lodes
These are the Suburbs of aquiescence silence rising fumelike from
the streets
This is the capital of money and dolor whose spires
flare up through air inversions whose bridges are crumbling
whose children are drifting blind alleys pent
between coiled rolls of razor wire
I promised to show you a map you say but this is a mural
then yes let it be these are small distinctions
where do we see it from is the question[17]

In these twenty-four tightly composed lines, Rich takes her readers by the hand, leading them through the map of her country, the difficult world, the USA.

She could be talking of South Africa.

Notes to the Afterword

[1] From "Heritage," by Countee in Cullen, *Color* (New York: Harper & Brothers, 1925), 36–41.

[2] Famously posed and expounded by W. E. B. Du Bois, *The Souls of Black Folk* (Chicago: A.C. McClurg & Co., 1903).

[3] From a poem, "SOWETO," by Sipho Sepamla, in *Voices from Within: Black Poetry from Southern Africa*, edited by Michael Chapman and Achmat Dangor (Johannesburg: AD Donker, 1986),127–128.

[4] One of the most revealing accounts from those years is Raymond Suttner, *The ANC Underground* (Johannesburg: Jacana Media, 2008), the memoir of an ANC operative.

[5] An entertaining fictional account of boyhood in the townships of Johannesburg is Chris van Wyk, *Shirley, Goodness and Mercy: A Childhood Memoir* (Johannesburg: Picador, 2004).

[6] Jhumpa Lahiri, *An Interpreter of Maladies: Stories* (New York: Houghton Mifflin, 1999).

[7] See Njabulo Ndebele, *Fools and Other Stories* (Johannesburg, Raven Press, 1983).

[8] Chinua Achebe. *The Education of a British Protected Child* (New York: Random House, 2009). See especially his "What is Nigeria to Me?" 39–46.

[9] See Ivor Chipkin, *Do South Africans Exist? Nationalism, Democracy and the Identity of "the People"* (Johannesburg: Witwatersrand University Press, 2007).

[10] Tinyiko Sam Maluleke, "Theology in My Life," *Reformed World* 56.3 (September 2006): 302–307.

[11] Njabulo Ndebele, "Arriving Home? South Africa beyond Transition and Reconciliation," in *In the Balance: South Africans Debate Reconciliation*, edited by Fanie Du Toit and Erik Doxtader (Pretoria: Jacana Media, 2010), 54–73.

[12] Shireen Hassim, Tawana Kupe, and Eric Worby, eds., *Go Home or Die Here: Violence, Xenophobia and the Reinvention of Difference in South Africa* (Johannesburg: Wits University Press, 2008).

[13] Tinyiko Sam Maluleke, "Justice in Post-Apartheid South Africa: Towards a Theology of Restitution," *Verbum et Ecclesia* 29.3 (2008): 681–696.

[14] Tinyiko Sam Maluleke, "Towards an HIV/AIDS Sensitive Curriculum," in *HIV/AIDS and the Curriculum. Methods of Integrating HIV/AIDS in Theological Programmes*, edited by Musa Dube (Geneva: World Council of Churches, 2003), 59–76.

[15] Jonathan D Jansen, *Knowledge in the Blood: Confronting Race and the Apartheid Past* (Cape Town: UCT Press, 2009).

[16] Nelson Mandela, *Long Walk to Freedom* (Lancaster: Abacus, 1994), 751.

[17] Adrienne Rich, "Here is a map of our country," in *An Atlas of the Difficult World: Poems 1988–1991* (New York: W. W. Norton, 1991), 6.

ENGAGE, REFLECT, AND COVENANT TO CHANGE

The Story of a Seminar

Bob and Alice Evans

Plowshares Institute has been conducting professional development seminars for more than three decades. We do this work because we hope to stimulate constructive change among leaders and in the places where they serve. We expect that these seminars will be catalysts for opening minds and hearts, creating new teaching and research, provoking strategic institutional change, and making new connections between leaders and their communities. Some observers will declare that these results are too much to hope for. Colleagues and institutional officers may oppose efforts to change what is comfortable and customary. Nevertheless, we have seen positive changes occur quite often when international "immersion" seminar members come home. We commonly hear our participants say:

"I think about it every day."
"It forced me to change the way I teach."
"I've radically changed my research focus."
"My school must revise its curriculum to engage the world."

"My church is not being responsive to the voices of the poor."
"Gender equity and HIV/ AIDS prevention and care are now
my missions."

Declarations like these persist long after the seminar is finished.

Independent research confirms that these seminars produce long-term
personal and institutional effects.[1]

Why do international seminars? We learned from Brazilian educator
Paulo Freire that people live in cultural bubbles, just as fish live in water. Fish
have no understanding of the significance of the water until they are flipped up
on the shore. Each of us is shaped by our cultural surroundings, but we seldom
see the power of our formative culture clearly until something draws us out of
it and allows us to look at our worldview in a new way. This process of moving
out of one's culture can be both terrifying and illuminating. An experiential
faculty development seminar provides an opportunity to land on the shore
of a radically different culture in order to gain insights about ourselves and
as well as the realms beyond our cultural waters. We are convinced that for
these kinds of insight to be sustainable and lead to personal transformation,
experiences outside of our cultural boundaries should be relatively safe, and
should be undertaken within a community of support and reflection.

The educational rhythm for this kind of seminar, says Joel Carpenter,
is "engage, reflect, and covenant to change." Immersion seminars for faculty development focus on linking direct engagement in a different society
to critical reflection about teaching, research, and engagement in one's local
community.

Why South Africa?

For the majority of our seminar participants, both from North America and
from various parts of Africa, South Africa was definitely a "different society."
The nation is in the midst of dramatic transition, moving from the oppression of apartheid toward the liberating potential of democracy. Desmond
Tutu invited Plowshares' directors to join him in this movement in 1972. Our
nearly forty years of engagement with South Africa and the massive social and
theological changes underway in this pivotal African nation made it an ideal

location for an immersive educational experience focused on Christian thinking about public affairs.

We hoped that seminar participants would be able to see and reflect on South Africans' struggle to build a renewed society: putting a new constitution into effect, publicly recognizing a painful past and moving toward the future, and developing prophetic models of the church in action. The team ranged across a variety of disciplines, including theologians, ethicists, social and political philosophers, political scientists, and professors of sociology, history, and the popular arts. They came from the United States, Canada, Ghana, Nigeria, Kenya, Uganda, Zimbabwe, and South Africa. The life of the community was enriched by fellowship, laughter, tears, arguments, worship, and prayer. And we took many opportunities to explore the diverse cultures and breathtaking beauty of South Africa.

The South African seminar engaged some of the country's most challenging issues in order to gain insights about Christian social and political witness. These engagements demanded disciplined reflection and conversation in an everyday rhythm. Continually we asked: what was the potential for applying new insights to our home countries, in North America and in sub-Saharan Africa? Could these visits not only transform our teaching and research but also lead to covenants of action for our own institutions, communities, and nations? The challenge, we came to realize, is that in education as in life, resistance is always easier than reconstruction.

An Experiential Approach

The educational process for the South African seminar began months before the scholars entered the country in June, 2009. A seminar-coordinating team emerged, and it included several distinguished South African theologians, notably Tinyiko Maluleke from the University of South Africa, John De Gruchy from the University of Cape Town, and Nico Koopman from the University of Stellenbosch. They consulted with Joel Carpenter of Calvin College and Plowshares seminar coordinators Bob and Alice Evans. The coordinating team selected five critical themes, which drove the selection of the seminar's primary engagements with South African society. Here are the themes and the representative institutions we visited:

1. Refugees, Migration, and Xenophobia	Central Methodist Church (Johannesburg)
2. Constitution, Democracy, and Human Rights	Constitutional Court (Johannesburg)
3. Parliament, Power, and Public Policy	Parliament (Cape Town)
4. HIV/AIDS and Health Policies	J.L. Zwane Church (Guguletu) and Metropolitan Life Insurance Corporation
5. Globalization, Economics, and Environment	Beyers Naude Center for Public Theology, (Stellenbosch)

Five thematic teams began to share their international research and reflect on their selected themes before their arrival in South Africa. Each team also agreed on a limited number of articles to send to the full group. This process of advance reading, group bibliographic research, and reflection set a pattern for both team and group interactions. Once on site, the team began its daily engagement in multifaceted dimensions of South African society, which had both emotional and intellectual impacts. Other integral daily components of our two weeks in South Africa were living together in retreat-style accommodations, group reflections led by different teams of participants, personal journal writing, and worship.

One of the agreements of the planning team was to honor the initial design but be continually open to where the Holy Spirit might be leading. During the seminar, the group expanded the seminar topics to include "History, Memory, Identity, and Land," which arose during four additional visits: at the Voortrekker Monument (Pretoria), Hector Pieterson Memorial (Soweto), Freedom Park (Pretoria), and District 6 Museum (Cape Town).

Our days typically included a visit or two to thematically significant sites and extended conversations with South Africans who were engaged in serving the relevant community. So for example at the Voortrekker Monument in Pretoria, which commemorates the great trek of the Afrikaner people into the South African interior and their conquest of African tribes, we talked to

Piet Miering, a Dutch Reformed theologian and professor at the University of Pretoria. Piet had served on the Truth and Reconciliation commission, and he said that the monument's linking of Afrikaner destiny to divine covenant had no place in his theology. He had seen firsthand the cruelty it provoked. But he reflected with us about people's need for a history, and we puzzled together over whether this memorial, with its deeply presumptive and prejudicial view of God's providence and the South African past, might ever be redeemed and transformed.

In like manner, we visited the Hector Pieterson memorial in Soweto, which honors the schoolboy who was one of the first to die in the Soweto uprising of 1976. The uprising started with a march of school children who were protesting the government's mandating that their instruction be in Afrikaans, a foreign tongue to most. Our guide, Jabulani Abraham Shoba, had known Pieterson and was a marcher that day when the police fired on the children. Now he is a Pentecostal pastor, engaged in community-serving ministries. The museum offers a "walk through," pictorial history of apartheid and the struggle against it. We were struck by what was becoming a recurring theme: South Africans' struggle to own an identity and to feel at home in their own country, where apartheid social engineering had been designed to alienate and divide people.

Team members typically came back to our residence and had some "down time" after visits to reflect, either singly or in casual conversations. Most evenings, we gathered for more formal discussion and closing prayers.

The Power of Shared Covenants

As facilitators of more than forty such Plowshares immersion seminars, we learned long ago that there is no way to predict or control what emerges from experiential encounters. They challenge participants to move out of their cultural cocoons and see the world from radically different perspectives. While we prepare the ground with a design for connecting people and visions, the fruits of an immersion seminar are a gift of grace, the remarkable, Spirit-filled alchemy of people, place, and open-hearted participation.

The rhythms of preparation, engagement, and reflection are crucial to transformational education. But another essential element is needed: a learning covenant. The group pursued this goal in a concluding retreat, two and a half days of life together at Volmoed Retreat Centre up in the hills behind Hermanus, a Western Cape coastal town. There the South African scholar/ guides who developed the original themes and helped identify the direct engagements encouraged the participants to share their most persistent questions and apply their personal insights to concrete actions.

Each participant committed from the outset to write a reflective essay that would merge prior scholarly pursuits with new insights. Essays envisioned during the retreat form the chapters of this publication. Beyond these essays, participants have also developed additional writings, conference presentations, and teaching resources.

To help participants apply and sustain their insights, we asked them to draft learning covenants. Scholars each selected a covenant partner with whom they shared a series of action commitments. Each of them identified how they would apply the insights or questions from the seminar to their teaching, research, and individual and institutional service. Covenant partners discussed how they could most effectively implement and sustain their respective commitments. They are expected to support and hold their partners accountable to these commitments after they have returned to the heavy demands of their scholarly and personal obligations within their own countries. Plowshares research over the years confirms that this covenanting process is one of the most powerful instruments for sustaining the impact of the international seminar experience. Making a covenant, and being held to it by a partner, may be the lynchpin that actually links the seminar experience to making changes in the months and years that follow.

We close this brief reflection with relevant comments from some of the scholar participants:

- A Canadian political scientist says: "This was really my first substantial trip overseas, certainly as a scholar, so this was particularly formative for me. The variety of the experiences was important: alternating between situations of great poverty and great power, great symbolism and the re-interpretation of symbols. These contrasts and juxtapositions and tensions really help stimulate thinking and action."

- An African woman theologian promises: "As a seal of commitment to a learning covenant, I commit myself to being a pragmatic and pro-active academic who will initiate and motivate action in all situations possible to facilitate the alleviation of poverty, degradation, and exploitation of humankind by the academic and corporate world."

- A U.S. philosophy professor also covenants: "I will re-orient core aspects of my life, including my teaching, scholarship, and service at my university, around the principal objective of promoting the moral dignity of all creatures.... This means regular service involvement with the poor in my city ... and meeting with administrators in academic affairs, campus ministries, and student life to explore ways to address the stigma of HIV/AIDS."

Experiential education has the potential to stimulate constructive change for individual scholars and for their universities, churches, and communities. The risk is high, and the financial commitment is substantial. But the consequences may be what we seek for all of our faculty and students. Cross-cultural, interdisciplinary, international immersions can bring wider and deeper perspectives to Christian higher education.

Note to the Appendix

1. David Roozen, *Changing the Way Seminaries Teach: Globalization and Theological Education* (Hartford: Hartford Seminary Center for Social and Religious Research, 1996).

Index

50 Cent, 71, 75–76
Aaboe, Julie, 240
Ackermann, Denise, 129
Act 55 (1949), 151
Adams, Nicholas, 293n98
Africa in Chaos (Ayittey), 216n3
Africa in Search of Democracy (Busia), 216n7
Africa Unchained: The Blueprint for Africa's Future (Ayittey), 217n16
"African," contentiousness of the term, 100n8
African Anglican Bishops, 131
African Christian Democratic Party (ACDP), 263n70
African Christianity: Its Public Role (Gifford), 216n6
African Independent Churches and Small Businesses: Spiritual Support for Secular Empowerment (Oosthuizen), 292n78
African Initiated/Independent Churches (AICs), 182, 250, 264n84; and apocalyptic eschatology, 275–78; and the claim of a sacred center in "Zion, city of our God," 270; classification of (Ethiopian churches and Zionist and Apostolic churches), 270–71; and the cultivation of social capital, 251; distinctive attire and lifestyle of AIC members, 272; and an ecclesiology of dispossession, 280–82; entrepreneurial currents in, 292n78; as *iiKonzo zo Moya* ("churches of the Spirit") as opposed to *iicawe zomthetho* ("churches of the law" or "churches recognized by government"), 271; and liturgy, 178–80; as part of an "insurgent" democracy, 282–84; the puzzle of to mainline theologians, 270–75; and the name "Zion," 276–77. *See also specific AICs*
African National Congress (ANC), 67, 147–48, 162n45, 246; and the Black Economic Empowerment (BEE) initiative, 148; and the National Interfaith Conference (NILC), 162n50
African penguin (*Spheniscus demersus*), 106–8; care of by the Southern African Foundation for the Conservation of Coastal Birds (SANCCOB), 107, 116n3; protection under the International Union for the Conservation of Nature and Natural Resources (IUCN), 107
"'African You Are on Your Own!'—The Need for African Reformed Christians to Seriously Engage Their Africanity in Their Reformed Theological Reflections" (Tshaka), 188n51
Afrikaner Reformed churches, 239, 259n23
Afrophobia, 166, 167–68
"AICs and the TRC, The: Resistance Redefined" (Petersen), 287–88n13
Akenson, Donald, 48, 51
Akper, Godwin I., 25, 100n7, 101n27
Alence, Rod, 257n4
alienation, 95–96, 98, 122, 133; of the poor, 287n2; in South African context, 94–95; in South African theology, 91–94; white alienation, 97
Allison, Dale C., 112
Amendment Act on Native Affairs (1957), 151
American pioneers: analogy between American pioneers and Voortrekkers, 39; and Native Americans, 39
ANC Underground, The (Suttner), 305n4

Anglican Aids & Healthcare Trust, 149
Anglican Church, 151
Anthonissen, Christine, 241
Anti-Apartheid Theology in the Dutch Reformed Family of Churches (Pauw), 259n23
apartheid, 32, 36, 48, 89, 90–91, 94–95, 101n13, 125, 146, 147, 151–52, 169, 177, 179, 193–94, 196, 220, 221, 234, 235, 239–42, 247–51, 252–53, 273–74, 209, 300, 308, 311; and the abuse of power, 194, 196; apartheid ideology, 55, 96, 152, 181, 188n54; apartheid theology, 53, 56; and the Balkanization of South African populations, 101n13; and the Group Areas Act (1950), 90; legacy of, 93, 158, 166; movements/struggles against, 62, 67, 109, 162n45, 187n34, 243, 244–45, 260n41, 274, 297; theological legitimacy of, 181, 182
"Arab spring," 27n1
Arendt, Hannah, 277
Ariel Rios Federal Building, 39–40; murals representing Native Americans in, 39
Ashcroft, Adam, 264n95
Augustine, 268, 285; on the *civitas Dei*, 268; on the *civitas terrena*, 268
authority, governmental: and the "divine right of kings" (Romans 13), 225; and "natural rights" (Locke), 225
Awasu, Charles, 25
Ayittey, George B. N., 216n3, 217n16
Bachelder, Robert, 150
Balcomb, Anthony, 97, 230n3, 247, 249, 257n5, 263n70
Ballard, Richard, 293n94
Banda, Hastings Kamazu, 197
Barth, Karl, 275, 283
Bebbington, David, 258n5
Bediako, Kwame, 198–99, 210, 211–12
Belhar Confession (1986), 133–34, 143n70, 167, 181–84, 185n4, 188n54, 188–89n56, 242, 260n37
Bell, Daniel, 291n70
Beloved (Morrison), the character "Stamp Paid" in, 69
Beyond Gated Politics: Reflections for the Possibility of Democracy (Coles), 292n90
Biko, Steve, 174, 175, 176, 178, 180, 181
Bismarck, Otto von, 175
Black Consciousness movement, 297
Black and Reformed (Boesak), 259n23
Blues Legacies and Black Feminism: Gertrude "Ma" Rainey, Bessie Smith, and Billie Holiday (Davis), 74–75; on "African queens," 75
Blyden, Edward, 296
Body of Power, Spirit of Resistance: The Culture and History of a South African People (Jean Comaroff), 258n11
Boesak, Allan, 161, 181, 241, 246, 259n23
Bompani, Barbara, 277–78, 280, 281
Bonilla-Silva, Eduardo, 172
Boom Shaka, 67, 72, 73
Botha, P. W., 251, 273–74, 289n38
Bouillon, Antoine, 176
Boyo, Bernard, 25, 122
Bratton, Michael, 257n4
Breidback, Angela, 65
Brink, Paul, 26
Bromiley, G. W., 203

CPSIA information can be obtained
at www.ICGtesting.com
Printed in the USA
LVOW08s1433040917
547474LV00006B/1107/P